Microsoft Word
for Windows® 95

Timothy J. O'Leary
Linda I. O'Leary

5 6 7 8 9 0 BAN BAN 9 0 9 8 7

ISBN 0-07-049104-6

Library of Congress Catalog Card Number 95-82266

Information has been obtained by The McGraw-Hill Companies, Inc. from sources believed to be reliable. However, because of the possibility of human or mechanical error by our sources, The McGraw-Hill Companies, Inc., or others, The McGraw-Hill Companies, Inc. does not guarantee the accuracy, adequacy, or completeness of any information and is not responsible for any errors or omissions or the results obtained from use of such information.

Contents

Word Processing Overview

One of the most widely used applications software programs is a word processor. Putting your thoughts in writing, from the simplest note to the most complex book, is a time-consuming process. Even more time-consuming is the task of editing and retyping the document to make it better. With the introduction of word processing, errors should be nearly nonexistent—not because they are not made, but because they are easy to correct. Word processors let you throw away the correction fluid, scissors, paste, and erasers. Now, with a few keystrokes, you can easily correct errors, move paragraphs, and reprint your document.

Definition of Word Processing

Word processing software is a program that helps you create any type of written communication. A word processor can be used to manipulate text data to produce a letter, a report, a memo, or any other type of correspondence. Text data is any letter, number, or symbol that you can type on a keyboard. The grouping of the text data to form words, sentences, paragraphs, and pages of text results in the creation of a document. Through a word processor you can create, modify, store, retrieve, and print part or all of a document.

Advantages of Using a Word Processor

The speed of entering text data into the computer depends on the skill of the user. If you cannot type fast, a word processor will not improve your typing speed. However, a word processor will make it easier to correct and change your document. Consequently, your completed document will take less time to create.

Another time saver is word wrap. As you enter text you do not need to decide where to end each line, as you do on a typewriter. When a line is full, the program automatically wraps the text down to the next line.

A word processor excels in its ability to change or edit, a document. Editing involves correcting spelling, grammar, and sentence-structure errors. As you enter characters using the keyboard, they are displayed on the screen and stored electronically in the computer's main memory. As you find errors, you can electronically delete or correct them. Once the document is the way you want it to appear, it can be permanently saved on a disk and printed on paper. Good-bye, correction fluid!

In addition to editing a document, you can easily revise or update it by inserting or deleting text. For example, a document that lists prices can easily be updated to reflect new prices. A document that details procedures can be revised by deleting old procedures and inserting new ones. This is especially helpful when a document is used repeatedly. Rather than recreating the whole document, you change only the parts that need to be revised.

Revision also includes the rearrangement of selected areas of text. For example, while writing a report, you may decide to change the location of a single word or several paragraphs or pages of text. You can do it easily by cutting or removing selected text from one location, then pasting or placing the selected text in another location. The selection can also be copied from one document to another.

Combining text in another file with text in your document is another advantage of word processors. An example of this is a group term paper. Each person is responsible for writing a section of the paper. Before printing the document, the text for all sections, which is stored in different files, is combined to create the complete paper. The opposite is also true: text that may not be appropriate in your document can easily be put in another file for later use.

Many word processors include additional support features to help you produce a perfect document. A spelling checker checks the spelling in a document by comparing each word to those in a dictionary stored in memory. If an error is found, the program suggests the correct spelling. A syntax checker electronically checks grammar, phrasing, capitalization, and other types of syntax errors in a document. A thesaurus displays alternative words that have a meaning similar or opposite to the word you entered.

You can also easily control the appearance or format of the document. Formatting includes such operations as changing the line spacing and margin widths, adding page numbers, and displaying page headers and footers. You can also quickly change how your text is aligned with the left or right margin. For example, text can be centered between the margins, or justified—evenly aligned on both the left and right margins. Perhaps the most noticeable formatting feature is the ability to apply different fonts (type styles and sizes) and text appearance changes such as bold and italics to all or selected portions of the document. Most word processing programs also have the ability to produce and display graphic lines and boxes. Graphic boxes can then be used to hold text or graphic images that you place into the document.

Most word processing programs include the WYSIWYG ("what you see is what you get") feature. This feature allows you to see onscreen exactly (or as close as possible) how your document will appear when printed. This means that the effects of your format changes are immediately displayed on the screen.

If, after reading the printed copy, you find other errors or want to revise or reformat the document, it is easy to do. Simply reload the document file, make your changes, and reprint the text. Now that saves time!

Word Processing Terminology

The following terms and definitions are generic in nature and are associated with most word processing programs.

Bold: Produces dark or heavy print.

Center: To center a line of text evenly between the margins.

Document: Text-based output created by a word processing program.

Edit: To change or modify the content of the document.

Font: Type style and size.

Format: Defines how the printed document will appear; includes settings for underline, boldface, print size, margin settings, line spacing, and so on.

Insert: To enter new text into a document in the middle of existing text.

Justified: Text that is evenly aligned on both the left and right margins.

Spelling checker: A support feature that checks words or the entire document for correct spelling.

Syntax checker: A support feature that checks grammar, phrasing, capitalization, and other types of syntax errors.

Text data: Any number, letter, or symbol you can type on a keyboard.

Thesaurus: A support feature that displays synonyms and antonyms for words in your document.

Word wrap: The automatic adjustment of the number of characters or words on a line that eliminates the need to press the [←Enter] (or [←Return]) key at the end of each line.

WYSIWYG: The feature that displays a document onscreen in a form as close as possible to how it will appear when printed.

Case Study for Labs 1–4

As a recent college graduate, you have accepted your first job as a management trainee for The Sports Company. The Sports Company is a chain of discount sporting goods shops located in large metropolitan areas throughout the United States. The program emphasis is on computer applications in the area of retail management and requires that you work in several areas of the company.

In this series of labs, you are working in the Southwest Regional office and are responsible for setting up the credit card enrollment program and for assisting with the monthly newsletter.

In Labs 1 and 2, you will create a letter to be sent to all new credit card recipients. You will learn how to use the word processing program to create, edit, format, and print the letter.

In Lab 3, the regional office has decided to send a monthly newsletter to credit card customers. You have been asked to design and prepare several articles for inclusion in the newsletter.

Lab 4 demonstrates how to personalize the credit card letter by creating a form letter and merging the recipients' personal information such as name and address into the form letter. You will also prepare a table that summarizes gross sales for the regional stores.

Before You Begin

To the Student

The following assumptions have been made:

- Microsoft Word version 7.0 or 7.0a for Windows 95 has been properly installed on the hard disk of your computer system.
- The data disk contains the data files needed to complete the series of Word 7.0 for Windows 95 labs and practice exercises. These files are supplied by your instructor.
- You have completed the McGraw-Hill Windows 95 lab module or you are already familiar with how to use Windows 95 and a mouse. A review of basic Windows 95 features is provided at the end of the lab module.

To the Instructor

Please be aware that the following settings are assumed to be in effect for the Word 7.0 or 7.0a for Windows 95 program. These assumptions are necessary so that the screens and directions in the manual are accurate.

- Language is set to English [US]. (Use Tools/Language and set English as default.)
- Navigation keys for WordPerfect users and Help for WordPerfect users are off. (Use Tools/Options/General.)
- The TipWizard is active. (Use Tools/Options/General.)
- The Normal view is on. Zoom is 100 percent. (Use View/Normal; View/Zoom/100%.)

- Wrap to Window setting is off. (Use Tools/Options/View.)
- All default settings for a normal template document are in effect.
- The Table Wizard is installed.
- In addition, all figures in the manual reflect the use of a standard VGA display monitor and a Panasonic KX-P2123 printer. If another monitor type is used, there may be more lines of text displayed in the windows than in the figures. This setting can be changed using Windows setup. The selected printer also affects how text appears on screen. If possible, select a printer and monitor type that will match the figures in the manual.

Microsoft Office Shortcut Bar

The Microsoft Office Shortcut Bar (shown below) may be displayed automatically on the Windows 95 desktop. Commonly, it appears in the upper right section of the desktop; however, it may appear in other locations, depending upon your setup. The Shortcut Bar on your screen may display different buttons. This is because the Shortcut Bar can be customized to display other toolbar buttons.

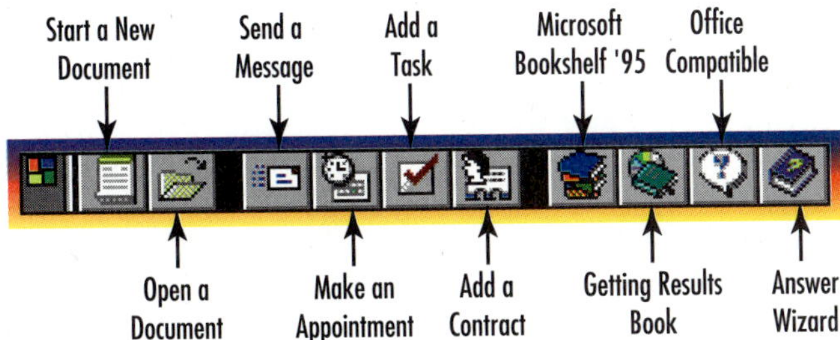

The Office Shortcut Bar makes it easy to open existing documents or to create new documents using one of the Microsoft Office applications. It can also be used to send e-mail, add a task to a to-do list, schedule appointments using Schedule+, or access Office Help.

Instructional Conventions

This text uses the same instructional conventions as described in the Introduction to the Labs at the beginning of the Windows 95 lab module.

In brief, they are:

- Command sequences you are to issue appear following the word "Choose:." Each menu command selection is separated by a /. If the menu command can be selected by typing a letter of the command, the letter will appear underlined.
- Commands that can be initiated using a button and the mouse appear following the word "Click:." The menu equivalent and keyboard shortcut appear in a margin note when the action is first introduced.
- Anything you are to type appears in bold text.

1 Creating and Editing a Document

Unlike most tools, the computer is multipurpose. It is designed to improve your efficiency and accuracy and help you solve problems. Because it can run many different types of software programs, it is a tool that can create a wide variety of products and solve many different kinds of problems.

COMPETENCIES

After completing this lab, you will know how to:

1. Load Word 7.0.
2. Use Toolbars.
3. Use Answer Wizard.
4. Create a new document.
5. Enter text.
6. Insert and delete blank lines.
7. Move around the document window.
8. Close and open files.
9. Move through a document.
10. Insert and delete text.
11. Display special characters.
12. Select text.
13. Undo editing changes.
14. Document and save a file.
15. Preview and print a document.
16. Exit Word.

Each application program your computer runs has a specific purpose. For example, a spreadsheet program helps you produce numerical-based documents, and drawing programs produce graphic art. The software tool you will learn about in this series of labs is the word processing application Word 7.0. Its purpose is to help you create text documents such as letters, reports, and research papers.

Concept Overview

The following concepts will be introduced in this lab:

1. Document Development	The development of a document follows several steps: Planning, Entering, Editing, Formatting, and Printing.
2. Document Template	A document template is a document file that includes predefined settings that can be used as a pattern to create many common types of documents.
3. AutoCorrect	A feature that makes some basic assumptions about the text you are typing and, based on these assumptions, automatically identifies and/or corrects the entry as you type.
4. Automatic Spell Check	A feature that identifies misspelled words as you type.
5. Word Wrap	The word wrap feature automatically decides where to end a line and wrap text to the next line.
6. Save Files	A permanent copy of your onscreen document is created by saving the document as a file on a disk.
7. Word Filenames	A Word filename follows the same naming rules as other Windows 95 programs. It is automatically saved with the filename extension .DOC.
8. Preview Documents	A feature that displays each page of your document in reduced size so you can see its layout.

CASE STUDY

The Sports Company is a chain of sporting goods shops located in large metropolitan areas across the United States. The stores are warehouse-oriented, discounting the retail prices of most items 15 percent. They stock sporting goods products for the major sports: team sports, racquet sports, aerobics, golf, winter sports, and so on.

As a recent college graduate, you have accepted a job in a management training program for The Sports Company. The training program emphasis is on computer applications in the area of retail management. The program requires that you work in several areas of the company. Your current assignment is in the Southwest Regional Office, where you are responsible for setting up the new credit card program and for assisting with the monthly newsletter.

During the next four labs you will be using Microsoft Word 7.0 or 7.0a for Windows 95 to edit a letter to be sent to the new credit card recipients, and to create the monthly newsletter. Specifically, in Lab 1, you will learn about entering, editing, previewing, and printing a document while you create the first draft of the letter.

Part 1

Loading Word 7.0 for Windows 95

If a shortcut to Word button Microsoft Word is displayed on your desktop, you can double-click on the button to start the program.

If the Microsoft Office Suite is on your system and the Office Shortcut Bar is displayed, you can click the Start a New Document button, select Blank Document, and choose OK, to load Word.

Refer to the Sizing Windows section in the Windows 95 Review for information on this feature.

If necessary, turn on your computer and put your data disk in drive A (or the appropriate drive for your system).

The Windows 95 desktop screen should be displayed. To start Word 7.0 for Windows 95,

Choose: **Start/Programs**

The Microsoft Word program should appear in the program list.

Choose: Microsoft Word

A title screen is briefly displayed while the computer loads the Word 7.0 program into memory. After a few moments, the Word application window is displayed and your screen should be similar to Figure 1-1.

If necessary, maximize the Word application window.

Examining the Word Window

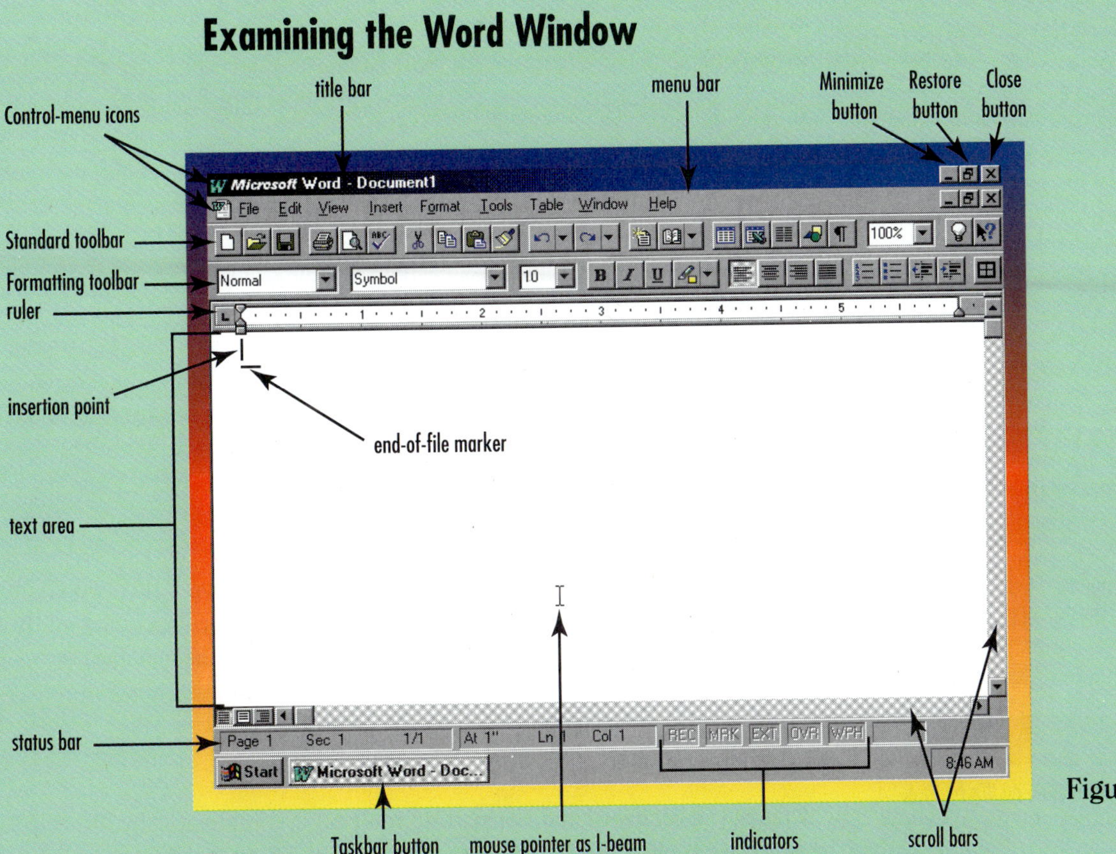

Figure 1-1

As you can see, many of the features in the Word window are the same as in other Windows 95 applications. Among those features are a title bar; a menu bar; buttons; icons; scroll bars; and mouse compatibility. You can move and size Word windows, select commands, use Help, and switch between files and programs, just as you can in Windows. The common user interface makes learning and using new applications much easier.

The Word window title bar displays the program name, Microsoft Word, followed by the filename Document1, the default name of the file displayed in the window. The left end of the title bar contains the Word application window Control-menu icon, and the right end displays the Minimize, Restore, and Close buttons. They perform the same functions and operate in the same way as in Windows 95.

If the title bar does not display the filename, the document window is not maximized. Maximize the document window.

The menu bar below the title bar displays the Word program menu, which consists of nine menus. The left end of the menu bar displays the document window Control-menu icon and the right end displays the document window Minimize, Restore, and Close buttons.

The two toolbars below the menu bar contain buttons that are mouse shortcuts for many of the menu items. The upper toolbar is the **Standard toolbar**, the bottom is the **Formatting toolbar**. There are nine different toolbars in Word.

The toolbar operates just like Windows 95 toolbars. You will learn more about the toolbar shortly.

The **ruler** is displayed below the Formatting toolbar. The ruler shows the line length in inches and is used to set margins, tab stops, and indents for selected paragraphs.

The large center area of the Word screen is the **text area**. This is where documents are displayed in open windows. Currently there is one open window, which is maximized and occupies the entire text area. The **insertion point**, also called the **cursor**, is the blinking vertical bar that marks your current location in the document. The solid horizontal line is the **end-of-file marker**. Because there is nothing in this document, the end-of-file marker appears at the first character space on the first line.

The **status bar** at the bottom of the Word window displays information about the location of the insertion point and the status of different settings as they are used. In addition, the status bar displays messages, such as button and command descriptions, to help you use the program more efficiently.

Mouse use is assumed throughout. Marginal notes will discuss keyboard tips as appropriate.

The mouse pointer may appear as an I-beam I or an arrow, depending on its location in the window. The mouse pointer changes shape depending on the task you are performing or where the pointer is located on the window.

If the mouse pointer is not an I-beam, move it into the text area.

Refer to the Mouse section in the Windows 95 Review for information on this feature.

Using Toolbars

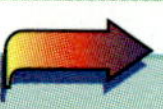

Refer to the Toolbar section of the Windows 95 Review for information on toolbar procedures.

By default, the Standard and Formatting toolbars are automatically displayed. The Standard toolbar contains buttons that are used to complete the most frequently used menu commands. The Formatting toolbar contains buttons that are used to change the appearance or format of the document. Many of the buttons are the same as those you have seen in toolbars in other Windows 95 applications. Many, however, are specific to the Word 7.0 application.

To quickly identify the toolbar buttons, point to each button in both toolbars to display the button name in the tooltip and a description in the status bar.

The last button on the Standard toolbar is the Help button. It is used to get Help on any command or window element.

Click:  **Help**

The mouse pointer shape changes to ?. Now, by clicking on any command or window element, you can get Help information directly related to the item you are pointing to.

Click on the button and read the Screen Tip that appears in the box. To clear the Screen Tip, click anywhere or press Esc.

As you learned from the Screen Tip, the TipWizard button turns the TipWizard toolbar on and off. To turn it on,

Click:  **TipWizard**

Your screen should be similar to Figure 1-2.

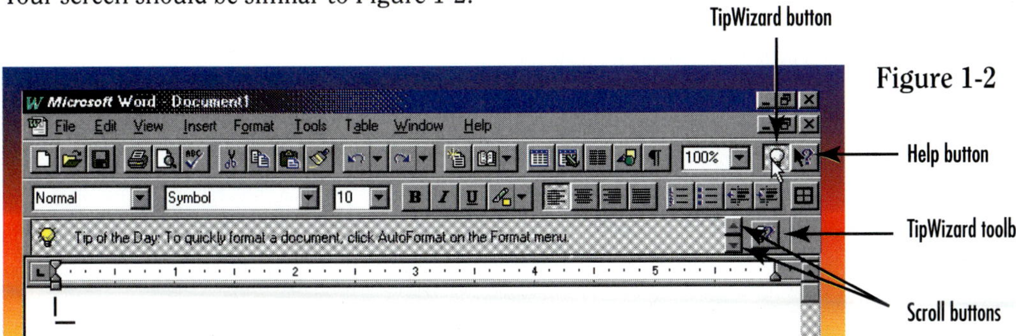

Figure 1-2

The TipWizard toolbar appears below the Formatting toolbar. It displays the tip of the day when first opened. As you use Word, the TipWizard toolbar will display a tip about the task you are performing if there is a more efficient or alternative method of doing it. However, once a tip has been displayed, it is not displayed again. To reset the TipWizard to display tips that may have already been seen,

Click: **while holding down** Ctrl

The TipWizard displays a new tip, indicating that it has been reset. It also stores all tips that have been displayed since you started the program. These tips can be viewed by using the TipWizard scroll buttons. To see the original tip,

Click: **(at the right end of the TipWizard box)**

The first tip is displayed.

Using Answer Wizard

While using Word, you will see that many of the toolbars open automatically as different tasks are performed. However, you can also open toolbars whenever you want. To find out how to open and close toolbars, you will use the Answer Wizard. A **wizard** is a feature that automatically shows you how to complete a task or provides step-by-step directions through the use of dialog boxes. The Answer Wizard is accessed through the Help menu.

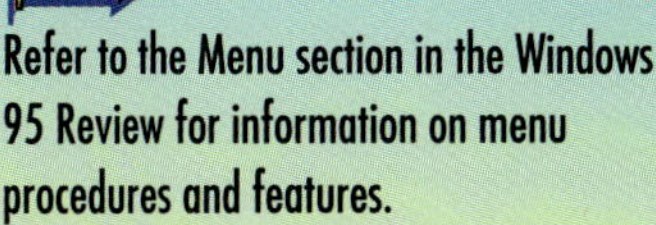

Refer to the Menu section in the Windows 95 Review for information on menu procedures and features.

The Help/Microsoft Word Help Topics command or the shortcut key F1 can also be used to access the Answer Wizard.

Choose: **Help/Answer Wizard**

The Help Topics dialog box displaying the Answer Wizard tab appears. In addition, the Help Topics dialog box includes the Contents, Index, and Find tabs, as found in all Windows 95 Help dialog boxes. The Answer Wizard tab includes two steps. In the Step 1 text box, you enter the word or phrase you want information on.

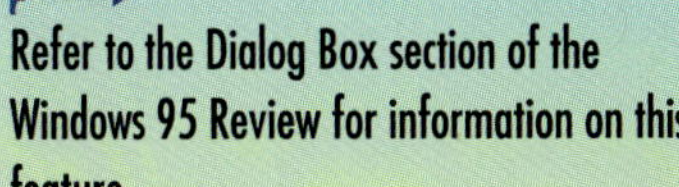

Refer to the Dialog Box section of the Windows 95 Review for information on this feature.

Type: **display toolbars**
Choose: **Search**

This text may already appear in the text box. If this is the case, you do not need to retype the request.

The Step 2 list box displays topics that contain information on your request.

Select: **Display or hide toolbars**

Your screen should be similar to Figure 1-3.

Figure 1-3

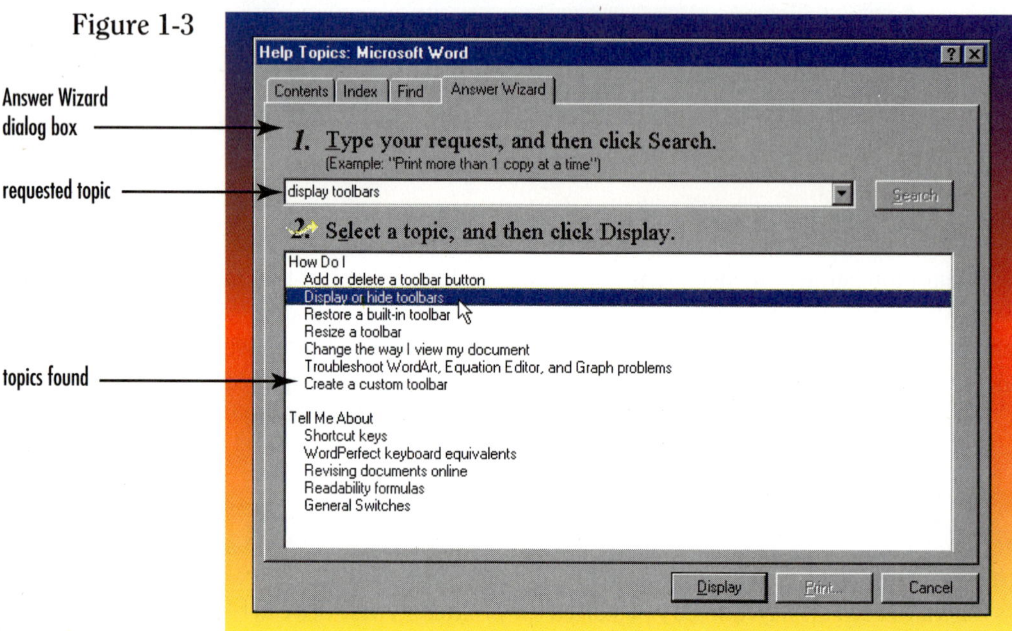

A dialog box may be displayed telling you that Word will step you through the task. To continue, choose Next >.

Choose: **Display**

Immediately, the Answer Wizard takes over to show you how to perform the task. As you watch, Answer Wizard performs the steps needed to answer your question. In this case, the View menu is opened and the Toolbars command selected. The Toolbars dialog box shown in Figure 1-4 is displayed, along with a Screen Tip explaining what you should do next.

Click on the Screen Tip to clear it.

Figure 1-4

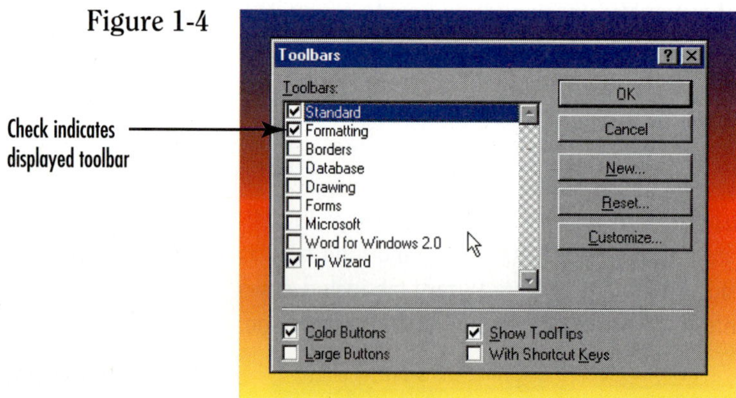

The dialog box lists the nine toolbar names. Those that are currently displayed are checked. Clicking on a toolbar from the list will display it on screen. Likewise, clicking on a checked toolbar will remove the toolbar from the screen. You can also create new toolbars or customize existing toolbars using this dialog box. Because you do not need to turn on any other toolbars,

Choose: **Cancel**

Refer to the Menus section of the Windows 95 Review for information on using Shortcut menus.

You can also quickly hide and display toolbars from the toolbar Shortcut menu. To open the toolbar Shortcut menu,

Right-click on any toolbar.

The Shortcut menu displays the same list of toolbars as in the Toolbar dialog box.

Clear the Shortcut menu.

Click anywhere outside the menu to clear it.

Developing a Document

Your first project with The Sports Company is to create a letter to be sent to all new credit card holders.

Concept 1: Document Development

The development of a document follows several steps: Planning, Entering, Editing, Formatting, and Printing.

Planning The first step in the development of a document is to understand the purpose of the document and to plan what your document should say.

Entering After planning the document, you can begin entering the content of the document by typing the text using the word processor.

Editing Making changes to your document is called **editing**. While typing, you are bound to make typing and spelling errors that need to be corrected. This is one type of editing. Another is to revise the content of what you have entered to make it clearer, or to add or delete information.

Formatting Enhancing the appearance of the document to make it more readable or attractive is called **formatting**. This step is usually performed when the document is near completion. It includes many features such as boldfaced text, italics, and bulleted lists.

Printing The last step is to print a hard copy of the document. This step includes previewing the document onscreen as it will appear when printed. Previewing allows you to check the document's overall appearance and to make any final changes needed before printing.

You will find that you will generally follow these steps in order for your first draft of a document. However, you will probably retrace steps such as editing and formatting as the final document is developed.

During the planning phase, you have spoken with the regional manager regarding the purpose of the letter and the content in general. The purpose of the letter is to thank the customer for opening a new charge account with The Sports Company. The content of the letter should include instructions to the customer about how to use the card and the benefits associated with being a charge card holder.

In this lab, you will create the letter shown in Figure 1-5.

Figure 1-5

Dear Preferred Customer:

Thank you for opening a new credit card account with The Sports Company and becoming one of our most valued customers. Here's your new credit card!

Please sign your new card in ink with your usual signature. If you have an old card, destroy it immediately. Always carry your new credit card with you. It will identify you as a Preferred Customer and guarantees you a quick and convenient shopping experience at any of The Sports Company stores located throughout the country.

We are the leading sports store in the Southwest with a tradition of personal, friendly service. As you use your new credit card, you will discover the many conveniences that only our credit customers enjoy.

We are very happy with the opportunity to serve you and we look forward to seeing you soon.

Sincerely,

Student Name
The Sports Company Manager

Entering and Editing Text

Now that you understand the purpose of the letter and have a general idea of the content, you are ready to enter the text.

A new Word document is like a blank piece of paper that already has many predefined settings. These settings are generally the most commonly used settings. They are called **default** settings and are stored as a document template.

Concept 2: Document Template

Every Word document is based on a document template. A document **template** is a document file that includes predefined settings that can be used as a pattern to create many common types of documents. The default document settings are stored in the Normal document template. Whenever you create a new document using this template, the same default settings are used.

There are many other template styles you can use that are designed to help you create professional-appearing documents. They include templates that create different styles of memos, letters, and reports.

The Normal document template sets the top and bottom margins to 1 inch and the left and right margins to 1.25 inch. Other default settings include a standard paper-size setting of 8 1/2 by 11 inches, tab settings at every half-inch, and single-line spacing.

To verify several of the default settings, you can look at the information displayed in the status bar.

Status Bar Elements

Page 1	Sec 1	1/1	At 1"	Ln 1	Col 1	REC	MRK	EXT	OVR	WPH	

The indicators on the status bar show both the location of the text displayed on the screen as well as the location of the insertion point in a document. The indicators are described below. The numbers following the indicators specify the exact location in the document.

Indicator	Meaning
Page	Indicates the page of text displayed on screen.
Sec	Indicates the section of text displayed on screen. A large document can be broken into sections.
1/1	Indicates the number of pages from the beginning of the document to the displayed page and the total pages in the document.
At	Indicates the vertical position of the insertion point from the top edge of the page.
Ln	Indicates the vertical position of the insertion point from the top margin of the page.
Col	Indicates the horizontal position of the insertion point from the left margin of the page.

As you can see from the first three indicators in the status bar, page 1 of section 1 of a document consisting of only 1 page (1/1) is displayed on your screen. The next three indicators show the position of the insertion point. Currently, the insertion point is positioned at the 1-inch location from the top of the page, on line 1 from the top margin and column 1 from the left margin.

You can also look at the ruler to verify several default settings.

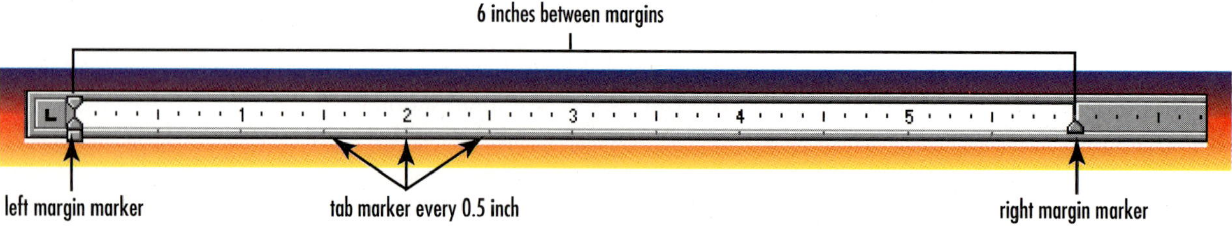

The symbol ⧗ at the zero position on the ruler marks the location of the left margin. The ▲ symbol on the right end of the ruler line at the 6" position marks the right margin. The ruler shows that the distance between the left and right margins is 6 inches. Knowing the default page size is 8 1/2 inches wide, this leaves 2 1/2 inches for margins: 1 1/4 inches for equal-sized left and right margins. The ruler also displays dimmed tab marks below each 1/2-inch position along the ruler, indicating a default tab setting of every 1/2 inch.

To create a new document, simply begin typing the text. On the first line of the letter you will enter the salutation "Dear Preferred Customer:". As you enter the text, it will include several intentional errors. Type the entries exactly as they appear.

Type: **dear**

Notice that as you type, the character appears to the left of the insertion point. The location of the insertion point shows where the next character will appear as you type. Also, the status bar reflects the new horizontal position of the insertion point on the line. It shows the insertion point is currently positioned on column 5 of line 1.

Press: Spacebar

Your screen should be similar to Figure 1-6.

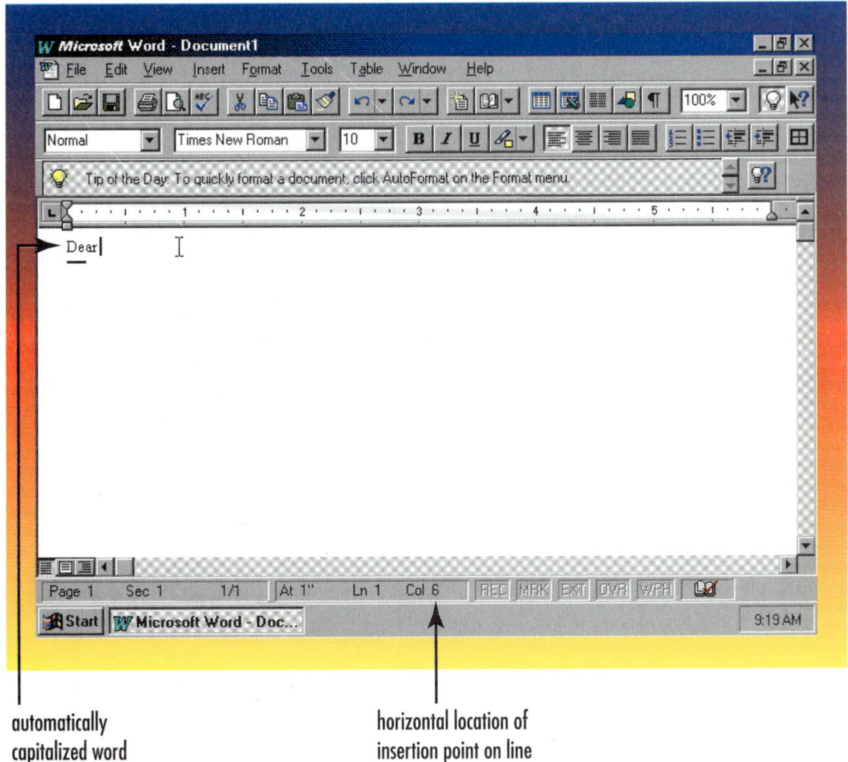

Figure 1-6

As soon as you complete a word, the program checks the word for accuracy. In this case, notice that Word automatically capitalized the first letter of the word. This is part of the automatic correcting feature of Word.

Concept 3: AutoCorrect

Word includes a feature called AutoCorrect, which makes some basic assumptions about the text you are typing and, based on these assumptions, automatically identifies and/or corrects the entry. The AutoCorrect feature automatically inserts proper capitalization at the beginning of sentences and the names of days of the week. It will also change to lowercase letters any words that were incorrectly capitalized due to the accidental use of the Caps Lock key. In addition, it also corrects common spelling errors automatically.

The program automatically corrects by looking for certain types of errors. This is part of Word's IntelliSense feature, which automatically gives you assistance while you work. For example, if two capital letters appear at the beginning of a word, Word changes the second capital letter to a lowercase letter. If a lowercase letter appears at the beginning of a sentence, Word capitalizes the first letter of the first word. If the name of a day begins with a lowercase letter, Word capitalizes the first letter.

In some cases, you may want to exclude an abbreviation or capitalized item from automatic correction. You can do this by adding the word to an exception list. Alternatively, you can add words to the list of words you want to be automatically corrected. For example, if you commonly misspell a word, you can add the word to the list and it will be automatically corrected as you type.

To continue entering the salutation,

Type: Prefered
Press: Spacebar

Your screen should be similar to Figure 1-7.

Figure 1-7

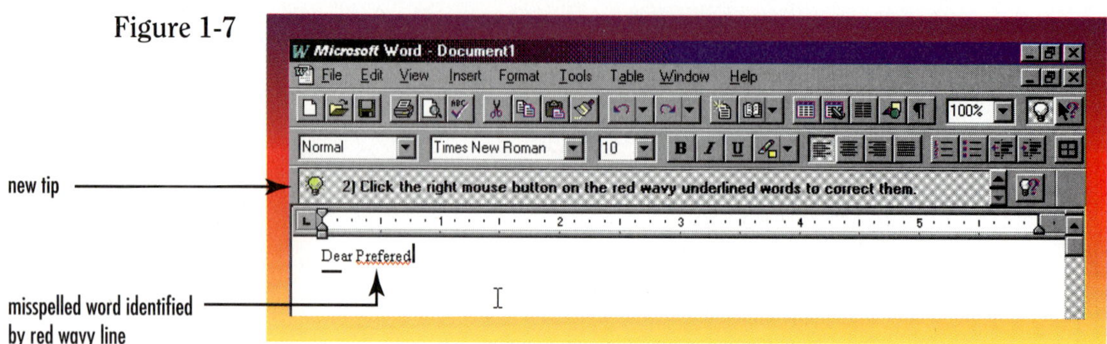

This time Word has identified the word as a misspelled word by underlining it with a wavy red line. Notice that the TipWizard now displays a tip about this feature.

Concept 4: Automatic Spell Check

Word automatically checks the spelling of each word as you type by checking the word against a dictionary of words. If the word does not appear in the main dictionary or in a custom dictionary, it is identified with a wavy red underline. The **main dictionary** is part of the Word program; a **custom dictionary** is one you can create to hold words you commonly use but that are not included in the main dictionary.

You can then correct the misspelled word by editing it. Alternatively, you can display a list of suggested spelling corrections for that word and select the correct spelling from the list to replace the misspelled word in the document.

Because you have discovered this error very soon after typing it, and you know that the correct spelling of this word is "preferred," you can quickly correct it using Backspace. The Backspace key removes the character or space to the left of the insertion point; therefore, it is particularly useful when you are moving from right to left (backward) along a line of text. To correct this word,

Press: Backspace 3 times

The space and the letters d and e are removed. Notice the wavy underline is also cleared. This is because the word is not yet complete. A word is complete when followed by a space. To complete the word correctly,

Type: red
Press: Spacebar

The word is now correct. To enter the last word of the salutation,

Type: Custommer
Press: Spacebar

Again, the word is misspelled. Another way to quickly correct a misspelled word, as indicated in the Tip Wizard toolbar, is to select the correct spelling from a list of suggested spelling corrections displayed on the Spelling Shortcut menu. To do this,

Right-click on the word to display the Spelling Shortcut menu.

Your screen should be similar to Figure 1-8.

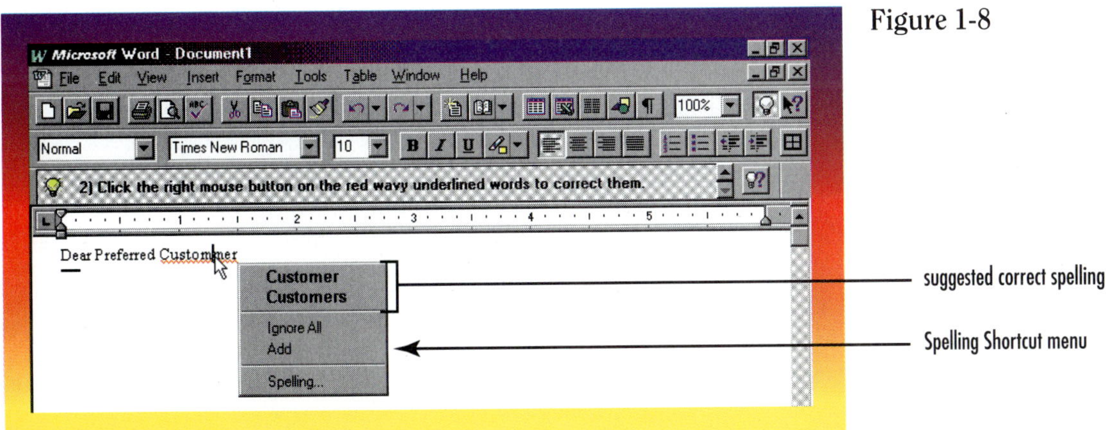

Figure 1-8

A Shortcut menu of suggested correct spellings is displayed. This menu displays two suggested correct spellings. The menu also includes several related menu options. Ignore All instructs Word to ignore the misspelling of this word throughout the rest of this session, and Add adds the word to the custom dictionary list. When a word is added to the custom dictionary, Word will always accept that spelling as correct. The last option, Spelling, starts the spell-checking program to check the entire document. You will learn about this feature in Lab 2.

Notice that the suggested replacements reflect the same capitalization as used in the document. The first suggestion is correct. To select it,

Click: Customer

The selected correct spelling replaces the misspelled word in the document. Sometimes there are no suggested replacements because Word cannot locate any words in its dictionary that are similar in spelling or the suggestions are not correct. If this happens, you need to edit the word manually.

Finally, to end the salutation with a colon,

Type: :

Inserting and Deleting Blank Lines

Next, you will enter the first paragraph of the letter. You want to begin the paragraph on a new line below the salutation, with a blank line between the two. The

[←Enter] key is used to insert a blank line into text or to end a short line. This is the same as if you pressed Return on a typewriter. To end the line,

Press: [←Enter]

The insertion point moves to the beginning of the next line. The status bar shows that the insertion point is positioned on line 2, column 1 of the page.

To separate the salutation from the first paragraph with a blank line,

Press: [←Enter]

Your screen should be similar to Figure 1-9.

Figure 1-9

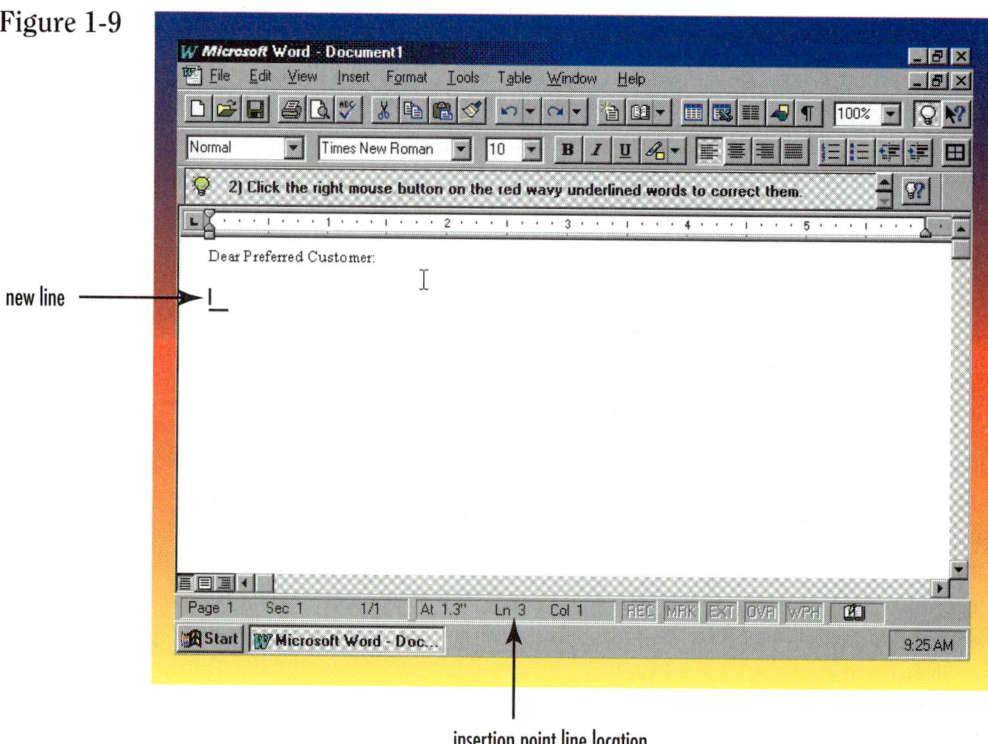

The insertion point is now positioned at the beginning of line 3. When [←Enter] is pressed at the beginning of a line, a blank line is inserted into the document. If the insertion point is in the middle of a line of text and you press [←Enter], all the text to the right of the insertion point moves to the beginning of the next line.

Now you can type the text for the first paragraph of the letter. Do not worry about making typing errors as you enter the text; you will learn how to correct them next.

Type: **Thank you for opening a new credit card account with The Sports Company and becoming one of our**

The line of text is very near the right margin. As you continue to type, when the text reaches the right margin, Word automatically wraps the text to the next line.

Concept 5: Word Wrap

The **word wrap** feature automatically decides where to end a line and wrap text to the next line based on the margin settings. This saves time when entering text, as you do not need to press ←Enter at the end of a full line to begin a new line. The only time you need to press ←Enter is to end a paragraph, to insert blank lines, or to create a short line such as the salutation. In addition, if you change the margins or insert or delete text on a line, the program automatically readjusts the text on the line to fit within the margin settings. Word wrap is common to all word processors.

Watch carefully as you continue the sentence to see how word wrap works.

Type: **most valued customers.**

Your screen should be similar to Figure 1-10.

Do not be concerned if the text on your screen wraps differently from that in Figure 1-10.

Figure 1-10

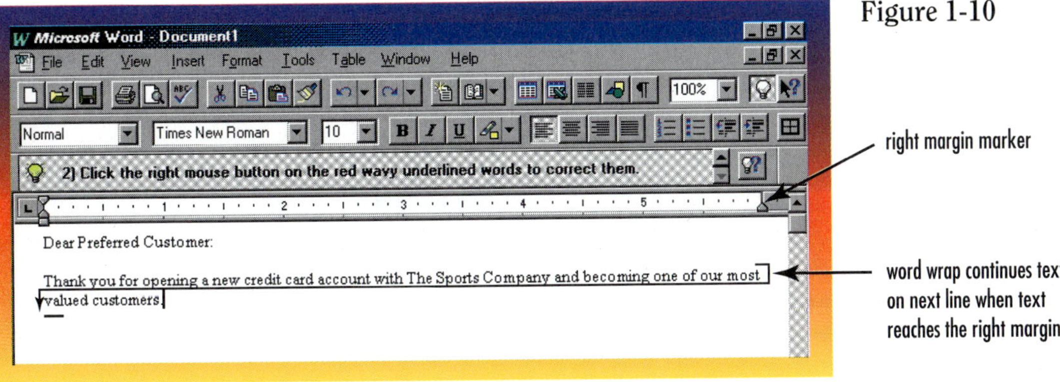

The program has wrapped the text that would overlap the right margin to the beginning of the next line. To continue the paragraph by entering a second sentence,

Press: Spacebar
Type: **Here's your new credit card!**

Generally, when using a word processor, separate sentences with a single space rather than a double space, which was common when using typewriters.

To end the paragraph,

Press: ←Enter

Once text is entered into a document, it is important to know how to move around within the text to correct errors or make changes. As soon as you learn about moving through a document, you will correct any errors you have made.

Moving Around the Document Window

Either the mouse or the keyboard can be used to move through the text in the document window. Depending on what you are doing, the mouse is not always the quickest means of moving. For example, if your hands are already on the keyboard as you are entering text, it may be quicker to use the keyboard rather than take your hands off to use the mouse. Therefore, you will learn how to move through the document using both methods.

You use the mouse to move the insertion point to a specific location in a document. When you can use the mouse to move the insertion point, it is shaped as an I-beam. However, when the mouse pointer is positioned in the unmarked area to the left of a line (the left margin), it changes to an arrow ⇗. This area is called the **selection bar** (see Figure 1-11). When the mouse is in this area, it can be used to highlight text.

Move the mouse pointer into the selection bar.

It changes to an ⇗.

Move it back to the document text.

You will learn about selecting text using this feature shortly.

To move the insertion point, position the I-beam at the location in the text where you want it to be.

Point to: **"y" of "you" (first line of first paragraph)**

Notice that the insertion point has not moved yet and the status bar information has not changed.

To actually move the insertion point, click the left mouse button. Move the mouse pointer out of the way so you can see the insertion point better.

Your screen should be similar to Figure 1-11.

Figure 1-11

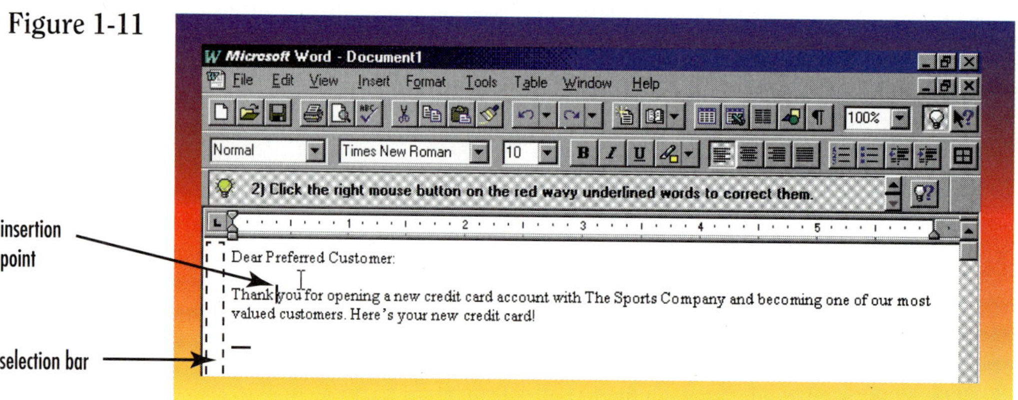

The insertion point should now be positioned on one side or the other of the "y," with the status bar showing the new location of the insertion point.

If it is positioned to the left of the "y," this means that the I-beam was positioned more to the left side of the character when you pressed the mouse button.

The letter to the right of the insertion point is the selected character—in this case the "y."

If it is positioned to the right of the "y," this means the I-beam was positioned more to the right side of the character when you clicked the mouse button. The letter to the right of the insertion point is the selected character, in this case the "o."

Throughout these labs you will be instructed to move to a specific letter in the text. This means to move the insertion point to the *left* side of the character so the character to the right is selected.

Make sure the pointer is an I-beam before clicking to move the insertion point. If text appears highlighted, click anywhere in the document where the mouse pointer is an I-beam to clear the highlighting.

Practice using the mouse to move the insertion point to the left side of a character by moving it to the following locations:

Move to: "S" in "Sports"
Move to: "P" in "Preferred"

The insertion point can also be moved around the window using the arrow keys located on the numeric keypad or the directional keypad. The arrow keys move the insertion point one character space in the direction indicated by the arrow.

If you are using the arrows on the numeric keypad, be sure the Num Lock key is off.

Press: → (10 times)

The insertion point moved 10 character spaces to the right and should be positioned to the left of the "C" in "Customer."

Press: ↓

The insertion point moved down one line. Because this is a blank line, the insertion point moves back to the left margin on the line.

Press: ↓

The insertion point moved down to the next line and to the "o" in "opening." It moved to that position because it was last located in a line containing text at that position. The insertion point will attempt to maintain its position in a line of text as you move up or down through the document.

When you hold down either → or ←, the insertion point moves quickly, character by character, along the line.

To see how this works, hold down → until the insertion point is positioned on the "C" in the word "Company." (If you moved too far to the right along the line of text, use ← to move back to the correct position.)

This saves multiple presses of the arrow key. Many of the Word insertion point movement keys can be held down to execute multiple moves.

As the new tip in the TipWizard indicates, you can also move the insertion point word by word in either direction on a line using Ctrl in combination with → or ←.

Press: Ctrl + → **(2 times)**

The insertion point moved two words to the right along the line. It should be positioned on the "b" in the word "becoming." To move back three words in this line,

Press: Ctrl + ← **(3 times)**

The Home and End keys can be used to quickly move the insertion point to the beginning or end, respectively, of a line of text. To move to the end of this line,

Press: End

To move to the beginning of the line,

Press: Home

The insertion point should be back on the "T" of "Thank."

Now that you know how to move within text on the window, move to any errors you may have made while entering the paragraph and correct them. You can use Backspace to delete characters to the left of the insertion point or Delete to delete characters to the right of the insertion point. You can also correct misspellings using the Spelling Shortcut menu.

Closing and Saving Files

The rest of the letter has been entered for you and saved in a file named Credit Card Letter on your data disk. Before opening this file, you will close the current document file using the Close command on the File menu.

Choose: **File**

Your screen should be similar to Figure 1-12.

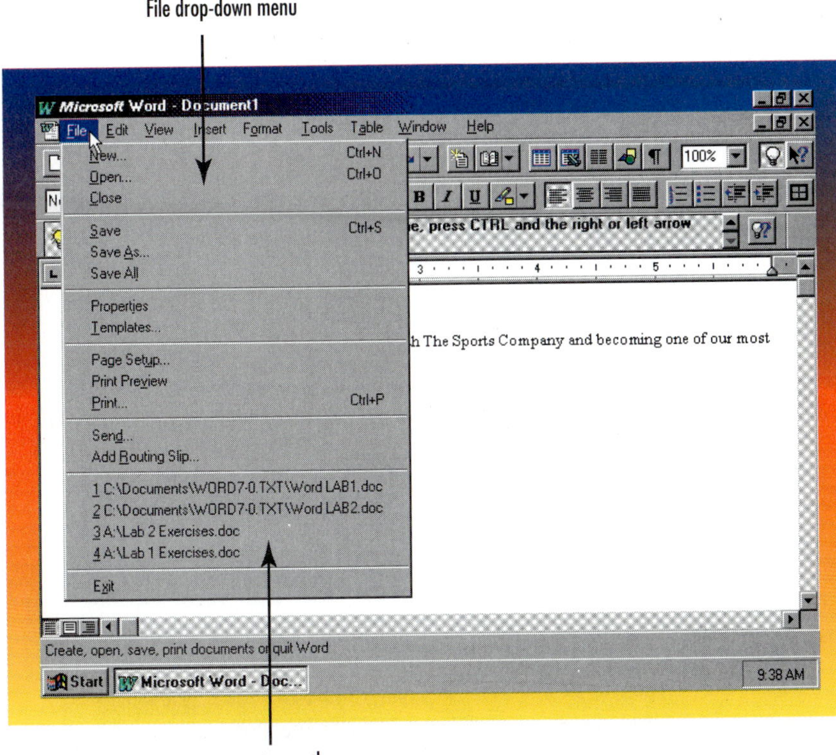

Figure 1-12

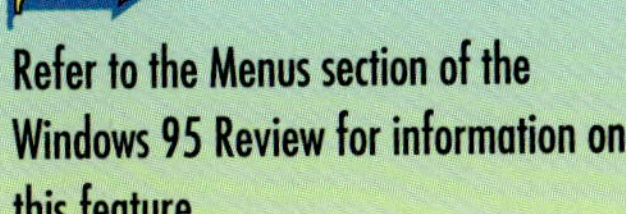

Refer to the Menus section of the Windows 95 Review for information on this feature.

Up to nine recently used documents may be displayed.

You could also click ☒ to close the document file.

The File drop-down menu consisting of 14 commands is displayed. In addition to the commands you would expect to see in the File menu, such as Save and Exit, there are several commands that are specific to Word. At the bottom of the File menu, a list of the names of the most recently used Word document files may be displayed. Clicking on the filename opens the file.

To close the document,

Choose: Close

Your screen should display the dialog box shown in Figure 1-13.

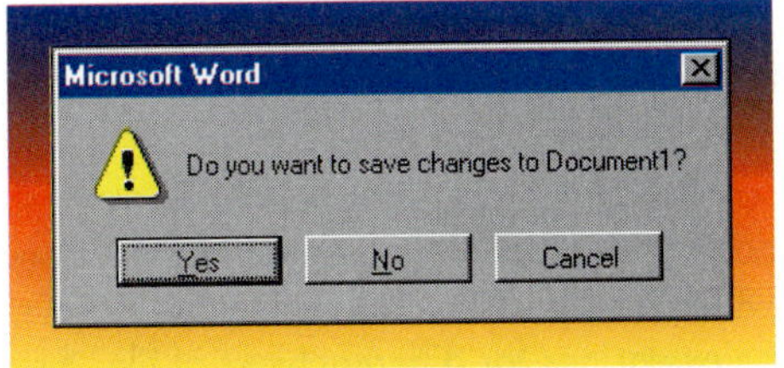

Figure 1-13

As a precaution against losing your work, Word displays this dialog box asking if you want to save the contents of the current document to disk. Selecting Yes saves the document as a file on a disk. No closes the document without saving, and Cancel returns you to the document.

Concept 6: Save Files

As you create a new document or edit an existing document, the changes you make are immediately displayed onscreen and are stored in your computer's memory. To create a permanent copy of your document, it must be saved as a file on a disk. As a safeguard against losing your work if your work is accidentally interrupted, Word automatically saves as you are working. Documents that are saved automatically are stored in a special format and location until you save them. When you restart Word after a power failure or other problem that occurred before you saved your work, Word opens all automatically saved documents so that you can save them. Although Word creates automatic backup files as you are working, it is still a good idea to save your work frequently.

To save the document you have created to a file on your data disk,

Choose: Yes

The dialog box shown in Figure 1-14 should be displayed.

Figure 1-14

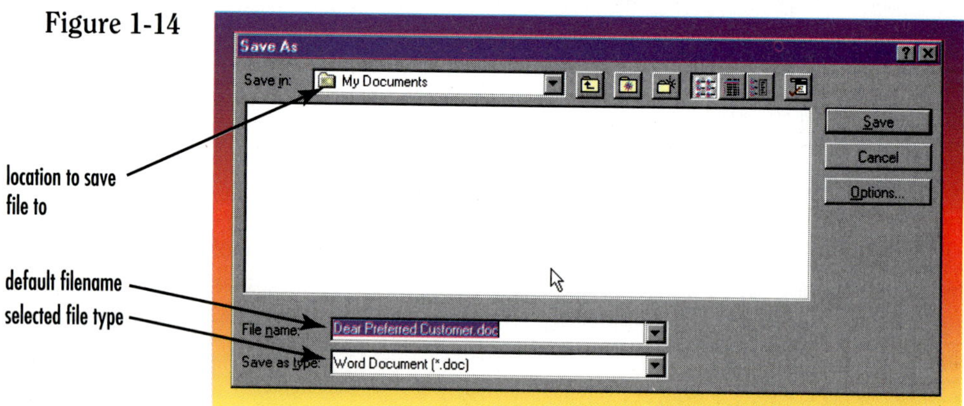

Refer to the Dialog Box section of the Windows 95 Review for information on this feature.

In the Save As dialog box, you specify the location where you want the file saved and the filename.

Refer to the Naming Files section of the Windows 95 Review for information on this feature.

Concept 7: Word Filenames

A Word filename can be up to 255 characters and follows the same naming rules as other Windows 95 products. It is automatically saved with the file extension .DOC, which identifies it as a Word document file. Word uses several different file extensions for different types of files that are created using the program.

The Save In drop-down list box displays the default folder as the location where the file will be saved. You need to change the location to the drive containing your data disk.

Place your data disk in drive A (or the appropriate drive for your system).

Select: Save In

The drop-down list displays the available drives on your system.

You could also type the location in the Save In text box.

Select: A (or the drive containing your data disk)

Now the large list box displays the names of all Word files on your data disk. Only Word document files are displayed because the Save As Type list box shows the currently selected type is Word Document.

If a system error message appears, check that your disk is properly inserted in the drive and that the disk drive door is completely closed. Reselect the option.

The File Name list box displays the default filename consisting of the first few words from the document. You will save the document as Letter Lab 1.

Select (highlight) the default filename in the File Name text box.

Refer to the Selecting Text section of the Windows 95 Review for information on this feature.

The selected filename will be cleared and replaced with the new text as it is typed.

Type: Letter Lab 1
Choose: Save

The filename can be entered in either upper- or lowercase letters and will appear exactly as you type it.

The document is saved on disk and the document window is closed. Now, the Word window displays an empty text area. Only two menus appear in the menu bar and the status bar indicators are blank because there are no open documents.

Opening a File

You are now ready to open the file named Credit Card Letter. As in all Windows 95 applications, the Open command on the File menu is used to open files. In addition, the toolbar shortcut Open can be used instead of the menu command.

The New button will open a blank new document using the Normal template.

Click:  Open

The menu equivalent is File/Open and the keyboard shortcut is Ctrl + O.

The Open dialog box shown in Figure 1-15 should be displayed.

Figure 1-15

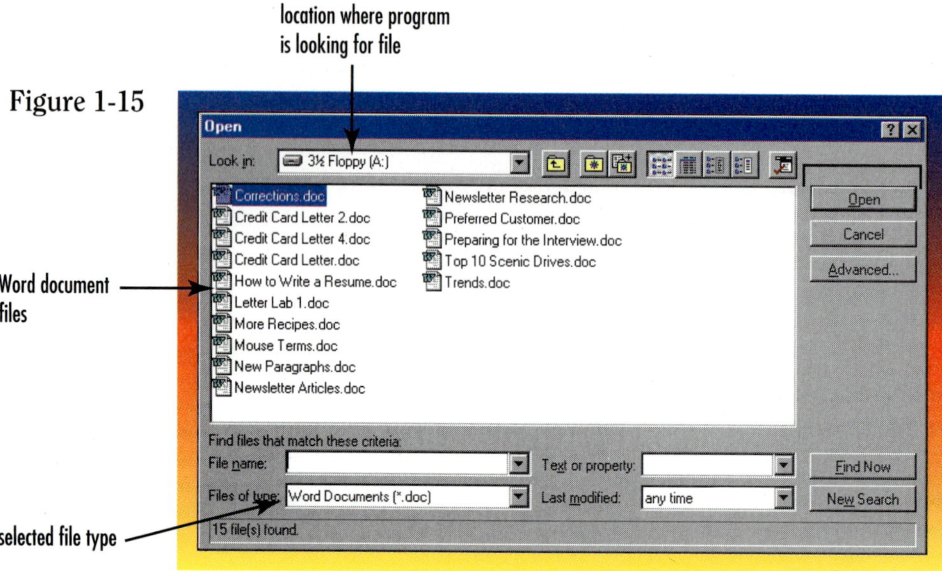

If the Look In location is not correct, select the appropriate location from the Look In drop-down list box.

In the Open dialog box, you specify the location and name of the file you want to open. The Look In drop-down list box displays the drive you specified when saving as the location where the program will look for files. The location should be the drive containing your data disk.

If necessary, scroll the list box until the filename Credit Card Letter is visible. If the filename is not displayed, ask your instructor for help.

The large list box displays the names of all Word files on your data disk. Only Word document files are displayed because the File of Type list box shows that the currently selected type is Word Documents.

Select: **Credit Card Letter.doc**

To complete the command,

You could also double-click the filename to both select it and choose Open.

Choose: **Open**

Your screen should be similar to Figure 1-16.

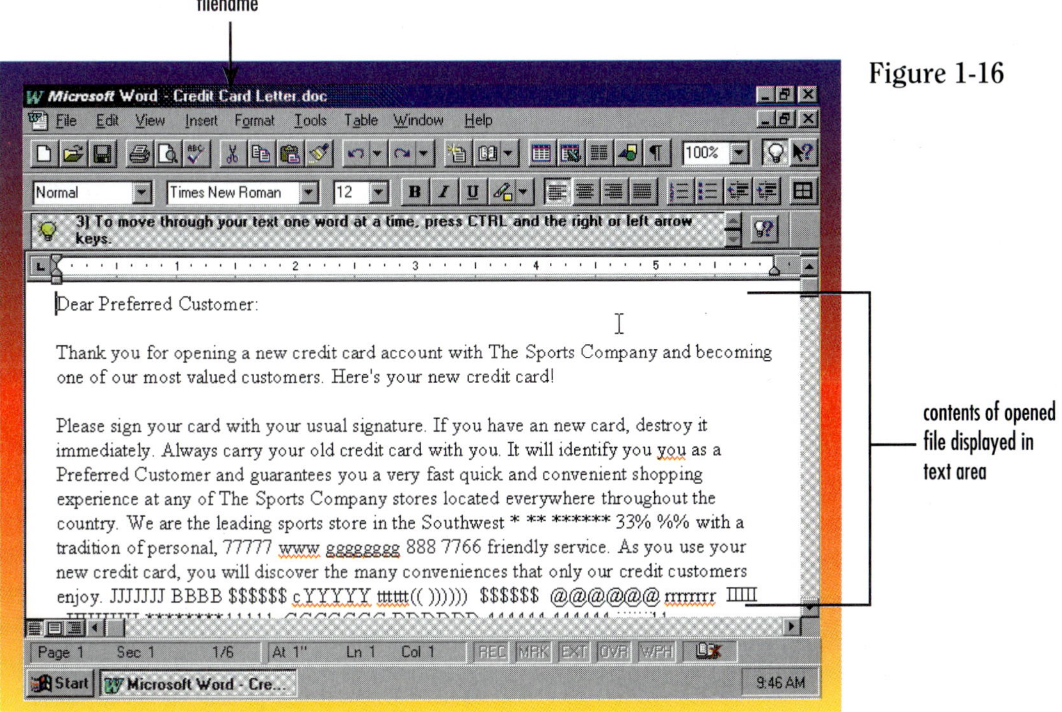

Figure 1-16

The file is loaded and displayed in the text area of the document window, and the filename is displayed in the Word title bar following the program name. The status bar briefly displays the filename and number of characters in the file. This file contains the rest of the first draft of the letter to new credit card customers. It contains many errors that need to be edited.

Note: If you end your lab session now, close the file and follow the instructions on page WP49 to exit the program. When you continue the lab at Part 2, load Word and open the Credit Card Letter file.

Part 2

Moving Through a Document

As you can see, the text area is not large enough to display the entire document. To bring additional text into view in the window, you can scroll the text using either the scroll bars or the keyboard. Again, both methods are useful, depending on what you are doing.

The scroll bar on the right border of the document window will scroll the document vertically, and the scroll bar on the bottom of the document window scrolls the document horizontally. Horizontal scrolling is useful when a large size of type makes the document so wide that it cannot be displayed on the screen. To view the end of the letter,

Refer to the Scroll Bars section of the Windows 95 Review for information on using this feature.

Scroll the window until the closing is displayed.

Your screen should be similar to Figure 1-17.

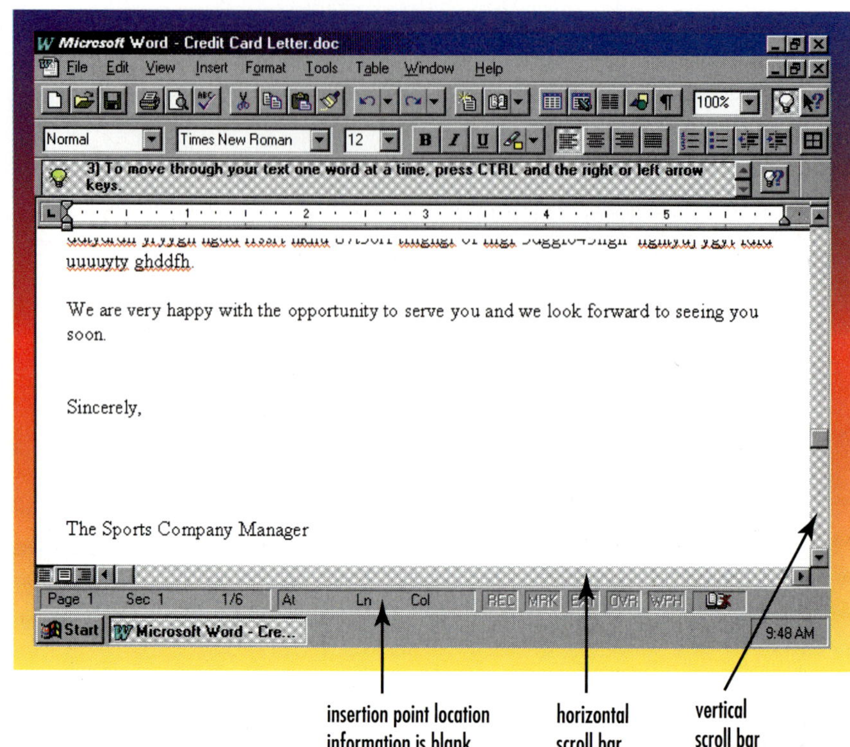

Figure 1-17

The text at the beginning of the letter has scrolled off the window, and the bottom of the letter is now displayed. Notice that the insertion point is no longer visible in the window, and the insertion point location information in the status bar is blank. To actually move the insertion point, you must click in a location in the window.

Move to: **"T" in "The" (last line of letter)**

The insertion point is now displayed in the document window.

You can also scroll the document using the keyboard. To return to the top of the letter,

The computer may beep to indicate you cannot move any farther in that direction.

Press: **↑ and hold down for several seconds until the insertion point is on the "D" in "Dear"**

While scrolling using the keyboard, the insertion point also moves.

You can also move quickly through a document in large jumps by moving a window or a page at a time, moving to a specific page, or moving to the end or beginning of the document.

To move up or down a full window of text on the document, use the Page Up or Page Down keys.

Press: Page Down **(2 times)**

The insertion point moved to the bottom line of the current window and then to the bottom line of the next window of text. You are still viewing page 1 of the document.

The insertion point can be moved to the top line of the previous page using the Alt + Ctrl + Page Up keys or to the top line of the next page using the Alt + Ctrl + Page Down key combination. To move to the top of the next page,

Press: Ctrl + Alt + Page Down

The insertion point is positioned on the first line of page 2. Notice that the status bar displays "Page 2."

To show where one page ends and another begins, Word displays a dotted line to mark the page break. To see this line,

Press: ↑

Your screen should be similar to Figure 1-18.

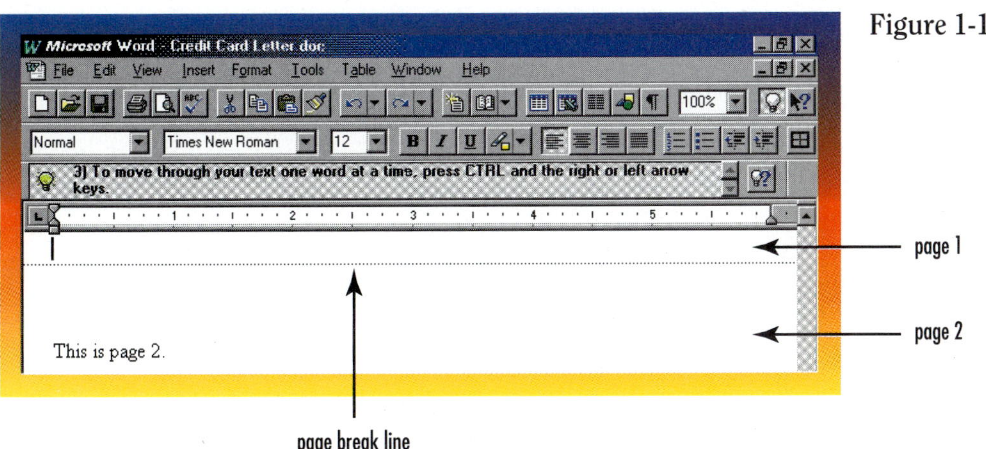

Figure 1-18

The insertion point is positioned on the last line of page 1, and the status bar displays Page 1. Word automatically enters a page break line in a document when the preceding page is full to show where a new page of text begins.

Clicking above or below the scroll box in the vertical scroll bar also moves window by window through the document. To move to the top of the document again,

Click above the scroll box four times.

Dragging the scroll box moves multiple windows forward or backward through the document. The location of the scroll box in the vertical scroll bar reflects your position in a document. When the scroll box is midway on this scroll bar, the displayed text is approximately in the middle of the document. As you drag the scroll box, the scroll tips indicator tells you the page that will be displayed in the window.

Click the vertical scroll box.

The scroll tips indicator tells you that page 1 is displayed in the window.

Drag the scroll box down the vertical scroll bar and release it when the scroll tip displays page 2.

Page 2 of the document is displayed in the window. You can confirm this by checking the status bar.

You can also move directly to a specific location in the document without scrolling through text you do not want to see using the Go To command in the Edit menu.

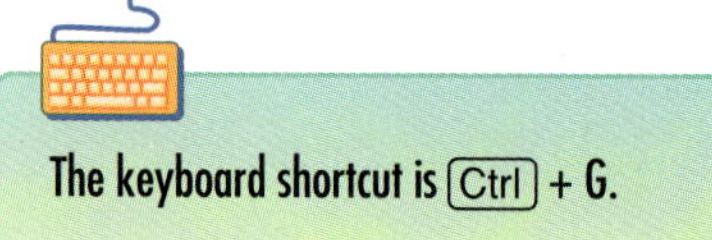

The keyboard shortcut is Ctrl + G.

Choose: **Edit/Go To**

The Go To dialog box shown in Figure 1-19 is displayed.

Figure 1-19

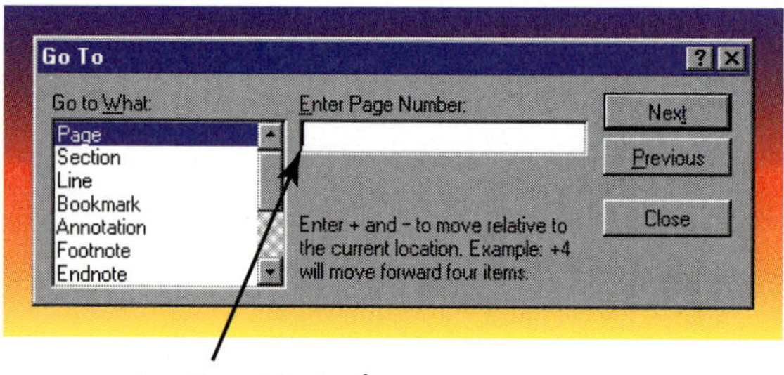

insertion point in text box

Refer to the Help section of the Windows 95 Review for information about this feature.

To learn more about the Go To command, use the What's This Help button to display Screen Tips about the list and text box.

By default, Word selects Page as the type of location to move to. To specify a page to move to, in the Enter Page Number text box,

Reminder: You can press ←Enter to choose the Go To command button.

Type: **5**
Choose: **Go To**

The insertion point is positioned on the first line of page 5.

The Go To dialog box stays open in case you want to move to a different location. To close the dialog box,

You could also click ☒ to close the dialog box.

Choose: **Close**

In a large document, using Go To is a lot quicker than pressing Alt + Ctrl + Page Down or using the scroll bar to move to a specific page.

The biggest jump the insertion point can make is to move to the beginning or end of a document. To move to the end of this document,

Press: Ctrl + End

Your screen should be similar to Figure 1-20.

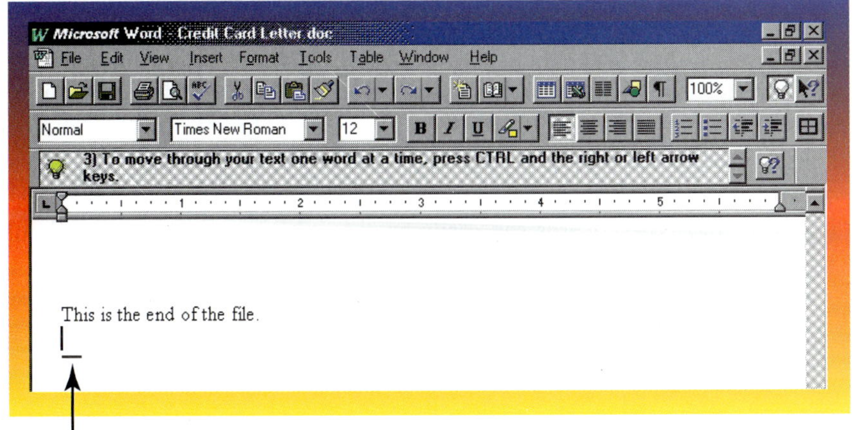

Figure 1-20

The insertion point should be positioned on a blank line on page 6 of this document. The status bar shows 6/6, indicating that you are viewing the sixth page of a six-page document. In addition, the end-of-file marker is displayed. This is the last line in the file.

To move quickly back to the beginning of the document,

Press: Ctrl + Home

You can also drag the scroll box to the bottom or top of the scroll bar to quickly move to the end or beginning of the document.

The insertion point should be positioned on the first line of page 1 of this document.

To review: The following features can be used to move through a document:

Mouse	Action
Click the new location	Positions insertion point
Click scroll arrow	Scrolls line by line or character by character in the direction of the scroll arrow
Click above/below scroll box	Scrolls the document window by window
Drag scroll box	Moves multiple windows up/down

Key	Action
→	One character to right
←	One character to left
↑	One line up
↓	One line down
Ctrl + →	One word to right
Ctrl + ←	One word to left
Home	Left end of line
End	Right end of line
Alt + Ctrl + Page Up	Top of previous page
Alt + Ctrl + Page Down	Top of next page
Page Up	Top of window
Page Down	Bottom of window
Ctrl + Home	Beginning of document
Ctrl + End	End of document
Edit/Go To	Moves to specified location

Inserting Characters

As you are using this file, the status bar may display the message "AutoSaving" and the hard drive may run. This indicates that the automatic save feature is on and the onscreen document is being saved as a backup file on the hard disk.

Now that you have learned how to move around the document, you are ready to learn how to correct errors in or edit the rest of the document.

After entering the text of a document, you should proofread it for accuracy and completeness. As you check the document, you see that the first sentence of the second paragraph is incorrect. It should read: "Please sign your new card in ink with your usual signature." The sentence is missing three words, "new," "in," and "ink." These words can easily be entered into the sentence without retyping it.

Text can be entered into a document in either Insert or Overtype mode. The default setting for Word is the Insert mode. As you type in **Insert mode**, new characters are inserted into the existing text. The text moves to the right to make space for the new characters, and the text on the line is reformatted as necessary.

To enter the word "new" before the word "card" in the first sentence,

Move to: **"c" in "card"**
Type: **new**
Press: Spacebar

Your screen should be similar to Figure 1-21.

Figure 1-21

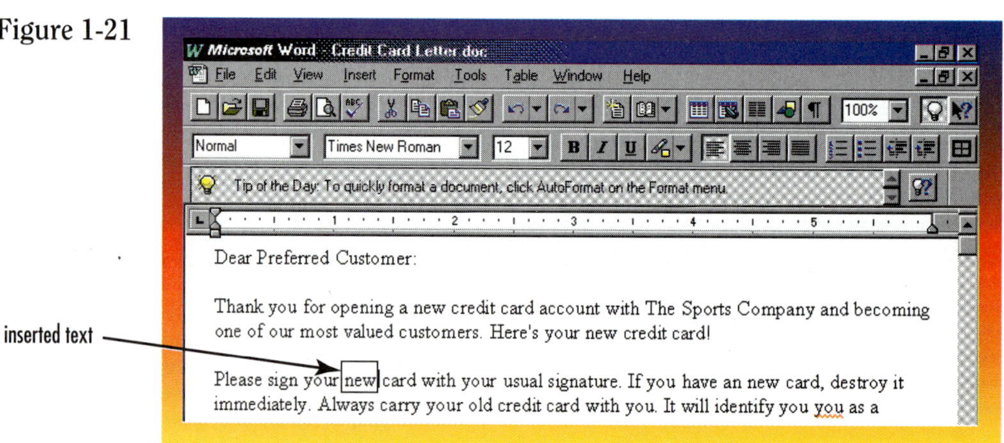

The word "new" has been entered into the sentence by moving everything to the right to make space as each letter is typed.

Continue to correct the sentence by entering the words "in ink" before the word "with."

In the second sentence, you notice that the word "new" should be "old."

Move to: **"n" of "new"**

You could delete this word and type in the new word, or you can use the Overtype mode to enter text in a document. When you use **Overtype mode**, new text types over the existing characters. Pressing [Insert] (the Insert key) changes the mode from Insert to Overtype.

> The OVR button is in the status bar.

Double-click: 

Notice the OVR status indicator button letters appears bright. This indicates the Overtype mode is on. See the following table for a description of the status bar mode indicators.

Indicator	Meaning
REC	Record macro feature is active.
MRK	Revision marking feature is on.
EXT	Extend selection mode is on.
OVR	Overtype mode is active.
WPH	Help for WordPerfect users is active.

To change the word "new" to "old,"

Type: old

Your screen should be similar to Figure 1-22.

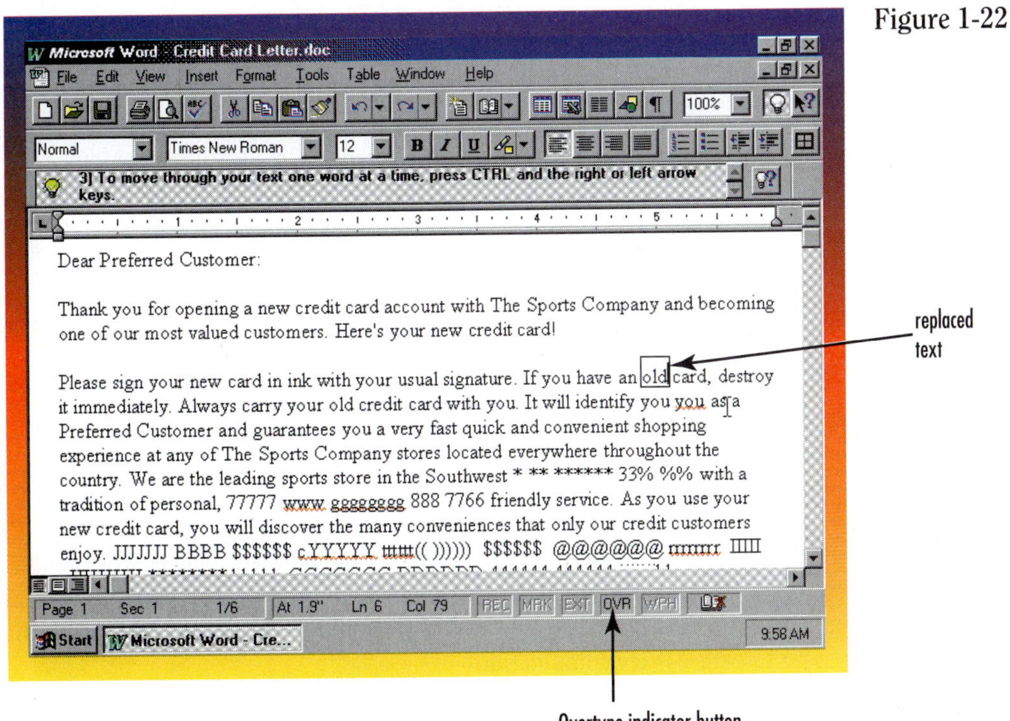

Figure 1-22

As each character was typed, the character (or space) under it was replaced with the character being typed.

Next, replace the word "old" in the third sentence of the paragraph with "new."

To turn off the Overtype mode,

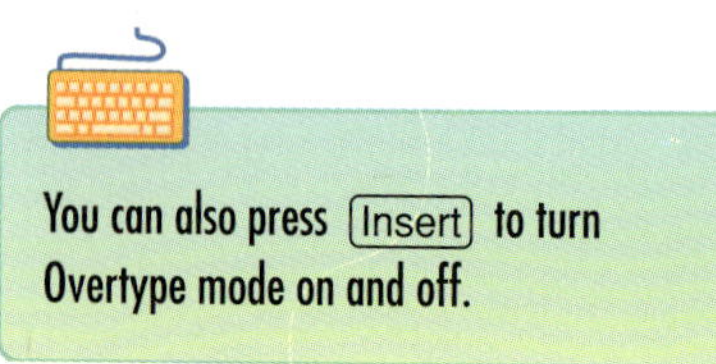

You can also press Insert to turn Overtype mode on and off.

Double-click: 

The OVR status indicator button letters are dimmed again.

Deleting Words

As you continue to read, you find that the fourth sentence of the second paragraph contains a repeated word and several unnecessary words. The repeated word "you" has been identified by the automatic spell checking feature.

To quickly delete a repeated word, display the Spelling Shortcut menu for the identified word "you" and select the Delete Repeated Word option.

Not all words you may want to delete, however, are repeated words. Other words may be unnecessary to the content. In the same sentence, the word "fast" is not needed because the following word "quick" conveys the same information. To delete the word "fast,"

Move to: "f" in "fast"
Press: Ctrl + Delete

Your screen should be similar to Figure 1-23.

Figure 1-23

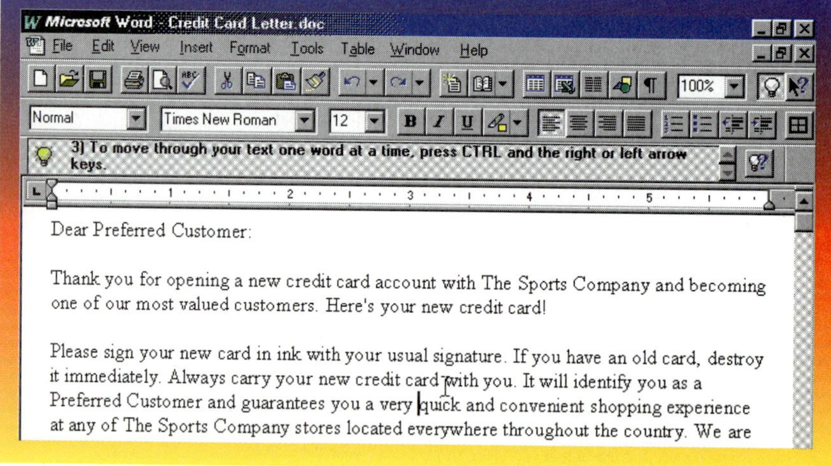

A "word" is any group of characters preceded and followed by blank space.

The word after the insertion point is deleted, including the blank space following the word. As you read the revised sentence, you also decide the word "very" is unnecessary. You can delete the word before the insertion point by using the Ctrl + Backspace key combination.

Press: 

The word "very" is deleted, including the blank space following the word.

In the same sentence, use either method to delete the word "everywhere."

If the insertion point is positioned in a word, rather than before or after a word, Ctrl + Delete removes the characters to the right of the insertion point to the end of the word, and Ctrl + Backspace removes the characters to the left of the insertion point to the beginning of the word.

Displaying Special Characters

As you continue to proof the letter, you decide that the second paragraph is too long and should be divided into two separate paragraphs. The new third paragraph should begin with the sentence "We are. . ."

Move to: **"W" in "We" (fourth line of second paragraph)**
Press: **←Enter (2 times)**

Each time you press ←Enter, Word inserts a special character called a **paragraph mark** at that location in the document. Other special character marks are also entered by the program to control the display of text onscreen. Word does not display these special characters because they clutter the screen, nor does it print them. However, there are times when you need to delete a special character, so you need to be able to see where it is.

Click: ¶ **Show/Hide**

The menu equivalent is Tools/Options/View/Spaces/Paragraph Marks

Your screen should be similar to Figure 1-24.

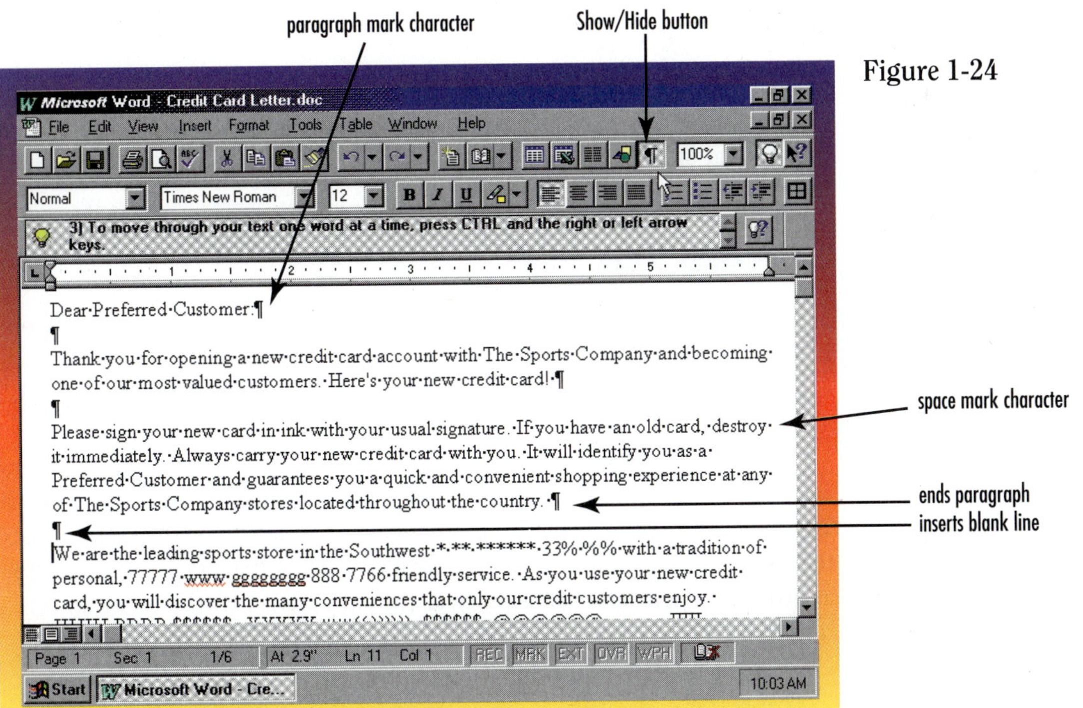

Figure 1-24

The document now displays the special characters. A paragraph mark character, ¶, is displayed wherever the ←Enter key was pressed. Between each word, a dot shows where the Spacebar was pressed. The ¶ character on the line above the insertion point represents the pressing of ←Enter that created the blank line between the second and third paragraphs. The ¶ character at the end of the line above that represents the pressing of ←Enter that ended the paragraph and moved the insertion point to the beginning of the next line.

To delete a special character, position the insertion point on the character, and press Delete, or position the insertion point to the right of the character and press Backspace. This works the same way as if you were deleting text in the document.

To delete the two ¶ characters that you just inserted,

Press: Backspace **(2 times)**

The blank line is removed and the text moves up to fill in the blank space at the end of the previous line and returns to a single paragraph.

To separate the text into two paragraphs again,

Press: ←Enter **(2 times)**

Two paragraph mark characters are inserted and the text moves down appropriately.

In many editing situations, it is necessary to display the special characters; however, this is not needed for simple text deletions. For normal entry of text, you will probably not want the characters displayed. To hide the characters,

Click: 

The screen returns to normal display. Now that you know how to turn this feature on and off, you can use it whenever you want when entering and editing text.

Selecting Text

Refer to the Selecting Text section of the Windows 95 Review for information on this feature.

You can also select text with the keyboard by holding down ⇧Shift while using the directional keys to expand the highlight in the direction indicated. Holding down Ctrl + ⇧Shift while using the → or ← keys selects word by word.

As you continue proofreading the letter, you see that the third paragraph contains several large areas of junk characters. To remove these characters, you could use Delete and Backspace to delete each character individually or Ctrl + Delete or Ctrl + Backspace to delete each "word." However, this is very slow.

Several characters, words, or lines of text can be deleted at once by first **selecting** the text and then pressing Delete. Text is selected by highlighting it. To select text, first move the insertion point to the beginning or end of the text to be selected. Then select the text by dragging using the mouse. You can select as little as a single letter or as much as the entire document.

The first area of characters to be removed follows the word "Southwest" in the first line of the third paragraph. To position the insertion point on the first character of the text to be selected,

Move to: **"*" (first line of third paragraph)**

Drag the mouse until the junk text is highlighted (including the space before the word "with").

Your screen should be similar to Figure 1-25.

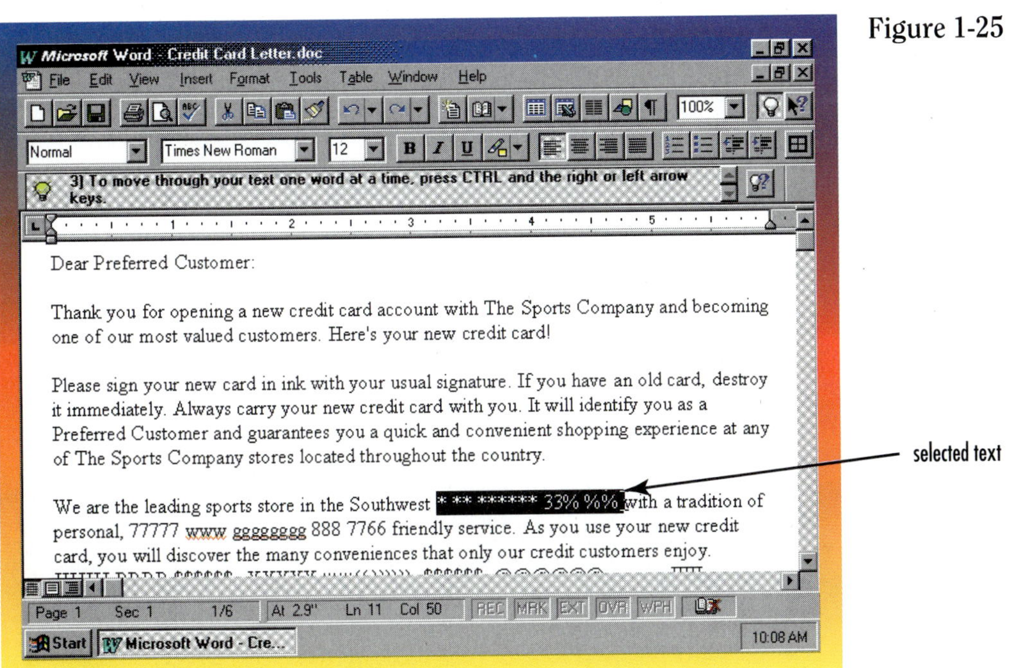

Figure 1-25

The highlight covers the junk text. Whenever text is highlighted, this indicates that it is selected. Text that is selected can then be modified using many different Word features. In this case, you want to remove the selected text. To do this,

Press: Delete

In a similar manner, select and delete the next set of junk characters following the word "personal," in this sentence.

Finally, as you continue reading, you see that the last two sentences of the paragraph consist entirely of junk characters.

Scroll the window to view the entire third paragraph.

You can also quickly select a standard block of text. A standard block consists of a sentence, paragraph, page, tabular column, rectangular portion of text,

> You can also select an area of text by clicking on the beginning of the text area and then holding down ⇧Shift while clicking on the end of the text area.

or the entire document. The following table summarizes the techniques used to select standard blocks.

To select a:	Procedure:
word	Double-click in the word.
sentence	Press Ctrl and click within the sentence.
line	Click in the selection bar next to the line.
multiple lines	Drag in the selection bar next to the lines.
paragraph	Triple-click on the paragraph or double-click in the selection bar next to the paragraph.
multiple paragraphs	Drag in the selection bar next to the paragraphs.
document	Triple-click in the selection bar or press Ctrl and click in the selection bar.

You will select and delete the first sentence of nonsense characters in this paragraph. To do so,

Move to: **anywhere in third sentence of third paragraph**
Press: Ctrl **and click**

Your screen should be similar to Figure 1-26.

Figure 1-26

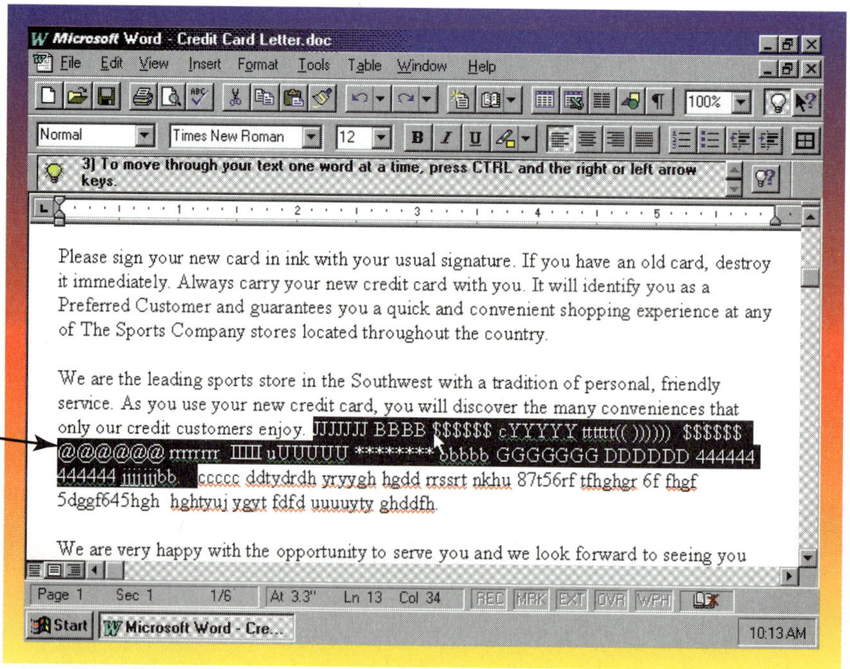

selected sentence

The entire sentence, including the space following the period, is selected. To delete this sentence,

Press: Delete

In a similar manner, delete the second sentence of junk characters.

Undoing Editing Changes

Finally, you are not too pleased with the last sentence of the letter and are considering removing it.

Double-click in the selection bar next to the last sentence of the letter to select it. Then delete the selection.

After thinking about this change, you decide the last sentence may not be so bad after all. As in all Windows 95 applications, you can use Undo to reverse your last action or command. Notice the Undo button includes a drop-down list button. Clicking this button displays a list of your most recent actions. When you select an action from the drop-down list, you also undo all actions above it in the list.

To restore the deleted text,

Click:  **Undo**

The menu equivalent is **E**dit/**U**ndo or Ctrl + Z.

Undo returns your last deletion and restores it to its original location in the text, regardless of the current insertion point location. Immediately after you Undo an action, the Redo command changes to a Redo Clear command. This allows you to restore your original revision.

Click:  **Redo**

The menu equivalent is **E**dit/Repeat or Ctrl + Y.

The sentence is removed again. To reverse this action again,

Click:  **Undo**

If the action cannot be reversed, Can't Undo is displayed in the Edit menu.

Now the letter should be correct.

Enter your name in the closing on the line above "The Sports Company Manager."

Finally, you also do not need the extra pages that were included in this document to demonstrate how to move around a document. To delete everything below the last line of the letter,

Move the insertion point to the line below the closing, "The Sports Company Manager."

To select and delete the text from the insertion point to the end of the file,

Press: ⇧Shift + Ctrl + End
Press: Delete

You could also scroll to the end of the file and hold ⇧Shift while clicking to select all text between the current insertion point location and the end location.

The status bar now shows that the insertion point is positioned on page 1 of a one-page document.

To review, the following editing keys have been covered:

Key	Action
Backspace	Deletes character to left of insertion point
Delete	Deletes character to right of insertion point
Ctrl + Backspace	Deletes word to left of insertion point
Ctrl + Delete	Deletes word to right of insertion point
←Enter	Ends a line and moves insertion point to next line or inserts a blank line
Edit/**U**ndo	Reverses your last action or command
Edit/**R**epeat	Repeats your last action or command

Documenting a File

Next, you will add your own documentation to the file properties. Each file automatically includes some basic summary information as well as property information. To see the information associated with this file,

Choose: File/Properties

If necessary, select the General tab.

The Properties tab dialog box shown in Figure 1-27 is displayed.

Figure 1-27

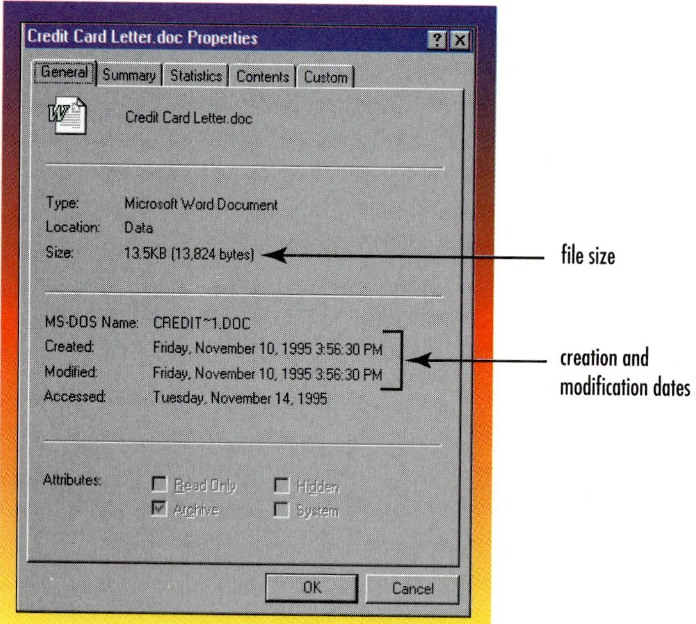

Each tab displays information about the document. The General tab displays basic information such as when the file was created and last modified, and the size of the file in bytes.

Select each tab and look at the recorded information.

To make it easier to find files, you can add your own properties to the file. Properties can include a descriptive title, the name of the author, the subject, and keywords that identify topics or other important information. The Summary tab is used to specify your own property information you want associated with the file.

Select the Summary tab.

The Summary Tab shown in Figure 1-28 should be displayed.

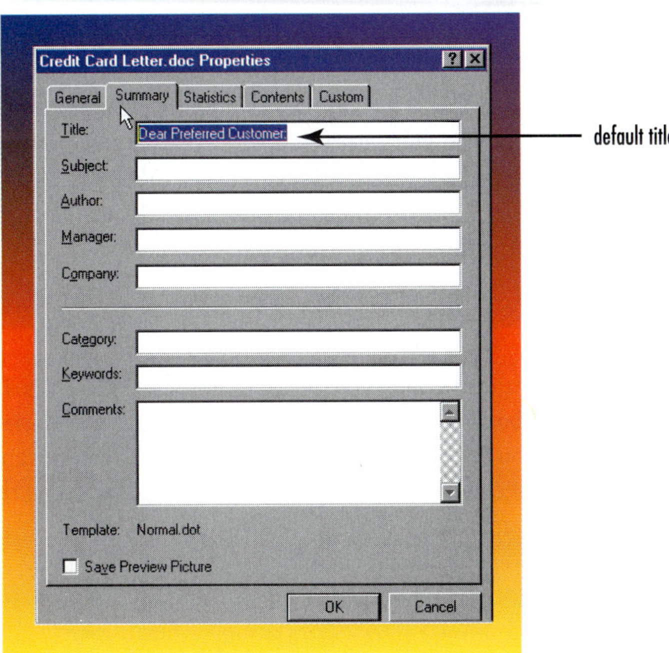

Figure 1-28

The Summary tab contains text boxes that allow you to enter a title, subject, author, keywords, and comments about the file. This information helps you locate the file you want to use as well as provides information about the objectives and use of the document. First, you will enter a descriptive title for the document. By default, Word displays the first few words from the document as the default title. To replace the default title with your own title,

The title can be different from the actual filename.

Select: **Dear Preferred Customer:**
Type: **Credit Card Letter**

Use Tab to both move and select the entry in a text box.

Next, you will enter a brief description of the document. In the Subject text box,

Type: **Letter to all new credit card holders**

To enter your name as the creator, in the Author text box,

Type: **[your name]**

The Author text box may be blank or show your school or some other name. Clear the existing contents first if necessary.

In the Company text box,

Type: **The Sports Company**

You could also add more detailed information in the Comments text box. To indicate that this is a first draft in the Comments text box,

Type: **First draft**
Choose: **OK**

Now, you are ready to save the changes you have made to the file on your data disk using the Save or Save As commands on the File menu. The Save command or the Save button will save the document using the same filename. The Save As command allows you to save the current file using a new filename. Because you may want to redo this lab and use the Credit Card Letter file again, you will save your edited version using a new filename.

Choose: **File/Save As**

The filename of the file you opened, Credit Card Letter, is displayed in the File Name text box of the Save As dialog box. To save the worksheet as Credit Card Letter 1, you can type the new filename entirely, or you can edit the existing name. In this case, it is easier to edit the filename by adding the number 1 to the end of the name.

If you do not clear the highlight the selected filename will be cleared and replaced with the new text as it is typed.

Click at the end of the filename (before the period) to both clear the highlight and place the insertion point at the end of the name.

Press: Spacebar
Type: **1**
Choose: **Save**

The new filename, Credit Card Letter 1, is displayed in the window title bar. The original document file is unchanged on your data disk.

Previewing a Document

Although you still plan to make several formatting changes to the document, you want to give a copy of the letter to the Regional Manager to get feedback regarding the content of the letter. Before printing, it is helpful to preview how the document will look when it is printed.

Concept 8: Preview Documents

To save time and unnecessary printing and paper waste, it is always a good idea to preview onscreen how your document will appear when printed. Previewing the document displays each page of your document in a reduced size so you can see the layout. You can also make last-minute editing and formatting changes while previewing and then print directly from the preview screen.

To preview the letter,

Click:  Print Preview

The menu equivalent is **File/Print Preview**.

Your screen should be similar to Figure 1-29.

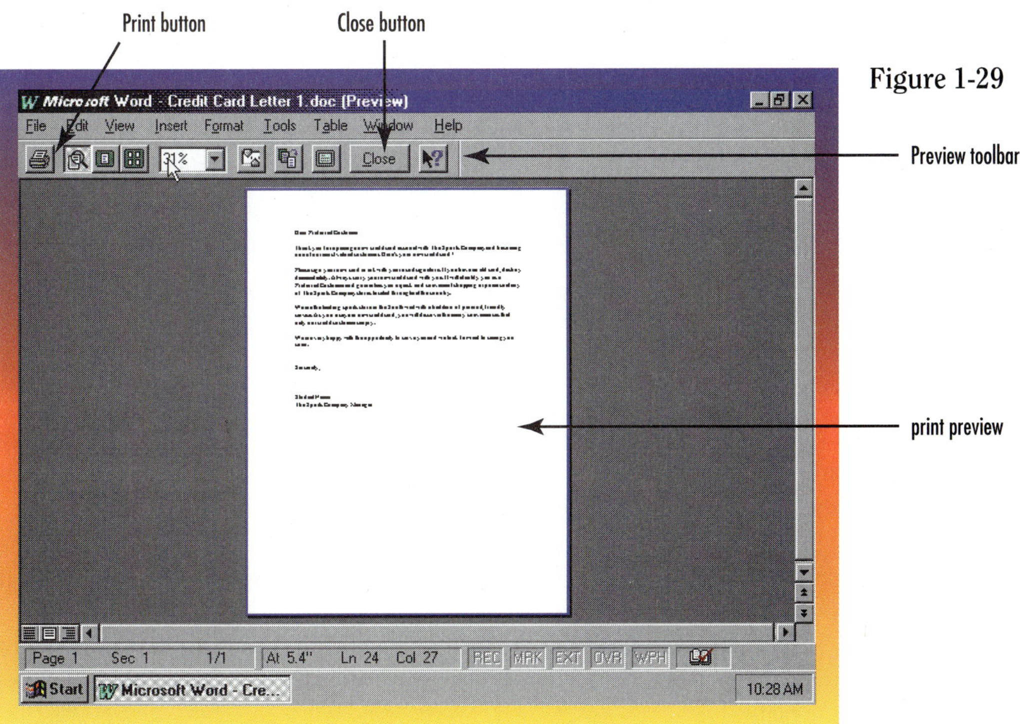

Figure 1-29

The Print Preview window displays a reduced view of how the current page will appear when printed. This view allows you to check your page layout before printing. The letter appears balanced within the left and right margins and does not appear to need any further modifications immediately.

This window also includes its own toolbar. You can print the letter directly from the Preview window using the Print button; however, this sends the document directly to the printer. Before printing, you need to check the print settings. To close the Print Preview window,

Click: 

Please consult your instructor for printing procedures that may differ from the following directions.

The keyboard shortcut for the Print command is Ctrl + P.

Printing a Document

The Print button on the Standard toolbar will also send the document directly to the printer. To check the print settings, you need to use the Print command on the File menu.

If necessary, make sure your printer is on and ready to print.

Choose: File/Print

The Print dialog box shown in Figure 1-30 is displayed.

Figure 1-30

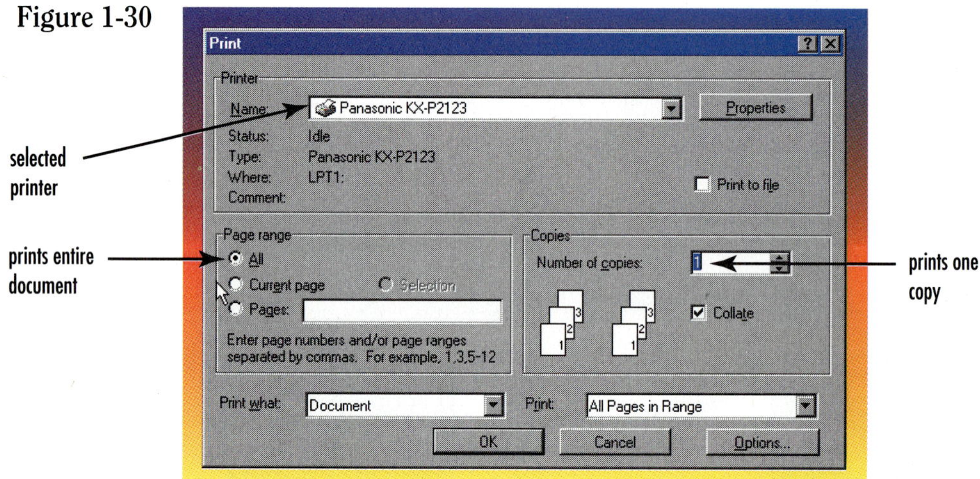

From the Print dialog box, you need to specify the printer you will be using and the document settings. The printer that is currently selected is displayed in the Name drop-down list box in the Printer section of the dialog box.

If you need to change the selected printer to another printer, open the Name drop-down list box and select the appropriate printer (your instructor will tell you which printer to select).

The Page Range area of the Print dialog box lets you specify how much of the document you want printed. The range options are described in the following table:

Option	Action
All	Prints the entire document
Current page	Prints selected page or the page the insertion point is on
Pages	Prints pages you specify by typing page number in text box
Selection	Prints selected text only

The default range setting, All, is the correct setting.

The other two areas of the dialog box are used to specify the number of copies and what parts of the document you want printed. The default setting of one copy of the document is acceptable.

To begin printing using the settings in the Print dialog box,

Choose: **OK**

Your printer should be printing out the current page of the document file. The printed copy of the credit card letter should be similar to Figure 1-5, shown at the beginning of the lab.

Note: Your printed copy may not match exactly if the printer you selected uses a different font size from the one used to display the document on the screen. You will learn about fonts in the next lab.

Exiting Word

Before exiting, you will turn off the TipWizard toolbar. The button is also used to hide the TipWizard toolbar when it is displayed.

If TipWizard is displayed when you exit the program, it will be displayed when the program is reloaded.

Click: 

The Exit command on the File menu is used to quit the Word program. Alternatively, you can click the Close button in the application window title bar.

The keyboard shortcut for the Exit command is Alt + F4.

Click: 

The Windows 95 desktop is visible again and the taskbar no longer displays the Word button.

To avoid losing data, always exit Word using the Exit command or the Close button.

LAB REVIEW

Key Terms

cursor (WP12)
custom dictionary (WP20)
default (WP16)
edit (WP15)
end-of-file marker (WP12)
formatting (WP15)
Formatting toolbar (WP11)
Insert mode (WP36)
insertion point (WP12)
main dictionary (WP20)
Overtype mode (WP37)
paragraph mark (WP39)
ruler (WP12)
selecting (WP40)
selection bar (WP24)
Standard toolbar (WP11)
status bar (WP12)
template (WP16)
text area (WP12)
wizard (WP13)
word wrap (WP23)

Command Summary

Command	Shortcut Key	Button	Action
File/New	Ctrl + N		Opens new file
File/Open	Ctrl + O		Opens selected file
File/Close			Closes file
File/Save	Ctrl + S		Saves file using same filename
File/Save As			Saves file using a new filename
File/Properties			Shows the properties of the active document
File/Print Preview			Displays document as it will appear when printed
File/Print	Ctrl + P		Prints file using selected print settings
File/Exit	Alt + F4		Exits Word program
Edit/Undo	Ctrl + Z		Restores last editing change
Edit/Redo or Repeat	Ctrl + Y		Restores last Undo or repeats last command or action
Edit/Go To	Ctrl + G		Moves insertion point to specified location in document
View/Toolbars			Displays or hides selected toolbars
Tools/Options/View/Spaces/Paragraph Marks			Displays or hides nonprinting characters
Help/Microsoft /Word Help Topics	F1		Displays Help Topics dialog box

Matching

1. [Print Preview button]	______	**a.** new text writes over existing text
2. document template	______	**b.** deletes word to the right of the insertion point
3. Overtype	______	**c.** moves to the top of the document
4. Ctrl + Backspace	______	**d.** constant adjustment of text to fill in extra space in a line without exceeding the margin setting
5. .DOC	______	**e.** a feature that shows you how to complete a task
6. Ctrl + Home	______	**f.** displays the Print Preview window
7. wizard	______	**g.** a predesigned document that is used as a pattern to create many common types of documents
8. [Save button]	______	**h.** deletes word to left of insertion point
9. word wrap	______	**i.** Word document file extension
10. Ctrl + Delete	______	**j.** Saves a document using the same filename

Fill-In Questions

1. Complete the following statements by filling in the blanks with the correct terms.

a. The ____________________ occupies the largest area of the Word screen.

b. A(n) __________________________ is a predesigned document.

c. Name the first three steps in developing a document: ________________________, ________________________, ________________________.

d. Text can be entered in a document in either the _______________ or _______________ mode.

e. The ______________ key erases the character to the right of the insertion point.

f. The automatic _____________________ feature makes entering text in a document faster than typing on a typewriter.

g. The Word document filename extension is _____________________ .

h. The ______________ displays a tip about a more efficient or alternative method directly related to the procedure you are trying to perform.

i. Word inserts hidden _______________ into a document to control the display of text.

j. The ______________ feature automatically identifies and corrects certain types of errors.

2. In the following Word screen, important elements are identified by letters. Enter the correct term for each screen element in the space provided.

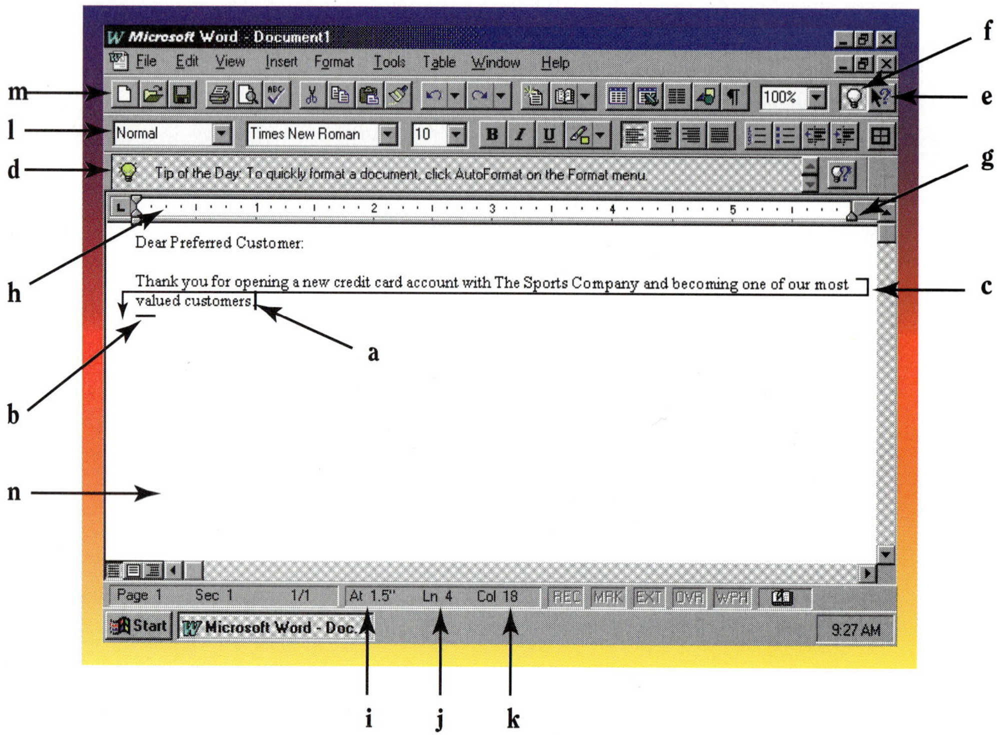

a. ______________________

b. ______________________

c. ______________________

d. ______________________

e. ______________________

f. ______________________

g. ______________________

h. ______________________

i. ______________________

j. ______________________

k. ______________________

l. ______________________

m. ______________________

n. ______________________

3. The following screen identifies several errors and changes that need to be made to the document. From the list below, match the letter to the procedure that will make the change.

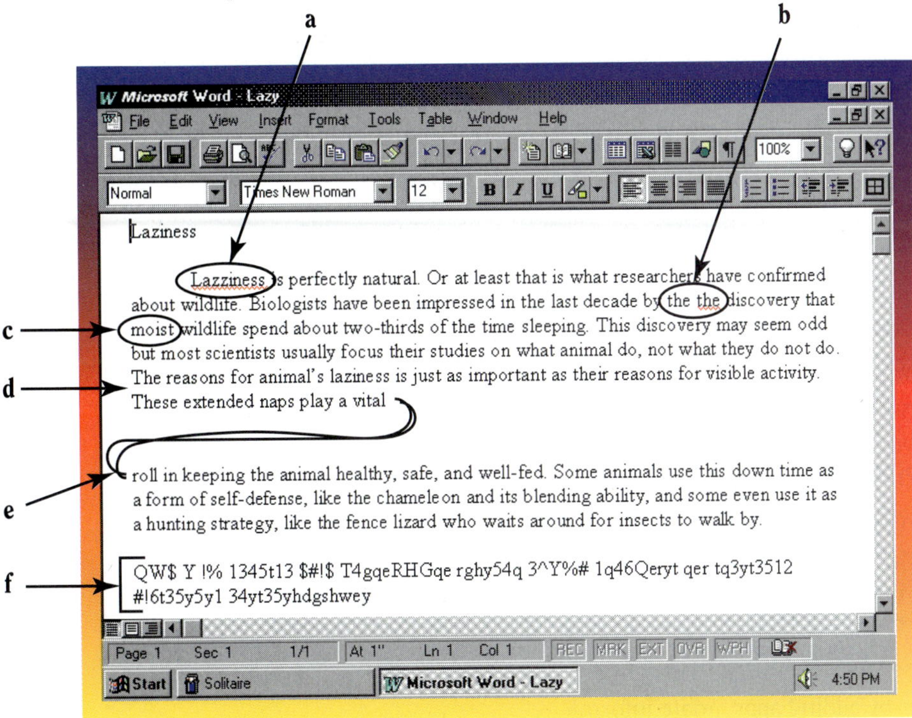

a) fix spelling	_____	Move to the letter "I" and press Delete
b) remove second "the"	_____	Display the Spelling Shortcut menu and select the correct spelling
c) Change moist to "most"	_____	Move to the letter "T" and press ←Enter twice
d) create new paragraph	_____	Triple-click in selection bar and press Delete
e) combine with previous paragraph	_____	Display the Spelling Shortcut menu and select Delete Repeated Word
f) delete paragraph	_____	Move to the letter "r" and press Backspace three times

Discussion Questions

1. Discuss several uses you may have for a word processor. Then explain the steps you would follow to create a document.

2. Discuss how the AutoCorrect and Auto Spellcheck features help you as you type. What types of corrections does the AutoCorrect feature make?

3. Discuss how word wrap works. What happens when text is added? What happens when text is removed?

4. Discuss three ways you can select text. Discuss when it would be appropriate to use the different methods.

5. Describe how the Undo and Redo features work. What are some advantages of these features?

Hands-On Practice Exercises

Step by Step

Rating System

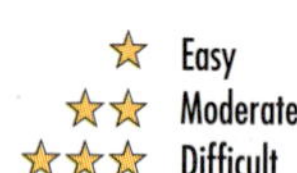

1. In this problem you will use the commands and features you learned in the lab to correct a document.

- **a.** Open the file CORRECTIONS on your data disk. Follow the directions to edit the file, and reveal a saying found on the wall of a fix-it shop.
- **b.** When you are finished, enter your name and the current date below the document. Save the file with the same name. Preview and print the document.
- **c.** Delete the lines of instructions to reveal only the lines of the saying, your name, and the date. Combine the first four lines to form one paragraph. Save the document as THREE KINDS OF JOBS on your data disk. Preview and print the saying.
- **d.** Document the file by adding appropriate information to the Summary tab of the Properties dialog box.

2. The mouse is a standard hardware device that makes performing many tasks much quicker. In this problem, you will edit a document about using a mouse.

- **a.** Open the file MOUSE TERMS on your data disk. Use the editing techniques you learned in Lab 1 to correct the errors in the document.
- **b.** Insert your name and current date below the document.
- **c.** Document the file by adding appropriate information to the Summary tab of the Properties dialog box. Save the document as MOUSE TERMS 1. Preview and print the document.

You will continue this exercise as Practice Exercise 1 in Lab 2.

3. Universal Industries has banned smoking in all buildings. Mr. Biggs, the CEO, has sent a memo informing employees of this restriction.

- **a.** Create the memo as shown below, and correct your spelling as you type. Press Tab after you type colons (:) in the To, From, Date, and RE lines. This will cause information following colons to line up evenly.

To:	[Student's Name]
From:	Mr. Biggs
Date:	[Current Date]
RE:	No Smoking Policy

Effective next Monday, smoking will be banned in all buildings. Ashtrays will be placed outside each door, and smoking material must be extinguished before you enter.

Thank you for your cooperation in this matter.

JBB/xxx

- **b.** Document the file by adding appropriate information to the Summary tab of the Properties dialog box. Save the document as NO SMOKING MEMO on your data disk. Preview then print the memo.

You will complete this exercise as Practice Exercise 3 in Lab 3.

4. You are in the process of compiling your grandmother's cookie recipes. You are going to pass the recipes on to several family members and friends who have requested them over the years. Following is a letter that you will enclose with the recipes. You will begin the cookie recipes in the next Practice Exercise, and continue to format and compile them in subsequent labs.

a. Enter the letter as shown below, and correct your spelling as you type.

[Student's Name]
[Street Address]
[City, State, Zip Code]
[Current Date]

Dear Friends and Family:

Enclosed, as promised, is a copy of Grandma Gertie's famous cookie recipes. We have all enjoyed them over the years, and it has been my pleasure to compile the recipes so you can continue to enjoy them for years to come.

For my next project, I would like to compile recipes from our own generation and pass them along, so we can pass them down. If you have any recipes that you would like to share with the rest of us, please send them to me at the above address.

Sincerely,

[Student's Name]

b. Document the file by adding appropriate information to the Summary tab of the Properties dialog box. Save the document as COOKIE LETTER on your data disk. Preview then print the letter.

You will complete this exercise as Practice Exercise 1 in Lab 4.

5. Here is the first of the cookie recipes that will be included in the collection referred to in the previous exercise.

a. Enter the recipe for Potato Chip Cookies as shown below. Correct your spelling as you type.

Potato Chip Cookies

Potato chips give these cookies a crunchy texture and eliminate the need for baking soda.

Ingredients:
2 sticks of butter (softened)
1/2 c. dark brown sugar (firmly packed)
1/2 c. crushed potato chips
1 tsp. vanilla extract
1/2 c. sifted flour
Confectioner's sugar

Directions:
Cream the butter and brown sugar together.
Add vanilla, chips, and nuts.
Gradually add the flour. Mix thoroughly.
Cover and chill the dough for at least 1 hour.
Roll dough into 1" balls, and roll in confectioner's sugar.
Place 1" apart on greased cookie sheet.
Bake in 350 degree oven for 12–15 minutes.
This recipe makes about 3-1/2 dozen cookies.

b. Insert a blank line between the crushed potato chips and the vanilla extract in the Ingredients section. Add "1/2 c. chopped pecans" to the list of ingredients.

c. Enter your name and the current date below the recipe.

d. Document the file by adding appropriate information to the Summary tab of the Properties dialog box. Save the document as POTATO CHIP COOKIES on your data disk. Preview then print the recipe.

You will continue to add more recipes to your collection in Practice Exercise 3 in Lab 2.

On Your Own

6. You are about to open a bed and breakfast in the Pocono Mountains. You are going to advertise the B&B in a local travel guide. Type the following information to create the first draft of the ad.

> Pocono Mountain Retreat
> 124 Mountain Laurel Trail
> Pocono Manor, PA 18349
>
> Phone: 1-717-839-5555
> Host: [Student's Name]
>
> Number of Rooms: 4
> Number of private baths: 1
> Maximum number sharing baths: 4
> Double rate for shared bath: $85.00
> Double rate for private bath: $95.00
> Single rate for shared bath: $65.00
> Double rate for shared bath: $75.00
> Open: All year
> Breakfast: Continental
> Children: Welcome, over 12
> Smoking: No
> Social Drinking: Permitted
>
> Located in the heart of the Poconos is this rustic country inn where you can choose to indulge yourself in the quiet beauty of the immediate surroundings or take advantage of the numerous activities at nearby resorts, lakes, and parks.
>
> In the winter, shuttle busses will transport you to the Jack Frost and Big Boulder ski resorts. We have trails for cross country skiing right on the property, and we will take you for a ride in our horse-drawn sleigh. In the summer, you can be whisked away to beautiful Lake Wallenpaupack for swimming and boating. The fall foliage is beyond compare, and you can hike our nature trails and take in the breathtaking scenery at this, or any time of year.
>
> In the evenings, you can relax in front of a cozy fire or take advantage of the swinging night life in the Poconos. The choice is yours!
>
> We have literature concerning all areas of interest in the Poconos. You can design your own custom tour, and Ed, our resident guide, will provide the transportation.
>
> Be sure to call well in advance for reservations during the winter and summer months.

Insert the text "Pets: No" below the "Breakfast: Continental" and "Children: Welcome, over 12".

Insert the current date below the ad.

Document the file by adding appropriate information to the Summary tab of the Properties dialog box. Save the document as B&B AD on your data disk. Print the ad.

You will continue this exercise as Practice Exercise 4 in Lab 2.

7. Toward the end of each set of Practice Exercises in each lab, you can complete a problem that will help you prepare for a job interview. This lab's exercise helps you create a cover letter. In Lab 2, you can create a list of tips on how to prepare for an interview. In Lab 3, you can create a document that tells what should be included in a resume and cover letter. In Lab 4, you merge the cover letter and create the resume.

Much of the information contained in these exercises was extracted from The Work Book by Barbara N. Price, Ph.D., Director of Career Planning and Placement, Luzerne County Community College, Nanticoke, PA.

Use the format below as a guide to creating a cover letter.

> [Student's Street Address]
> [City, State, Zip Code]
>
> Date of Writing

Mr. John Doe
Job Title
Company
Street Address
City, State, Zip Code

Dear Mr. Doe:

Tell why you are writing; name the position, field, or general occupational area which you are asking about; if you know of a specific job opening, mention it. When responding to an advertisement, be sure to include the name and date of the publication in which it was placed. If referred by a contact person, mention the fact and include the person's name in your opening sentence.

Mention one or two qualifications you think would be of greatest interest to the employer, slanting your remarks to his/her point of view. Tell why you are particularly interested in his/her company, location, or type of work. If you have had related experience, or specialized training, be sure to point it out.

Refer the reader to the enclosed resume, application, or the medium which gives information concerning your qualifications. Close by making specific request for an interview. Make sure your closing is not vague, but makes a specific action from the reader likely.

Sincerely,

(Your handwritten signature)

[Student's Name]

ENCL.

Document the file by adding appropriate information to the Summary tab of the Properties dialog box. Save the document as COVER LETTER on your data disk. Print the document.

You will continue this exercise as Practice Exercise 7 in Lab 4.

1 Creating and Editing a Document

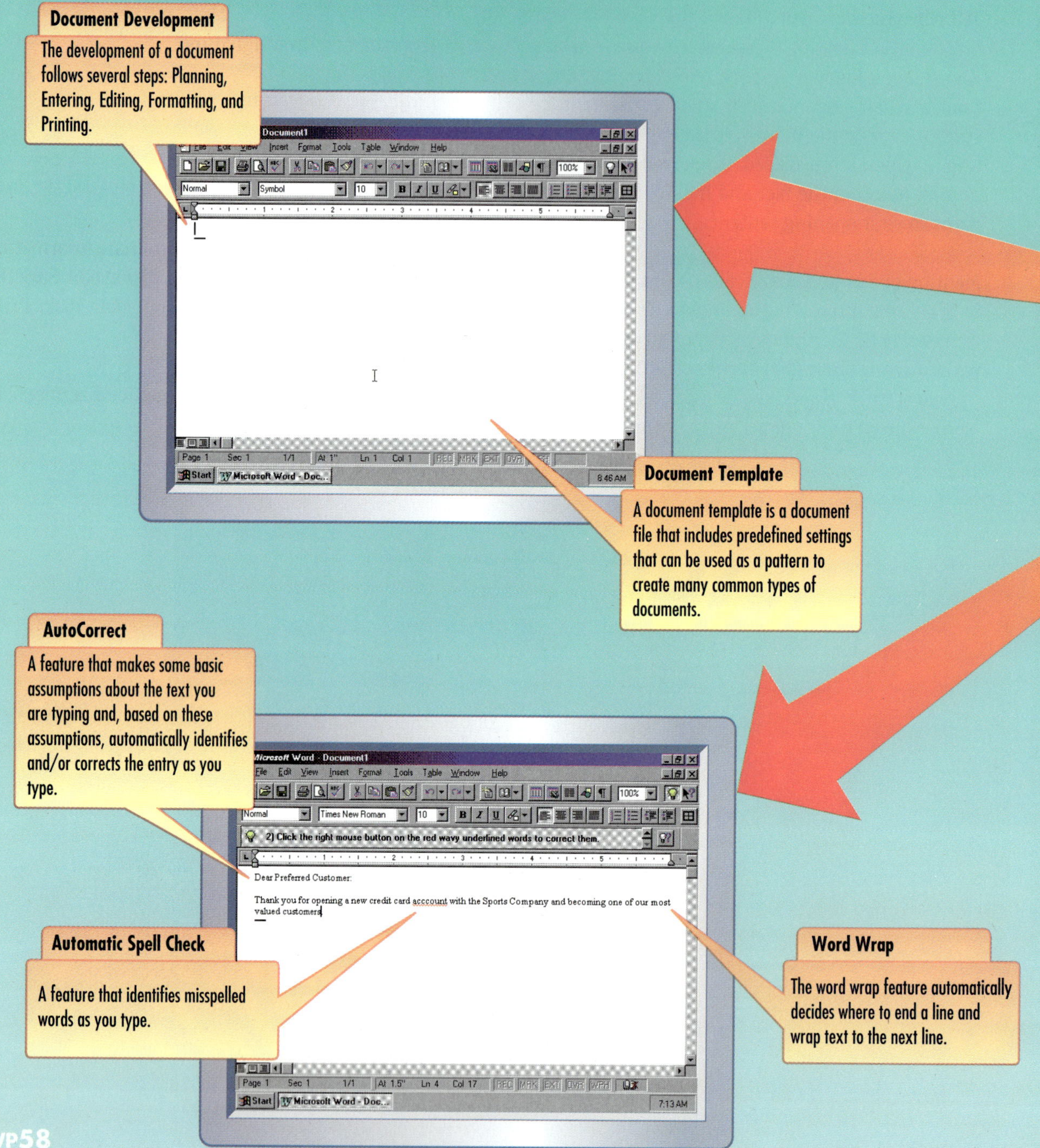
Document Development
The development of a document follows several steps: Planning, Entering, Editing, Formatting, and Printing.
Document Template
A document template is a document file that includes predefined settings that can be used as a pattern to create many common types of documents.
AutoCorrect
A feature that makes some basic assumptions about the text you are typing and, based on these assumptions, automatically identifies and/or corrects the entry as you type.
Automatic Spell Check
A feature that identifies misspelled words as you type.
Word Wrap
The word wrap feature automatically decides where to end a line and wrap text to the next line.
Microsoft Word - Document1
2) Click the right mouse button on the red wavy underlined words to correct them.
Dear Preferred Customer:
Thank you for opening a new credit card acccount with the Sports Company and becoming one of our most valued customers

Concepts

- Document Development
- Document Template
- AutoCorrect
- Automatic Spell Check
- Word Wrap
- Save Files
- Word Filenames
- Preview Documents

Save Files

A permanent copy of your onscreen document is created by saving the document as a file on a disk.

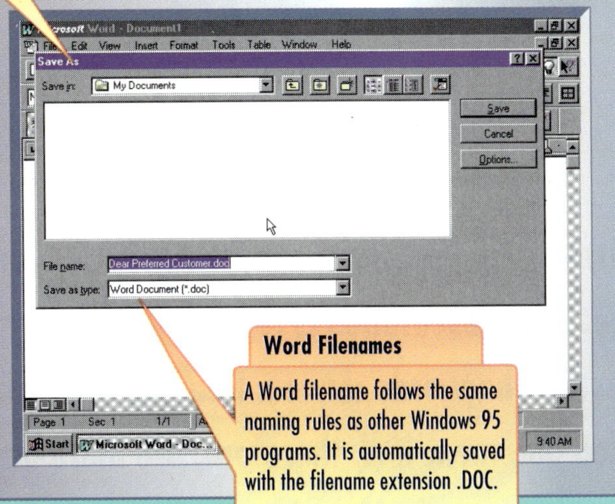

Word Filenames

A Word filename follows the same naming rules as other Windows 95 programs. It is automatically saved with the filename extension .DOC.

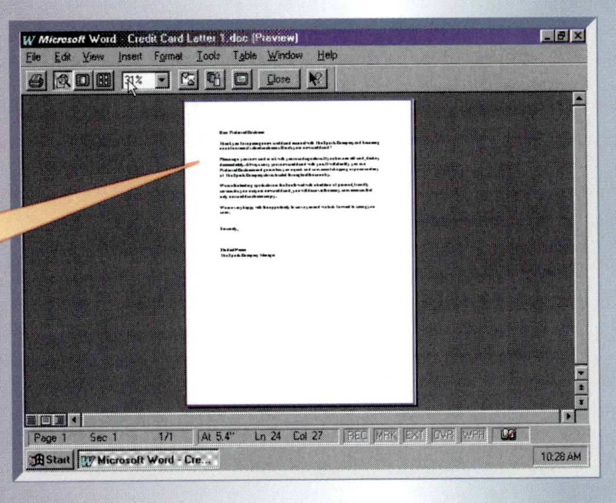

Preview Documents

A feature that displays each page of your document in reduced size so you can see its layout.

Formatting a Document

2

Written communication is more than just words on a page. The presentation is just as important as the message the words convey. Readers are drawn to a well-styled document and, therefore, are more inclined to read it. So, to leave the right impression on the person you are communicating with, add a little personal style to your document.

COMPETENCIES

After completing this lab, you will know how to:

1. **Spell-check a document.**
2. **Open a second document window.**
3. **Copy text between documents.**
4. **Move text.**
5. **Replace selected text.**
6. **Use the Thesaurus.**
7. **Find and replace text.**
8. **Use the date command.**
9. **Set margins.**
10. **Indent paragraphs.**
11. **Create an itemized list.**
12. **Bold, italicize, and underline text.**
13. **Set paragraph alignment.**

In this lab, you will use some of the formatting features included in Word 7.0 to stylize or format the credit card letter. You will see how using these features greatly improves the appearance and design of the letter. The result is that the letter not only looks better—it also conveys the message more clearly.

Concept Overview

The following concepts will be introduced in this lab:

1. Multiple Document Windows	Opening multiple document windows lets you switch easily between documents to cut, copy, and paste, as well as to see reference information in other documents.
2. Thesaurus	A thesaurus is a reference tool that contains synonyms, antonyms, and related words for commonly used words. Use the Thesaurus to add interest and variety to your writing.
3. Find and Replace	To make editing easier, you can use the Find and Replace feature to find a word in a document and automatically replace it with another word.
4. Margins	The margin is the distance from the text to the edge of the paper. Specifying different margin settings for a document changes the appearance of the document on the printed page.
5. Document Views	There are six different ways that you can view a document. Each view offers different features for creating and editing your documents.
6. Indents	To help your reader find information quickly, you can indent paragraphs of similar content. Indenting paragraphs sets them off from the rest of the document.
7. Bulleted and Numbered Lists	Use bulleted or numbered lists to organize information and make the message clear and easy to read.
8. Text Formats	Different text formats can be applied to selections to add emphasis or interest to a document.
9. Paragraph Alignment	To give your documents more visual interest, you can change the alignment of paragraphs. Alignment is how text is positioned on a line between the margins or indents.

CASE STUDY

After editing the rough draft of the credit card letter, you showed it to The Sports Company regional manager. The manager has made several suggestions on how to improve the letter's style and appearance (shown on the next page in the marked-up copy). In addition, the manager wants the letter to include some additional information about The Sports Company newsletter and a first purchase discount when customers use their new credit card. You will copy the new information provided by the manager into the credit card letter, and then add the style and formatting changes to the letter.

ADD DATE

Dear Preferred Customer:

INDENT PARAGRAPHS

Thank you for opening a new credit card account with The Sports Company and becoming one of our most valued customers. Here's your new credit card!

ADD "Sports Company"

MAKE 3 SENTENCES INTO BULLETED LIST

Please sign your new card in ink with your usual signature. If you have an old card, destroy it immediately. Always carry your new credit card with you. It will identify you as a Preferred Customer and guarantees you a quick and convenient shopping experience at any of The Sports Company stores located throughout the country.

REWORD

ADD 2 NEW PARAGRAPHS FROM THE FILE NEW PARAGRAPHS

We are the leading sports store in the Southwest with a tradition of personal, friendly service. As you use your new credit card, you will discover the many conveniences that only our credit customers enjoy.

JUSTIFY

We are very happy with the opportunity to serve you and we look forward to seeing you soon.

FIND A BETTER WORD

INDENT TEXT

Sincerely,

Student Name
The Sports Company Manager

ADD CUSTOMER SERVICE TELEPHONE NUMBER

Part 1

Spell-Checking a Document

Load Word 7.0. Put your data disk in drive A (or the appropriate drive for your system).

The Sports Company regional manager hastily entered into a new file the two paragraphs about the newsletter and discount to be incorporated into the credit card letter.

To see the paragraphs, open the file New Paragraphs.

The two paragraphs are displayed in a document window. As you are reading the document, you notice a typing error on the first line: "Sprots" should be "Sports." As you learned in Lab 1, Word automatically spell-checks as you type. When you first open a document, a spelling-check is automatically performed and Word identifies the misspelled words. To correct the misspelled words, you can use the Shortcut menu to correct each individual word, as you learned in

Lab 1. However, in many cases you may find that it's more efficient to wait until you are finished writing before you correct any spelling errors. Rather than continually breaking your train of thought to correct spelling errors as you type, you can use the **Spelling tool** to correct all the words in the document at once.

Click: Spelling

The menu equivalent is Tools/Spelling and the keyboard shortcut is F7.

Your screen should be similar to Figure 2-1.

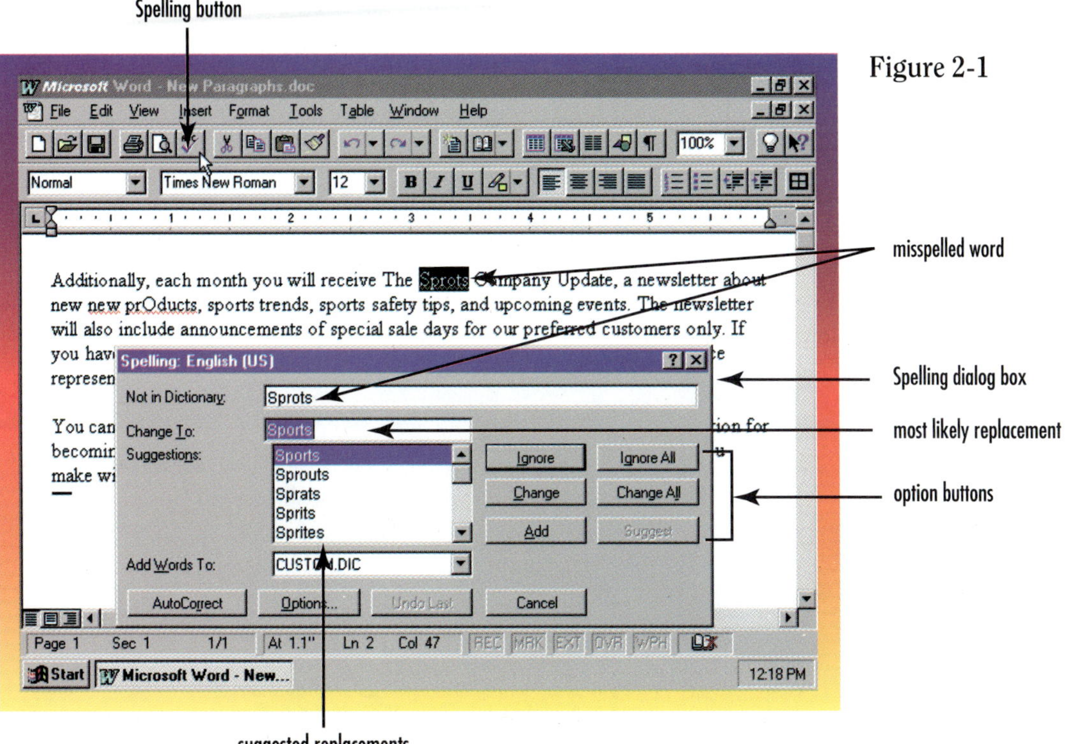

Figure 2-1

The Spelling dialog box is displayed and the Spelling tool has immediately located the first word that may be misspelled. It displays the word "Sprots" in the Not in Dictionary text box and highlights it in the document.

The Change To text box displays the word the Spelling tool has located in the dictionary that most closely matches the misspelled word. The Suggestions list box displays other words that are similar to the misspelled word. The first word is highlighted and is the word that is displayed in the Change To text box. Sometimes the Spelling tool does not display any suggested replacements because it cannot locate any words in its dictionary that are similar in spelling. If there are no suggestions, the Change To text box displays the word that is highlighted in the text.

To tell the Spelling tool what to do, you need to choose from the six option buttons. They have the following effects:

Button	Action
Ignore	Accepts word as correct for this occurrence only.
Ignore All	Accepts word as correct throughout the spelling-check of the document.
Change/Delete	Replaces word with the word in the Change To text box. Deletes duplicate word.
Change All	Replaces same word throughout the document with the word in the Change To text box.
Add	Adds word to the custom dictionary. Spelling will always accept an added word as correct.
Suggest	Displays suggested replacement words if Suggest option is off.

In addition, the dialog box includes four command buttons. They have the following effects:

Button	Action
AutoCorrect	Adds word to the AutoCorrect list so Word can correct misspellings of it automatically as you type.
Options	Allows you to specify rules that Word uses to check spelling.
Undo Last	Reverses most recent actions made during spelling check.
Close	Closes Spelling dialog box without saving any changes made.

To change the spelling of the word to one of the suggested spellings, highlight the correct word in the list and then choose Change. If there were no suggested replacements, and you did not want to use any of the option buttons, you could edit the word yourself by typing the correction in the Change To text box. Because "Sports" is already highlighted and is the correct replacement,

You can also press ←Enter or double-click on the word with the correct spelling in the Suggestions list to both select it and choose Change.

Choose: Change

The Spelling tool replaces the misspelled word with the selected suggested replacement and moves on to locate the next error.

This time a repeated-word error has been located. To remove the second duplicate word,

Choose: Delete

The next error that is located is an inconsistent capitalization error. Word locates words that contain capital letters within lowercase letters as possible errors. To edit the word to the suggested change,

Choose: Change

The word "products" is corrected.

There should be no other misspelled words. However, if the Spelling tool encounters others in your file, correct them as needed. When no others are located, Spelling will display a message box telling you that the spelling check is complete. To close the message box,

Choose: OK

You want to save and replace the original two paragraphs with the newly corrected text. To do this,

Click:  Save

The menu equivalent is File/Save and the keyboard shortcut is Ctrl + S.

Word does not prompt you for a filename because the file was already named. After a few moments, the document is saved on the disk.

Opening a Second Document Window

Next, you will open the credit card letter. A copy of the credit card letter that you edited in Lab 1 is on your data disk in a file named Credit Card Letter 2.

Open the file Credit Card Letter 2.

You now have two document files open in two separate document windows.

Concept 1: Multiple Document Windows

You can open multiple documents in separate windows in the text area at the same time. Opening multiple document windows lets you switch easily between documents to cut, copy, and paste, as well as to see reference information in other documents. The memory your computer has available may limit the number of documents you can have open.

Although you can have multiple document windows open at one time, only one can be active. The **active window** is the window you can work in and that is affected by any commands you use. To make a window active, you switch to the window of your choice from the Window menu. You can also press Ctrl + F6 to cycle forward through all open documents, or Ctrl + ⇧Shift + F6 to cycle backward. When there are only two windows open, Ctrl + F6 will switch from one document window to the other.

The Credit Card Letter 2 document window is the active window and completely covers the New Paragraphs document window. To make the New Paragraphs document window active,

Choose: Window

Your screen should be similar to Figure 2-2.

Figure 2-2

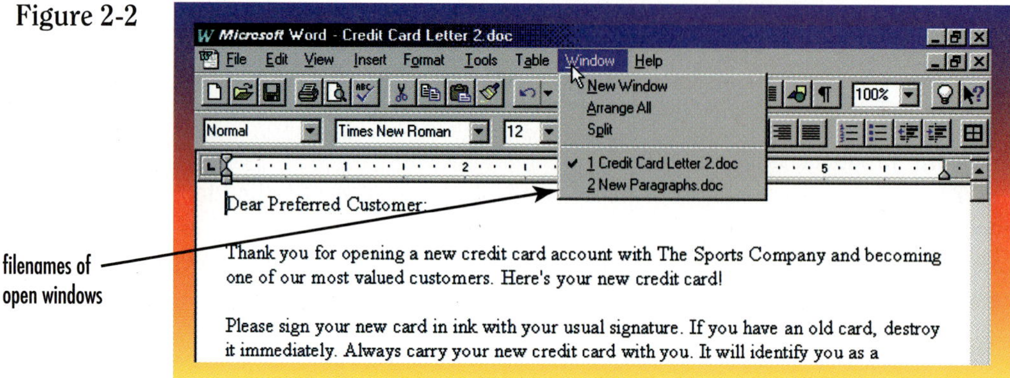

The Window menu lists the filenames of all open document windows in the order they were opened. The window displaying the checkmark is the active window. To make the New Paragraphs window active,

Choose: **2 New Paragraphs**

The window containing the New Paragraphs file is now the active window and covers the Credit Card Letter 2 window. To make the Credit Card Letter 2 document window active again,

Press: 

> You can also size document windows individually by dragging the window border.

To make it easier to view the document windows, you can display both document windows in the text area at once.

Choose: **Window/Arrange All**

Your screen should be similar to Figure 2-3.

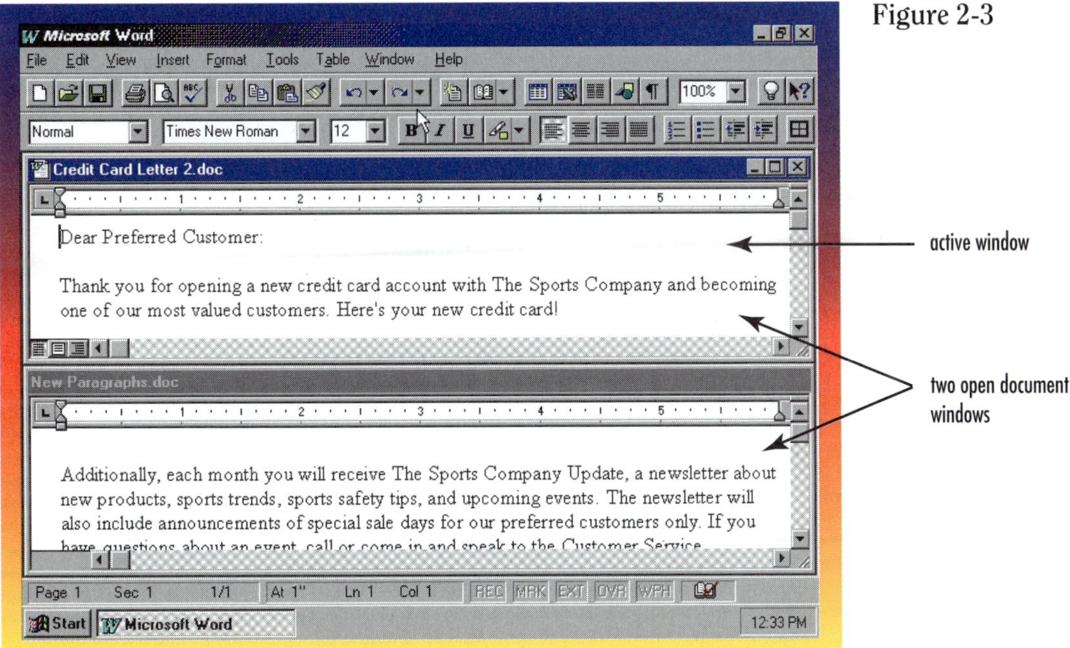

Figure 2-3

The text area now displays two document windows, one above the other. The active document window is Credit Card Letter 2, in the upper half of the screen. You can tell it is the active window because the title bar is a different color or highlighted, and it contains the insertion point. Any text you type or commands you choose affect the document in the active window only. The status bar provides information for the active document window.

Make the New Paragraphs document window active.

Click anywhere on a visible document window to make it active.

Copying Text Between Documents

After looking at the letter, you decide you want the two new paragraphs from the New Paragraphs document to be entered following the second paragraph of the credit card letter.

You can easily copy text from one file to another by selecting the text, copying it to the Clipboard, and then pasting the text from the Clipboard into another document file.

To select all the text in the New Paragraphs document,

Choose: **Edit/Select All**

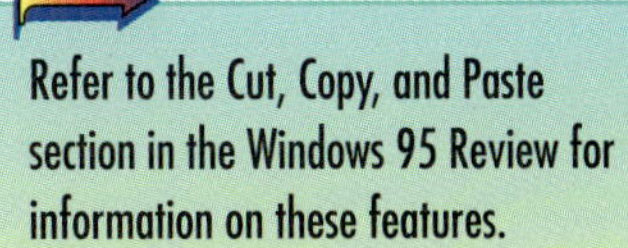

Refer to the Cut, Copy, and Paste section in the Windows 95 Review for information on these features.

The shortcut key is Ctrl + A, or hold down Ctrl and click in the selection bar.

Your screen should be similar to Figure 2-4.

Figure 2-4

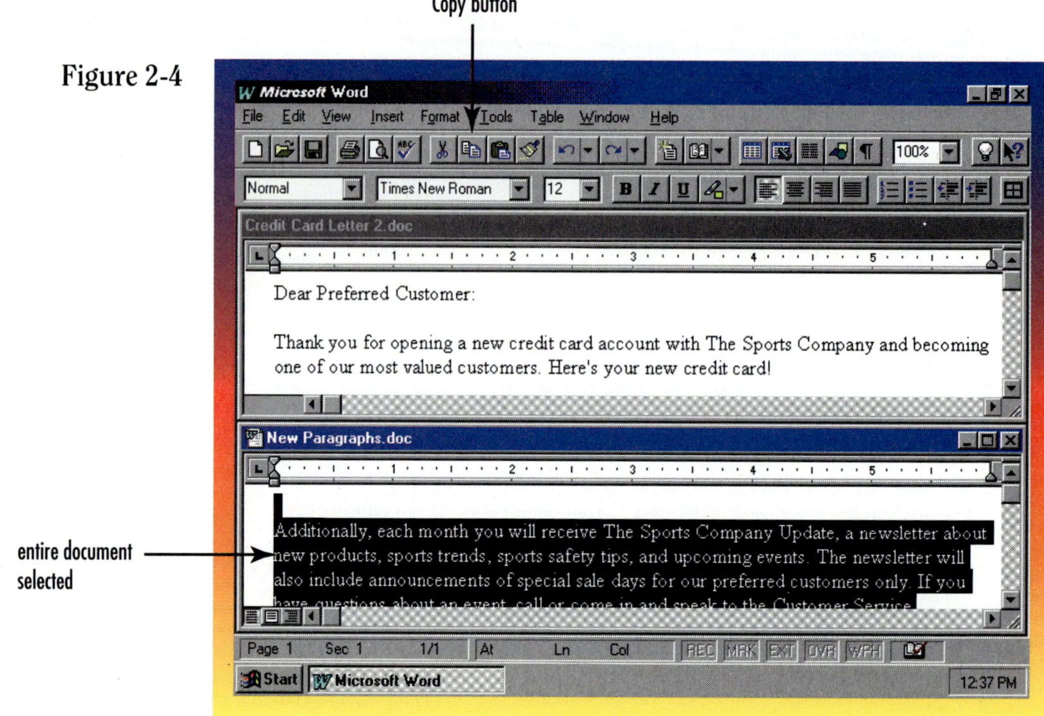

Once text is selected, it can be copied to another location in the same document or another document.

To copy the selected text,

The menu equivalent is Edit/Copy and the shortcut key is Ctrl + C.

Click:  **Copy**

Next, you want to specify where you want the copy of the selection to appear.

Make the Credit Card Letter 2 window active.

Move to: **blank line separating the second and third paragraphs (above the paragraph that begins with "We are the leading...")**

Then, to insert, or paste, the copy into the active document,

The menu equivalent is Edit/Paste and the shortcut key is Ctrl + V.

Click:  **Paste**

The two copied paragraphs from the New Paragraphs file have been inserted into the Credit Card Letter 2 file at the location of the insertion point.

You no longer need to view both document windows.

Reminder: Click ▣ on the active window to maximize it.

To make it easier to work with the Credit Card Letter 2 document window, maximize the window. Move to the top of the document.

Your screen should be similar to Figure 2-5.

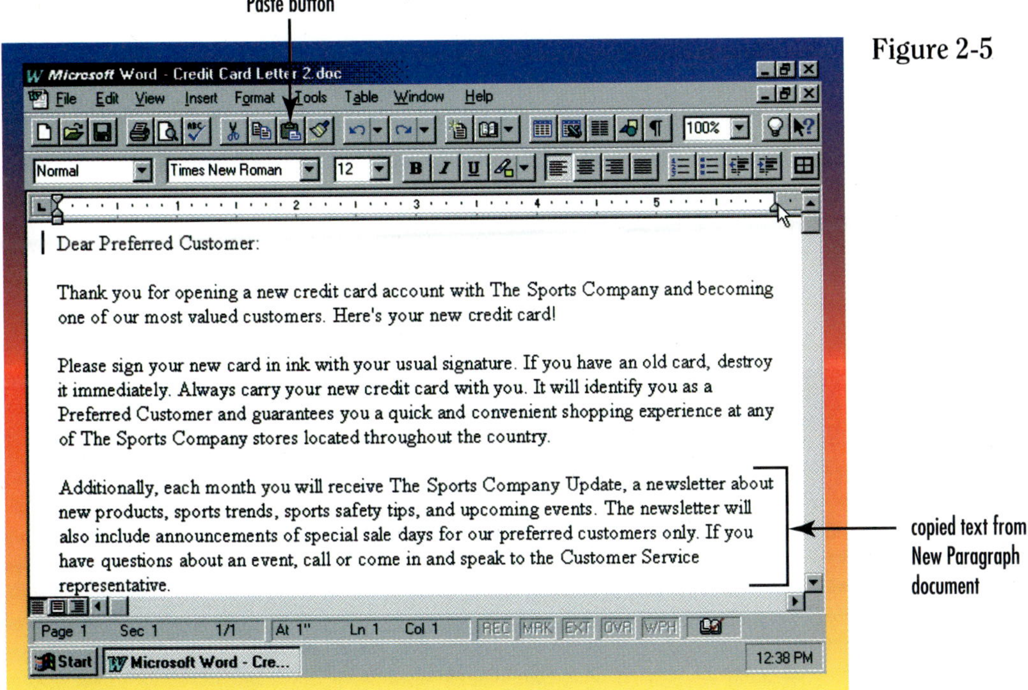

Figure 2-5

Look over the entire letter. When you finish viewing it, move to the top of the letter.

Moving Text

After looking over the credit card letter, you decide to change the order of the paragraphs. You want the paragraph about the 10 percent discount (fourth paragraph) to follow the second paragraph. To do this, you will cut the paragraph from its current location and paste it into the letter at the new location.

Select the paragraph beginning with "You can."

Reminder: Drag or double-click in the Selection bar next to the paragraph to select it.

The entire paragraph should be highlighted.

As you have learned, you can use the Shortcut menu to select many of the most common commands. This menu displays options related to the current selection.

Display the Shortcut menu for the selected paragraph.

Point to the selected text while right-clicking or press ⇧Shift + F10.

The Shortcut menu of options that can be used with selected text is displayed.

Choose: **Cut**

You can also click Cut, or choose Edit/Cut, or press Ctrl + X to cut text to the Clipboard.

The selected paragraph is removed from the document.

Delete the extra blank line.

Next you need to move the insertion point to the destination location where the text will be inserted.

Move to: **"A" in "Additionally" (first sentence, third paragraph)**

To paste the text into the document from the Clipboard,

> You can also choose Paste from the Shortcut menu.

Click: **Paste**

Insert a blank line between the paragraphs.

Your screen should be similar to Figure 2-6.

Figure 2-6

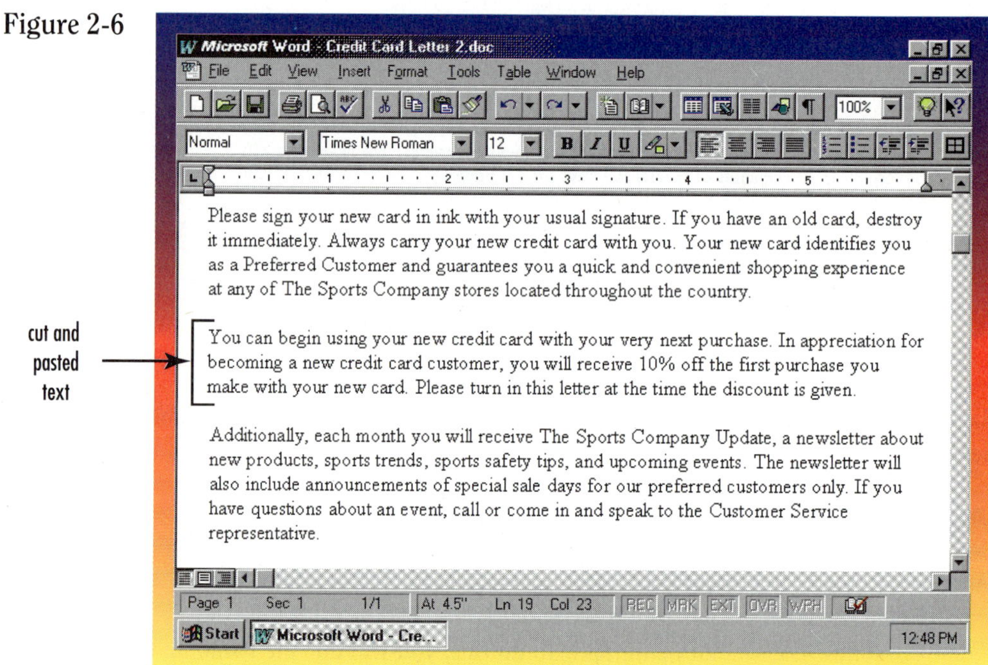

The deleted paragraph is reentered into the document at the insertion point location. That was a lot quicker than retyping the whole paragraph!

Replacing Selected Text

As you continue checking the letter, you want to make several text changes suggested by the regional manager. First you will reword the last sentence of the second paragraph. Instead of "It will identify you as a..." you would like it to say, "Your new credit card identifies you as a. . . ." Because the part you want to replace is shorter than the new text, Overtype mode will cut off some of the text you want to keep. By first selecting the text you want to remove and then typing in the new text, the part you want to keep will not be affected.

Select: **"It will identify" (second paragraph, fourth sentence)**
Type: **Y**

The "Y" is entered on the line, and the selected text has been deleted. You could also press Delete before typing the new text. However, as you just saw, this is unnecessary if you want to enter new text at the current location.

To continue entering the new text,

Type: **our new card identifies**

The new text is inserted into the sentence and the text following has been reformatted.

Finding and Replacing Text

The next item you want to change is to replace all occurrences of the words "new credit card" in the letter with "new Sports Company credit card" where appropriate. This process is very quick and easy using the Find and Replace feature.

Concept 3: Find and Replace

To make editing easier, you can use the Find and Replace feature to find a word in a document and automatically replace it with another word. For example, you created a lengthy document that describes the type of clothing and equipment you need to set up a world-class home gym. You decide to change "sneakers" to "athletic shoes." Instead of deleting every occurrence of "sneakers" and typing "athletic shoes," you use the Find and Replace feature to perform the task automatically. This feature is fast and accurate; however, use care when replacing so that you do not replace unintended matches.

In addition, you can use the options shown below to refine how the find and replace feature works.

Option	Effect on Text
Match Case	Replaces words and retains the capitalization.
Find Whole Words Only	Finds *cat* only and not *cat*astrophe too, for example.
Use Pattern Matching	Finds special characters, such as a question mark or a hyphen.
Sounds Like	Finds words that sound like the word you type; very helpful if you don't know the correct spelling of the word you want to find.
Find All Word Forms	Finds and replaces all forms of a word, such as *buy* for purchase and *bought* for purchased.

These options can be combined in many ways to help you find and replace text in documents. You will find this to be another helpful feature that word processing software packages offer to make editing easier. You can also find occurrences of special formatting, such as replacing bold text with italicized text, and special characters.

The Replace command on the Edit menu is used to find and replace text. Word will begin the search for all occurrences of words at the insertion point. If the search does not begin at the top of the document, when Word reaches the end of the document it asks if you want to continue searching from the beginning of the document. You can also highlight text to restrict the search to the selection.

To start the search at the beginning of the letter,

The **E**dit/**F**ind command locates specified text only.

Press: Ctrl + Home
Choose: **Edit/Replace**

Word may display the last text entered in the Find What text box. In addition, the four most recent text entries can be displayed by opening the drop-down list box.

The Replace dialog box is displayed. In the Find What text box, you enter the text you want to locate. When you enter the text to find, you can type everything lowercase, because Word is not **case-sensitive**. This means that lowercase letters will match both upper- and lowercase letters in the text.

If the existing entry is already correct, you do not need to retype it.

Type: **new credit card** (do not press ←Enter)

After entering the text to find, do not press ←Enter or this will choose Find Next and the search will begin.

The Replace dialog box on your screen should be similar to Figure 2-7.

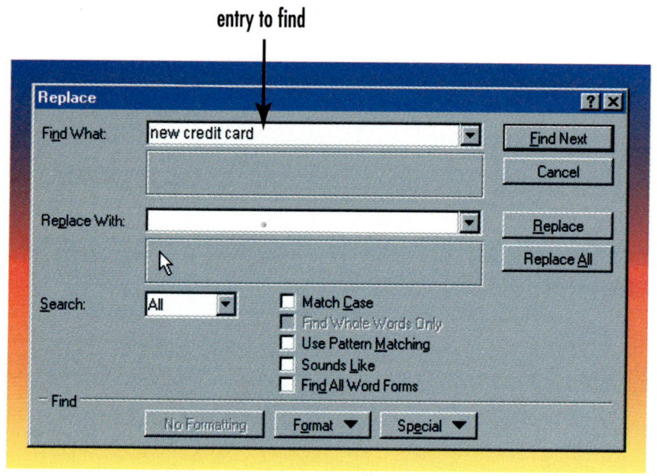

Figure 2-7

The last entered replacement text may be displayed in the Replace With text box

You want to replace "new credit card" with "new Sports Company credit card". The replacement text must be entered exactly as you want it to appear in your document. If necessary, to enter the replacement text,

Press: Tab
Type: **new Sports Company credit card**

The Search drop-down list box displays All as the default setting. You also can search down or up from the insertion point. Because you want to search the entire document, All is the appropriate setting. To begin the search,

Choose: **Find Next**

Immediately, the insertion point moves to the first occurrence of text in the document that matches the Find text and highlights it.

If necessary, move the dialog box so you can see the located text.

Your screen should be similar to Figure 2-8.

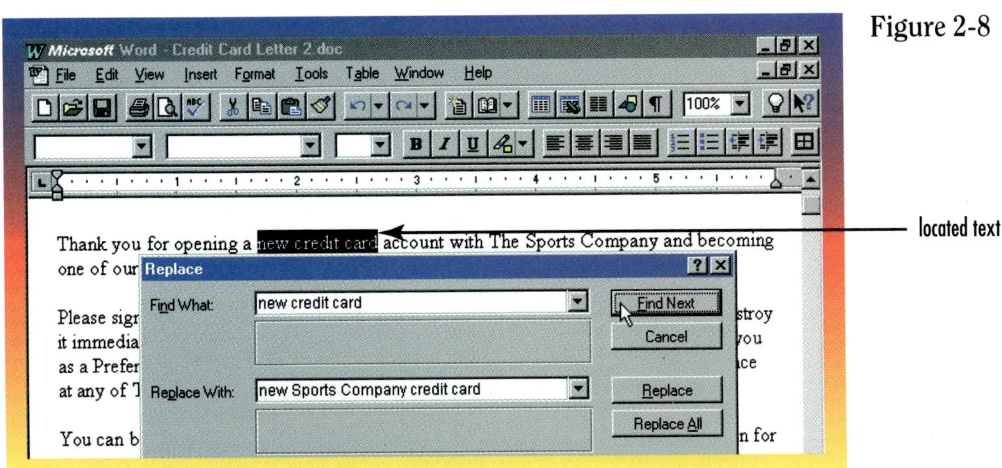

Figure 2-8

You do not, however, want to replace this text because the company name would appear twice in the same sentence. To tell the program to continue the search without replacing the highlighted text,

Choose: **Find Next**

Word immediately continues searching and locates a second occurrence of the Find text. To replace this text with the replacement text,

Choose: **Replace**

Do not use Replace All, because it will replace all occurrences including the one you skipped.

The highlighted text has been replaced, and the third occurrence of matching text is located.

In the same manner, replace the rest of the occurrences.

If you are changing all the occurrences it is much faster to use Replace All. Exercise care when using Replace All, because the search text you specify might be part of another word and you may accidentally replace text you want to keep.

When Word has completed the search, you will see the message "Word has finished searching the document." To close the message box,

Choose: **OK**

Close the Replace dialog box.

Using Drag and Drop

Next, you want to add the telephone number of the Customer Service Department to the letter. You want it to follow the reference to the Customer Service representative in the last sentence of the fourth paragraph.

Move to: **period of last sentence in fourth paragraph**
Press: Spacebar
Type: **(1-800-555-9838)**

After looking at the sentence, you decide you would like to move the telephone number to follow the word "call" in the same sentence.

Select the telephone number, excluding the parentheses.

Word also includes a **drag-and-drop** editing feature that can be used to move or copy selections. To use drag and drop to move a selection, point to the selection and drag the pointer to the location where you want the selection inserted. A thin I-beam appears to show you where the text will be placed.

Point to the selection. Drag to the space after "call" in the same sentence. Click anywhere outside the selected text to clear the highlight.

Delete the parentheses at the end of the sentence and correct the spacing as necessary around the telephone number.

Your screen should be similar to Figure 2-9.

Refer to the Drag and Drop section in the Windows 95 Review for information on this feature.

To use drag-and-drop to copy a selection, hold down Ctrl while dragging.

Drag-and-drop also can be used between documents and applications if both documents are visible on the screen.

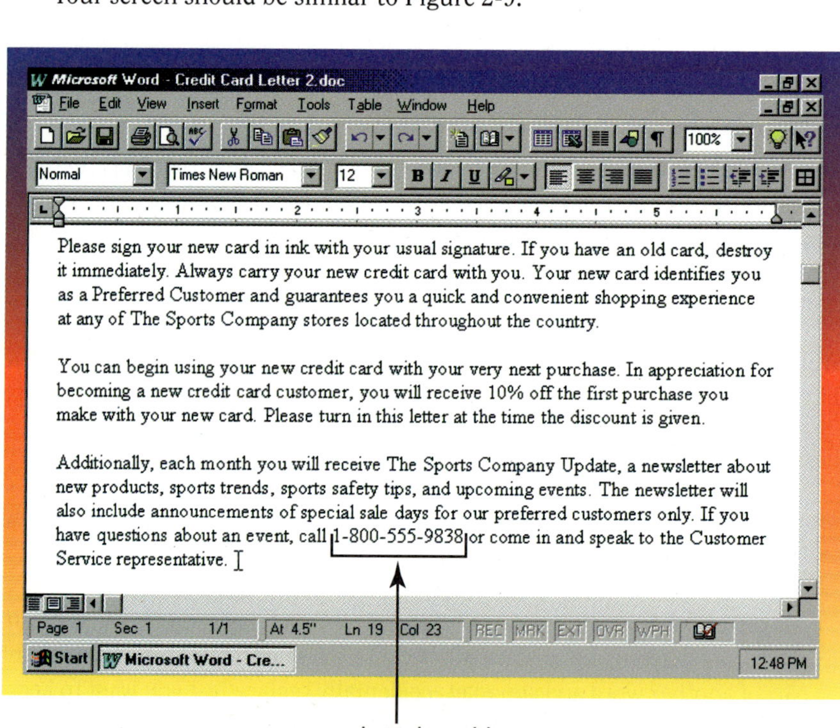

Figure 2-9

Drag and drop is most useful for copying or moving short distances in a document.

Using the Thesaurus

The next text change you want to make is to find a better word for "happy" in the last sentence of the letter. To help find a similar word, you will use the thesaurus tool.

Concept 2: Thesaurus

The Word **thesaurus** is a reference tool that provides synonyms, antonyms, and related words for a selected word or phrase. Synonyms are words with a similar meaning, such as "cheerful" and "happy." Antonyms are words with an opposite meaning, such as "cheerful" and "sad." Related words are words that are variations of the same word, such as "cheerful" and "cheer."

The Word Thesaurus can help to liven up your documents by adding interest and variety to your text.

To identify the word you want looked up,

Move to: "happy" (last paragraph)

To use the Thesaurus,

Choose: Tools/Thesaurus

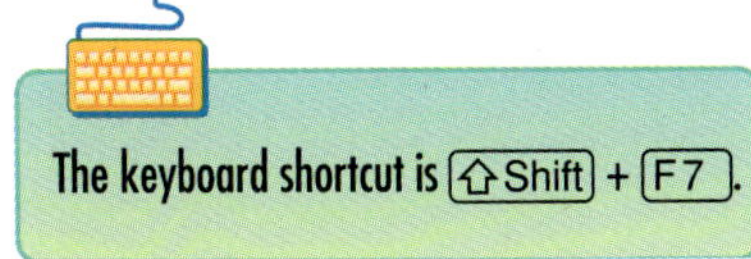

Your screen should be similar to Figure 2-10.

Figure 2-10

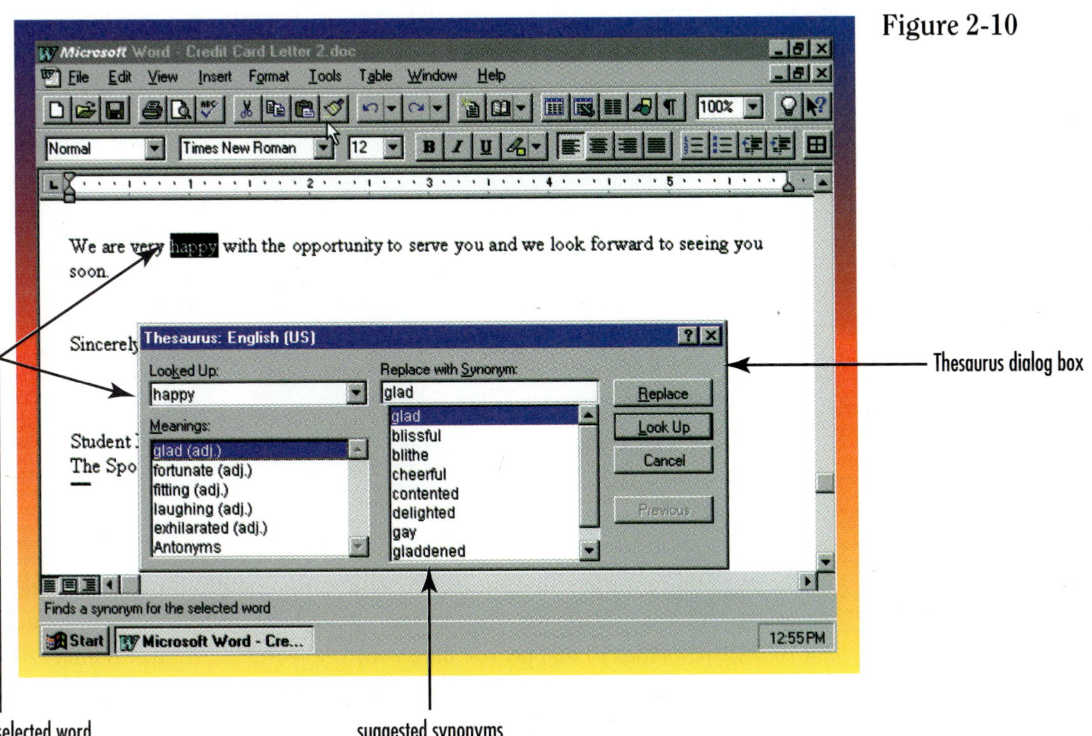

If a synonym, antonym, or related word is not found, the Thesaurus displays an alphabetical list of entries that are similar in spelling to the selected word.

The Thesaurus dialog box displays a list of possible meanings for the looked-up word. From this list you can select the most appropriate meaning for the word. The highlighted word "glad" is appropriate for this sentence. The list of words in the Replace with Synonym box are synonyms for the word "happy" with a meaning of "glad. The best choice from this list is "delighted."

Select: **delighted**
Choose: **Replace**

The word "happy" is replaced with "delighted" in the paragraph.

Remove the word "very" from the sentence.

Now the sentence reads much better.

Using the Date Command

The last text change you need to make is to add the date to the letter. You want to enter the date on the first line of the letter four lines above the salutation.

Move to the "D" in "Dear" at the top of the letter. Then, insert four blank lines and move to the first blank line.

The insertion point should be at the top of the letter where the date will be entered.

The Date and Time command on the Insert menu inserts into your document the current date as maintained by your computer system.

Choose: **Insert/Date and Time**

The Date and Time dialog box shown in Figure 2-11 should be displayed.

Figure 2-11

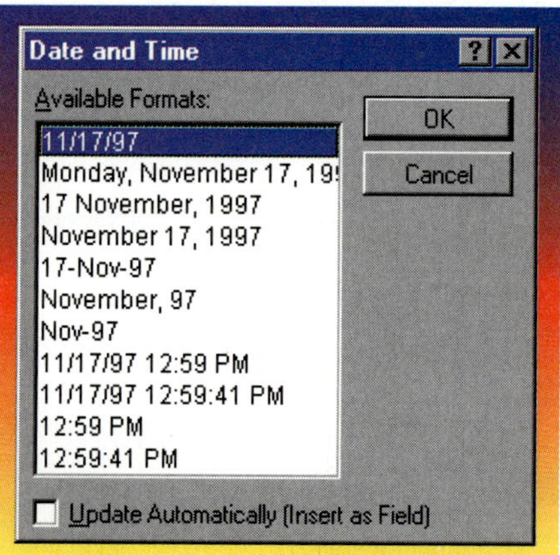

The Available Formats list box displays the format styles for the date and time using the current date and time on your computer system as samples. You want to set the format to display the date with the complete month name, followed by the date and year (Month XX, 199X). The option that will display the date in this format is the fourth setting in the list.

Select the fourth format setting.

The second option, Update Automatically, is used to enter the date as a field. A **field** is a special code that instructs Word to insert information into a document. The **field code** contains the directions that tell Word what type of information to insert. The information that is displayed as a result of the field code is called the **field result**. Many field codes are automatically inserted when you use certain commands. Others you can create and insert yourself. Many fields update automatically when the document changes. Using fields makes it easier and faster to perform many common or repetitive tasks.

In this case, if you insert the date as a field, whenever the letter is printed, the field result will display the current date in the selected format. Because the letter will be sent to new customers as they apply for a credit card, you want to insert the date as a field. To do this,

> Alt + ⇧Shift + D will insert the current date as a field in the format MM/DD/YY.

Select: **Update Automatically (Insert as Field)**
Choose: **OK**

The field result displays the current date, as maintained on your computer system, at the location of the insertion point. Although the date appears as text, it is a field. To see this,

Press: ←

Your screen should be similar to Figure 2-12.

> The date in Figure 2-12 will be different from the date that appears on your screen.

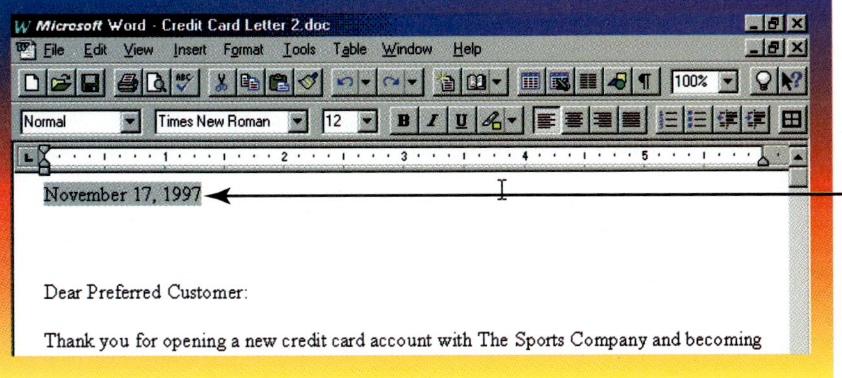

Figure 2-12

The entire date is shaded, indicating that the insertion point is positioned on a field entry. Next, you will look at the underlying field code.

Display the field's Shortcut menu.

Choose: **Toggle Field Codes**

The field code {TIME \@ "MMMM d, yyyy"} is displayed. To redisplay the field result, from the field's shortcut menu,

Choose: **Toggle Field Codes**

Whenever this file is printed, Word will print the current system date using this format.

Note: If you are ending your session now, replace Student Name with your name in the closing and save the file as Credit Card Letter 3. Print the letter. When you begin Part 2, open this file.

Part 2

Improving the Appearance of a Document

Next, the regional manager has suggested that you make the following formatting changes to improve the appearance of the letter.

- Decrease the margin width
- Indent the paragraphs
- Make a list with bullets out of the text in the second paragraph
- Change the alignment to justified

When complete, your revised letter will look like Figure 2-13.

Figure 2-13

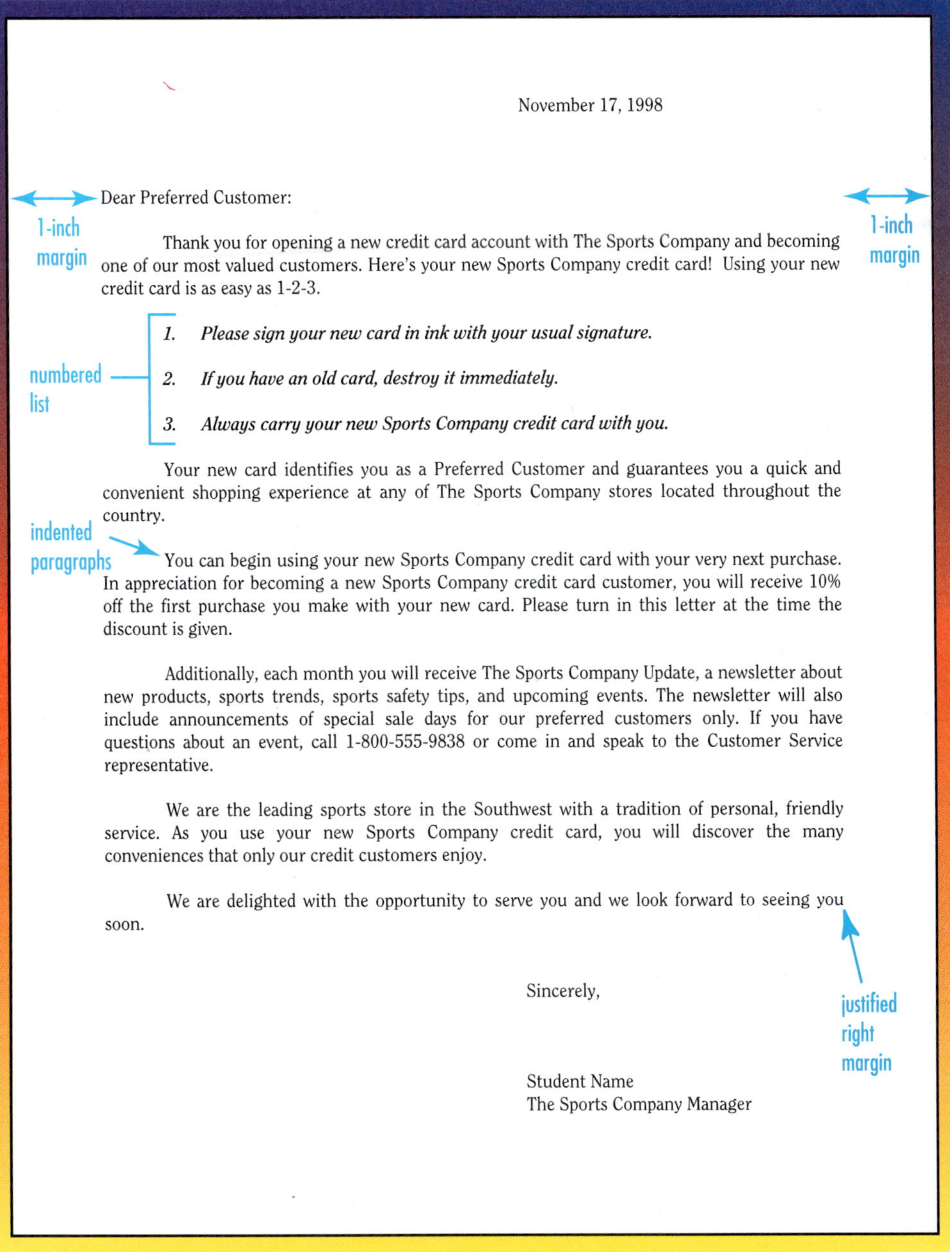
November 17, 1998

Dear Preferred Customer:

Thank you for opening a new credit card account with The Sports Company and becoming one of our most valued customers. Here's your new Sports Company credit card! Using your new credit card is as easy as 1-2-3.

1. *Please sign your new card in ink with your usual signature.*
2. *If you have an old card, destroy it immediately.*
3. *Always carry your new Sports Company credit card with you.*

Your new card identifies you as a Preferred Customer and guarantees you a quick and convenient shopping experience at any of The Sports Company stores located throughout the country.

You can begin using your new Sports Company credit card with your very next purchase. In appreciation for becoming a new Sports Company credit card customer, you will receive 10% off the first purchase you make with your new card. Please turn in this letter at the time the discount is given.

Additionally, each month you will receive The Sports Company Update, a newsletter about new products, sports trends, sports safety tips, and upcoming events. The newsletter will also include announcements of special sale days for our preferred customers only. If you have questions about an event, call 1-800-555-9838 or come in and speak to the Customer Service representative.

We are the leading sports store in the Southwest with a tradition of personal, friendly service. As you use your new Sports Company credit card, you will discover the many conveniences that only our credit customers enjoy.

We are delighted with the opportunity to serve you and we look forward to seeing you soon.

Sincerely,

Student Name
The Sports Company Manager

Setting Margins

The first formatting change you want to make is to change the margin widths.

Concept 4: Margins

The margin is the distance from the text to the edge of the paper. Standard single-page documents have four margins: top, bottom, left, and right. Double-sided documents also have four margins: top, bottom, inside, and outside.

Single-Sided Document Margins

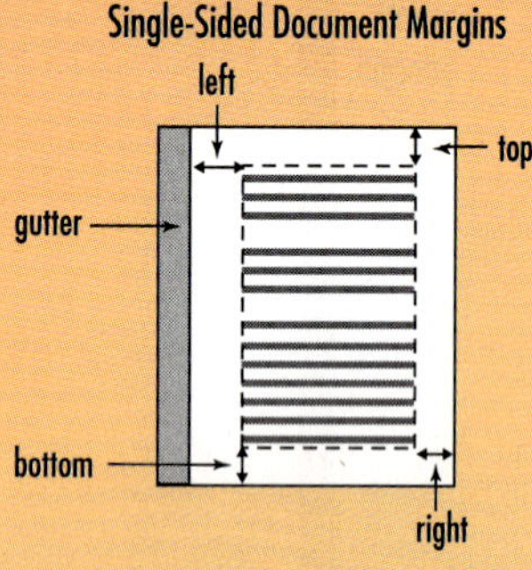

Double-Sided Document Margins

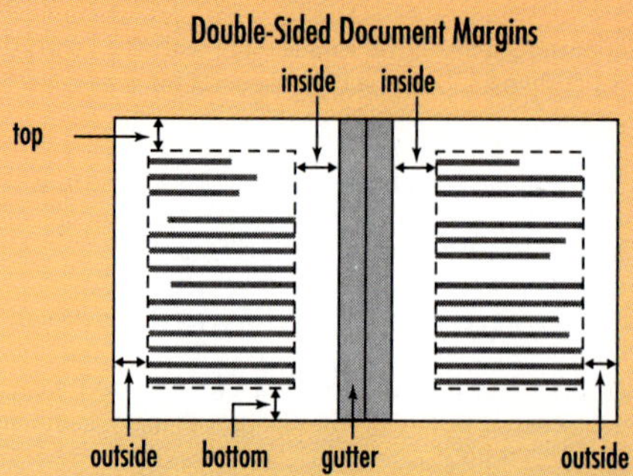

Setting	Measurement Affected
Top	Distance from the top edge of the paper to the first line of text on the page
Bottom	Distance from the bottom edge of the paper to the last line of text on the page
Left	Distance from the left edge of the paper to the left edge of the text on the page
Right	Distance from the right edge of the paper to the right edge of the text on the page
Inside	Distance from the inside edge of the paper to the inside edge of the text on the page (double-sided documents)
Outside	Distance from the outside edge of the paper to the outside edge of the text on the page (double-sided documents)
Gutter	Additional space in left or inside margin to accommodate binding
Header	Distance from the top edge of the paper to the first line of header text
Footer	Distance from the bottom edge of the paper to the last line of footer text

You set margins to alter the appearance of the document on the printed page. For example, you have paper with a preprinted border 2 inches from the top of the paper. To print your document on this paper, you would set the top margin to 3 inches. You want your header text to print 0.5 inch above the border, so you set the Header margin to 1.5 inches.

Preprinted Border at 2.0 Inches

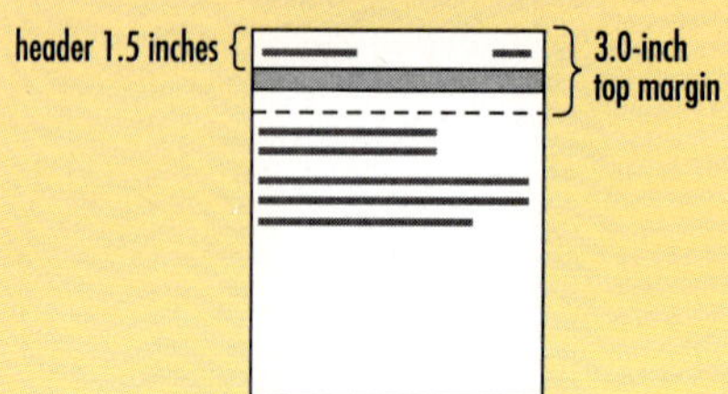

You would like to see how the letter would look if you changed the right and left margin widths from the default setting of 1.25 inches to 1 inch. The Page Setup command on the File menu is used to change settings associated with entire pages.

Choose: **File/Page Setup**

The Page Setup tab dialog box is used to modify four groups of setting: Margins, Paper Size, Paper Source, and Layout.

If necessary, choose the Margins tab.

The Margins tab (shown in Figure 2-14) displays the seven margin settings that can be changed. The default margin settings are for single-sided pages and are displayed in the text boxes to the right of each option. The Preview box shows a sample of how the current margin settings will appear on a page. New margin settings can be entered by typing the value in the text box or by clicking the ▲ and ▼ buttons or pressing the ↑ or ↓ keys to decrease or increase the setting by tenths of an inch.

To set margins for double-sided documents, choose Mirror Margins.

Using any of these methods, set the left margin to 1 inch.

The Preview box shows the results of the change to the left margin setting.

In a similar manner, change the right margin setting to 1.

Your Page Setup dialog box should be similar to Figure 2-14.

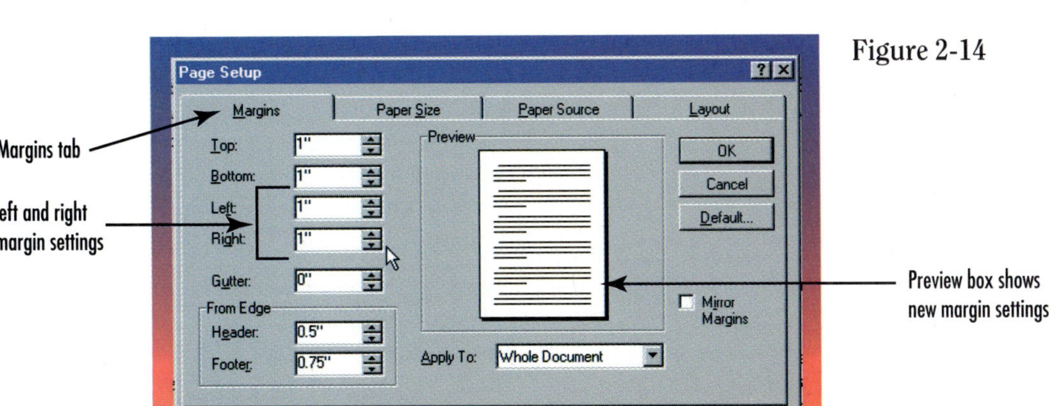

Figure 2-14

To complete the command,

Choose: **OK**

The letter has been reformatted to fit within the new margin settings. Because the margins are smaller, more text can be entered on a line. However, now the line is too long to fit within the window.

Scroll the window to the right to view the end of the line.

The ruler shows that the text space is 6.5 inches rather than 6 inches.

Changing Document Views

Because you have to scroll the window, it is difficult to see how the margins have changed the layout of the document. To make it easier to see how the document lays out on the page, you will change the document view.

Concept 5: Document Views

You can view a document in six different ways. Each view offers different features for creating and editing your documents. It's best to start your document in Normal view, then to add finishing touches like headers, footers, and graphics, switch to Page Layout view. Finally, use Print Preview to check the document before you print.

Document View	Command	Button	Effect on Text
Normal View	View/Normal		Shows text formatting but not the layout of the page. This is the best view to use when typing, editing, or formatting text.
Page Layout View	View/Page Layout		Shows how the text and objects are positioned on the printed page. This is the view to use when editing headers and footers, adjusting margins, working in columns, drawing objects, and placing graphics and frames.
Outline View	View/Outline		Shows the structure of the document. This is the view to use to move, copy, and reorganize text in a document. You can collapse the document to view just the headings or expand to view the entire document.
Full Screen View	View/Full Screen		Shows the document without Word's toolbars, menus, scroll bars, and other screen elements. You can still use the Shortcut menus and keys to access commands. To return to the view you were using, click Full Screen or press Esc.
Master Document View	View/Master Document		Shows several documents organized into a master document. This is the view to use to organize and maintain a long document that is divided into several documents. You can generate a table of contents and an index from all the documents in the master document.
Print Preview	File/Print Preview		Shows multiple pages of a document in a reduced size. This is the view to use to check the layout of a document and make editing and format changes before you print.

To display the document in Page Layout view,

Click:  Page Layout View

The menu equivalent is **V**iew/**P**age Layout.

The Page Layout View button is located on the left edge of the horizontal scroll bar.

Your screen should be similar to Figure 2-15.

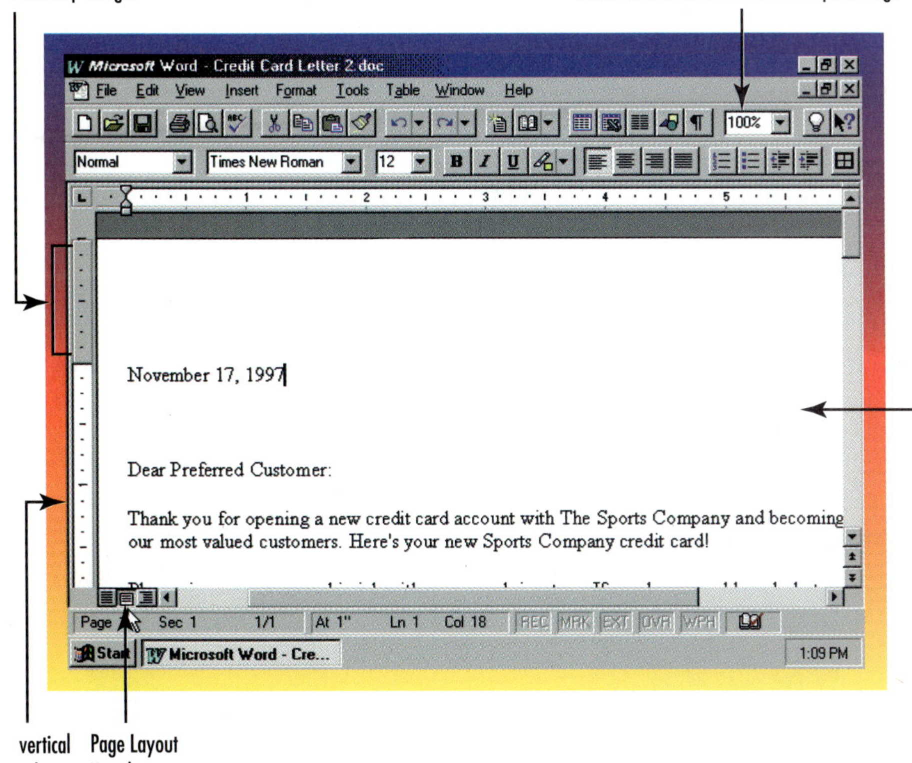

Figure 2-15

Your screen may display more or less text than is shown in Figure 2-15. This is because your zoom setting may be different. You will learn about this feature next.

This view displays the current page of your document as it will appear when printed. The text still extends off the window space to the right.

The screen now displays a vertical ruler that shows the vertical position of text. Notice that the date will be printed 1 inch from the top of the paper (the default top margin setting). It shows the text as it would appear on the paper.

To see more of the text in the window at one time, you can decrease the onscreen character size using the Zoom command.

The menu equivalent is **V**iew/**Z**oom.

Click:  Zoom Control

Your zoom percentage may be different than 100%. Word uses the zoom percentage that was in use when you last exited the file or program.

The default display, 100%, shows the characters the same size as they will be when printed. You can increase the character size up to two times normal display (200%) and reduce the character size to 10%.

Select 50%.

The text is fully displayed across the width of the window, and you also can see three sides of paper.

You can also set the zoom to display the full width, a whole page, or multiple pages. The Whole Page option automatically sets the percent value to display the entire page on the screen. To use this option,

The menu equivalent is View/Zoom/Whole Page.

Click: 50% Zoom Control
Choose: Whole Page

Your screen should be similar to Figure 2-16.

Figure 2-16

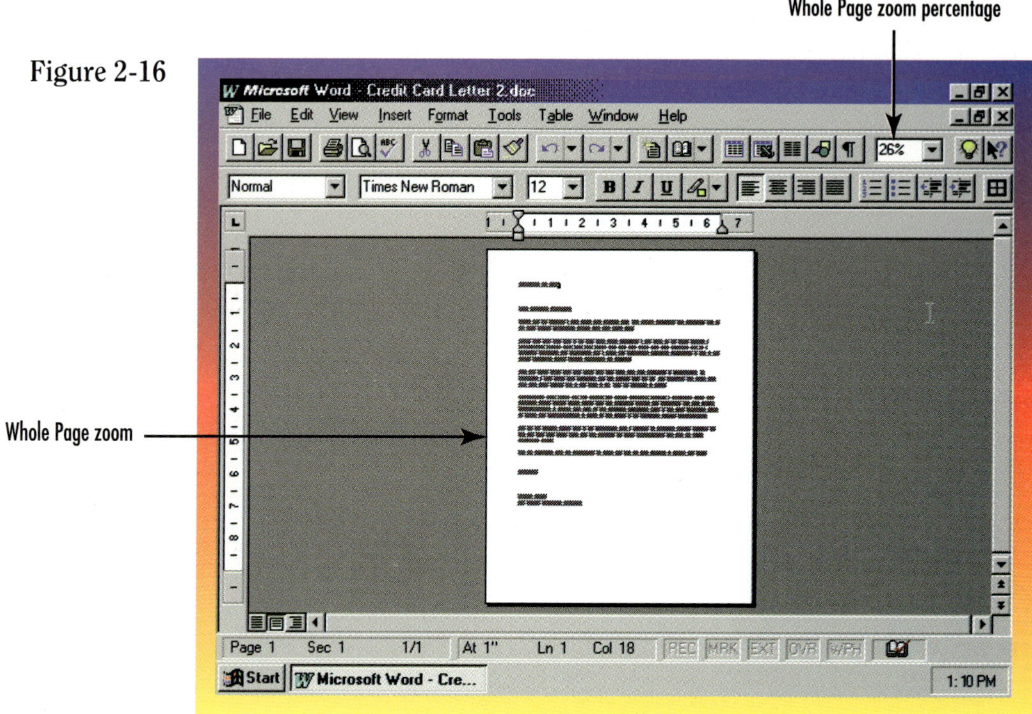

Your zoom percentage may be slightly different.

The zoom percent is 26 (displayed in the Zoom button). Now the entire page is visible but the text is too small to read. This view is similar to Print Preview. You can now easily see how the change in margin width has affected the document.

Return the Zoom percent to 100%.

To return the document display to Normal view,

The Normal View button is located on the left end of the horizontal scroll bar.

The menu equivalent is View/Normal.

Click:  Normal View

Indenting Paragraphs

Next, you want to change the letter style from the block paragraph style to an indented paragraph style. To do this, you will indent the first line of each paragraph and the closing.

Concept 6: Indents

To help your reader find information quickly, you can indent paragraphs of similar content. Indenting paragraphs sets them off from the rest of the document. There are four types of indents you can use to stylize your documents.

<table>
<tr><th>Indent</th><th>Effect on Text</th></tr>
<tr><td>Left
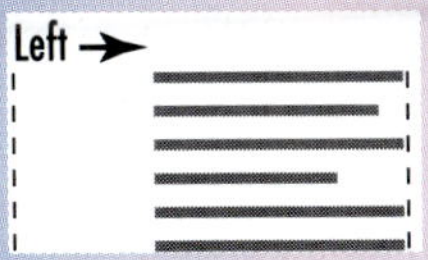
</td><td>Indents the entire paragraph from the left margin. To extend the paragraph into the left margin, use a negative value for the left indent.</td></tr>
<tr><td>Right
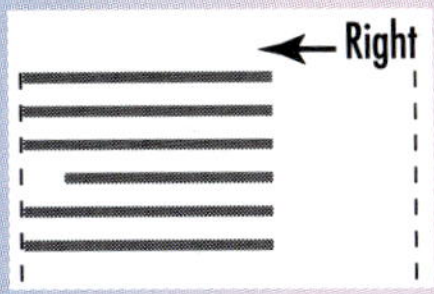
</td><td>Indents the entire paragraph from the right margin. To extend the paragraph into the right margin, use a negative value for the right indent.</td></tr>
<tr><td>First Line
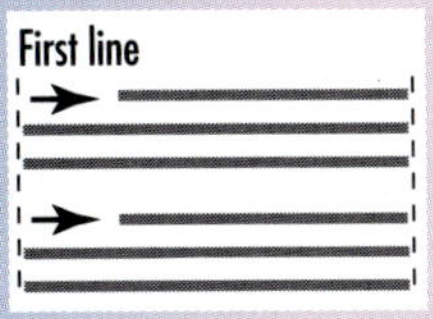
</td><td>Indents the first line of the paragraph. All following lines are aligned with the left margin.</td></tr>
<tr><td>Hanging

</td><td>Indents all lines after the first line of the paragraph. The first line is aligned with the left margin. A hanging indent typically is used for bulleted and numbered lists.</td></tr>
</table>

To indent the first line of the first paragraph,

Move to: "T" in "Thank" (first sentence, first paragraph)
Choose: Format/Paragraph/Indents and Spacing

The Indents and Spacing tab of the Paragraph dialog box shown in Figure 2-17 is displayed.

Figure 2-17

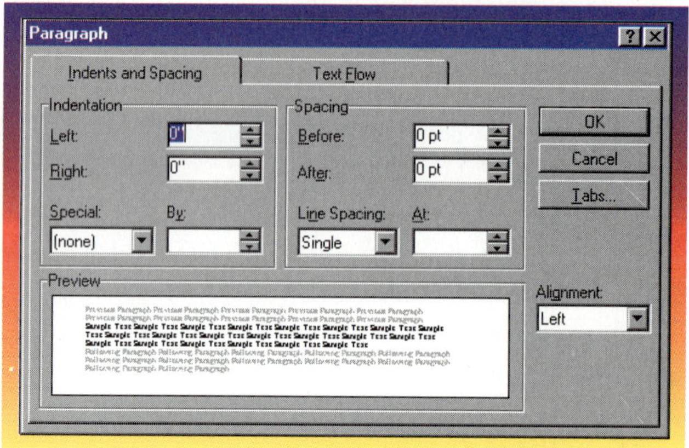

The left and right indentation settings for the current paragraph are 0. This setting aligns each line of the paragraph with the margin setting. Specifying an indent value would indent each line of the paragraph the specified amount from the margin. To indent the first line only,

Choose: **Special/First Line**

The default indent setting of .5" for this option is displayed in the By text box.

Choose: **OK**

Your screen should be similar to Figure 2-18.

Figure 2-18

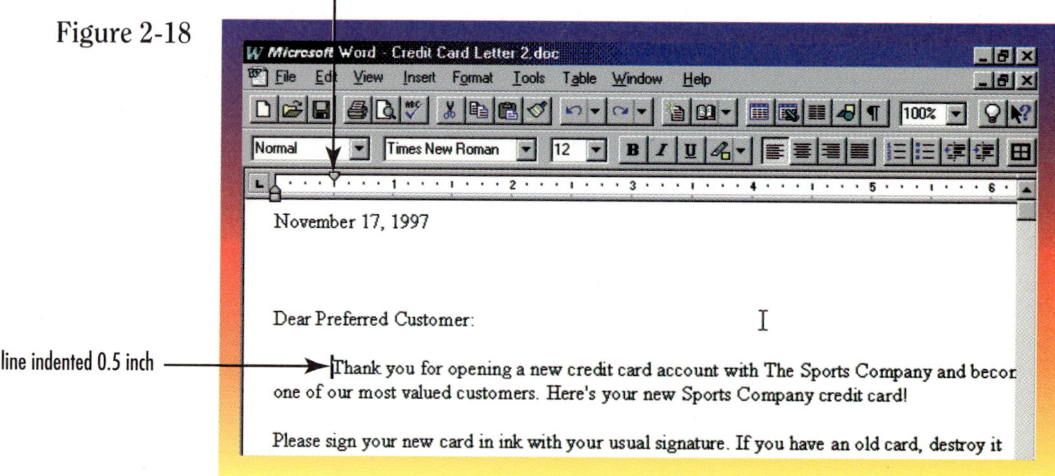

You can also indent the first line of a paragraph by dragging the upper indent marker to the position on the ruler.

The first line of the paragraph indents 0.5 inch from the left margin to the first tab setting. The text in the paragraph wraps as needed. The text on the following line begins at the left margin. Notice the upper indent marker on the ruler moved to the 0.5 position.

A much quicker way to indent the first line of a paragraph is to press Tab at the beginning of the paragraph.

Move to: **"P" in Please**
Press: Tab

Pressing Tab indents the first line of the paragraph to the first tab stop from the left margin.

You will learn about setting tab stops in Lab 3.

You can indent the remaining four paragraphs individually, or you can select the paragraphs and indent them simultaneously by either using the Format menu or dragging the indent marker on the ruler.

Select the remaining four paragraphs. Drag the upper indent marker on the ruler to the 0.5-inch position.

A dotted vertical line is displayed as you drag to show where the indent will appear in the text.

The lower indent marker controls the indent for all lines in a paragraph after the first line.

In the same manner, select the closing lines and indent them to the 3.25-inch position on the ruler.

Move to the top of the document.

Creating an Itemized List

You want to add a new sentence to the first paragraph to tell the reader what the list is about.

Now you want to display the first three sentences in the second paragraph as a list. When you complete the adjustment of the paragraph, it will look like Figure 2-19.

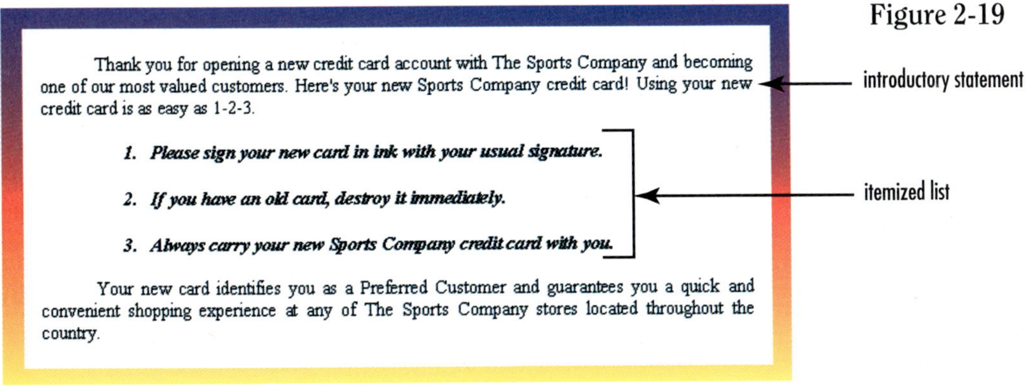

Thank you for opening a new credit card account with The Sports Company and becoming one of our most valued customers. Here's your new Sports Company credit card! Using your new credit card is as easy as 1-2-3.

1. ***Please sign your new card in ink with your usual signature.***
2. ***If you have an old card, destroy it immediately.***
3. ***Always carry your new Sports Company credit card with you.***

Your new card identifies you as a Preferred Customer and guarantees you a quick and convenient shopping experience at any of The Sports Company stores located throughout the country.

Figure 2-19

Add the introductory sentence, "Using your new credit card is as easy as 1-2-3." to the end of the first paragraph.

Next, you will create the itemized list using the first three sentences of the second paragraph.

Concept 7: Bulleted and Numbered Lists

Whenever possible, to make your writing clear and easy to read, use bulleted or numbered lists to organize information. A list can be used whenever you present three or more related pieces of information.

Use a bulleted list when you have several items that logically fall out from a paragraph into a list. A bulleted list displays one of several styles of bullets before each item in the list. You can select from several types of symbols to use as bullets and you can change the color, size, and position of the bullet. Here are a few examples.

Use a numbered list when you want to convey a sequence of events, such as a procedure that has steps to follow in a certain order. A numbered list displays numbers or letters before the text. Word automatically increments the number or letter as you start a new paragraph. You can select from several different numbering schemes to create your numbered lists. Here are a few examples.

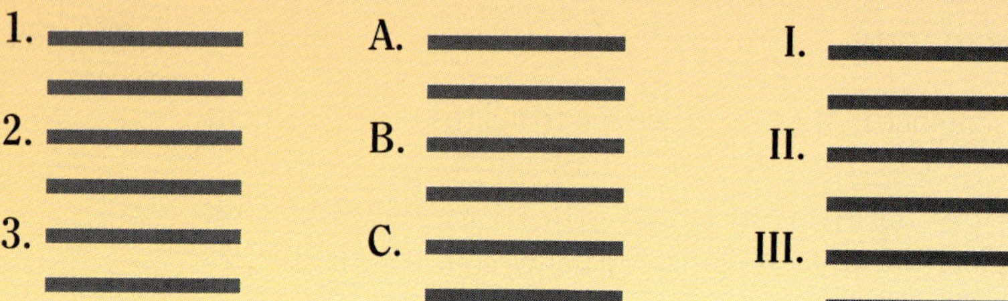

First, you need to remove the indent at the beginning of the second paragraph and then place each sentence on a separate line that you want to be itemized in the list. To remove the tab,

> You can also drag the upper indent marker to the 0 position on the ruler to clear the indent.

Move to: "P" of "Please"
Press: ⇧Shift + Tab

Then, to place the next sentence on a separate line beginning at the left margin,

Move to: "I" of "If" (second sentence, second paragraph)
Press: ←Enter (2 times)

In a similar manner, place the next sentence on a separate line.

Make the last sentence, beginning with "Your new . . .", a new paragraph. (Remember to indent the first line of the paragraph.)

You should now have a list of three items, each separated with a blank line. Leaving a blank line between items in a list makes the list easier to read. Next you will add a bullet before each of the items.

Select the three items.

The bullet feature of Word will add a bullet automatically before the first line of a paragraph and indent the text following the bullet. To use the bullet feature,

Choose: **Format/Bullets and Numbering**

If necessary, select the Bulleted tab.

The Bulleted tab of the Bullets and Numbering dialog box shown in Figure 2-20 is displayed.

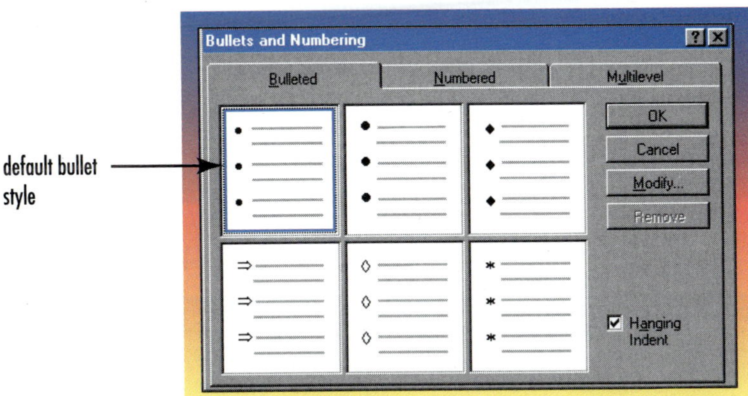

Figure 2-20

Six styles of bullets are available. The first style is the default style and is the style you will use.

If it does not appear highlighted, select the first bullet style.

Choose: **OK**

You can click Bullets to apply the last-used bullet style.

Your screen should be similar to Figure 2-21.

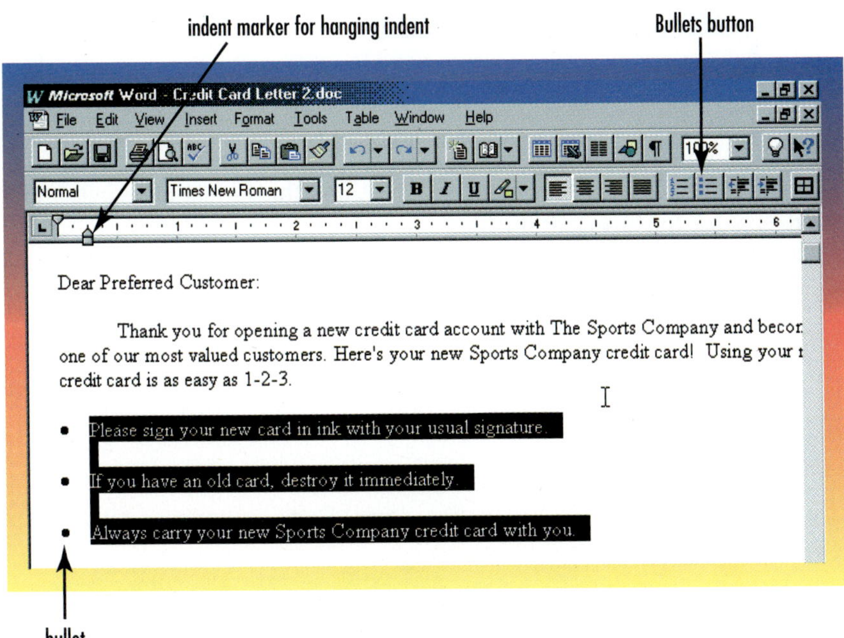

Figure 2-21

To create bulleted lists as you type, type an asterisk (*), press Tab, and then type the text. When you press ←Enter, Word 7.0 automatically changes the asterisk to a bullet and adds a bullet to the next line. To turn off the bullets, press ←Enter twice.

To create numbered lists as you type, type a number, type a period, press Tab, and then type the text. When you press ←Enter, Word 7.0 automatically creates a numbered list and numbers the next line. To turn off the numbered list, press ←Enter twice.

You can click Numbering to apply the last-used numbering style.

A small bullet is inserted at the left margin before each sentence, and the text following the bullet is indented to the 0.25-inch position. The ruler displays the lower indent marker at the 0.25-inch position to show the hanging indent setting for text in the selection. If the text following each bullet was longer than a line, the text on the following lines would also be indented to the 0.25-inch position.

You want to see how the same items would appear with numbers rather than bullets. To change the style to numbers,

Choose: **Format/Bullets and Numbering/Numbered**

Select the top left number style option.

Choose: **OK**

Your screen should be similar to Figure 2-22.

Figure 2-22

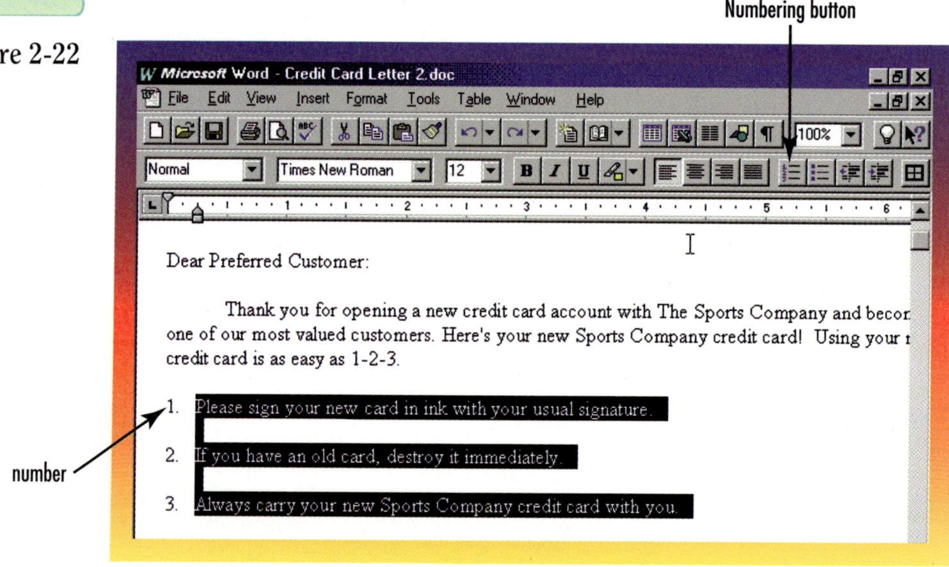

To remove bullets or numbers, choose Format/Bullets and Numbering/Remove/OK or click the or button again.

The bullets are replaced with numbers. You think this format looks better and decide to leave the format as it is.

Finally, you want to change the indent for the three items so that the number aligns with the 0.75-inch position.

The three items should still be highlighted.

If they are not, select them.

To indent the selection,

Press: Tab **(2 times)**

Your screen should be similar to Figure 2-23.

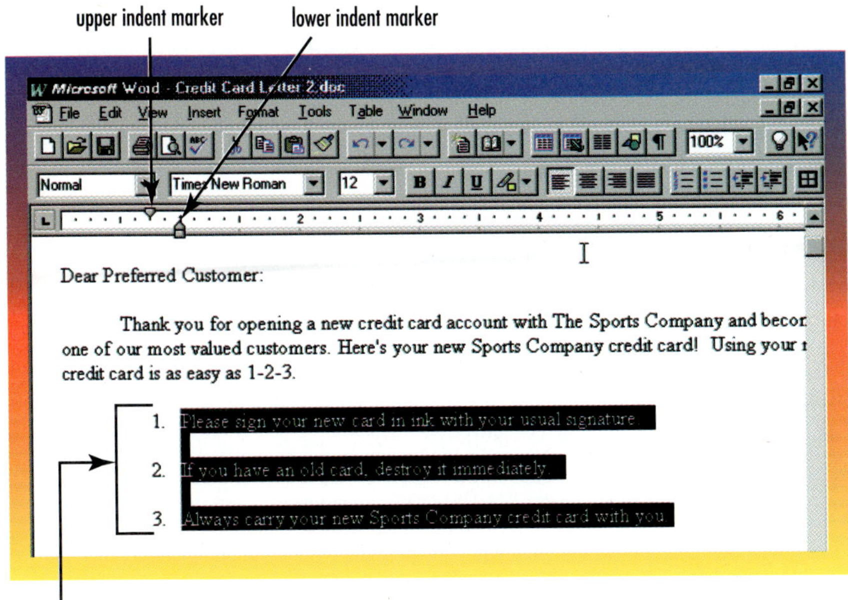

Figure 2-23

The numbers align with the 0.75-inch position and the text with the 1-inch position in the document. In an itemized list, the upper indent marker on the ruler controls the position of the number or bullet and the lower indent marker, the position of the item following the number.

Itemizing and indenting the selection has made it stand out from the text in the letter.

Applying Text Formats

You would like to make these sentences stand out even more in the document. One way to do this is to change the text appearance by applying different styles and effects to a selection.

Concept 8: Text Formats

Different text formats can be applied to selections to add emphasis or interest to a document. The table below describes the text formats and their uses.

Format	Example	Use
Bold, Italic	**Bold** *Italic*	Adds empahsis
Underline	Underline	Adds emphasis
Strikethrough	~~Strikethrough~~	Indicates words to be deleted
Superscript	"To be or not to be."[1]	Used in footnotes and formulas
Subscript	H_2O	Used in formulas
Hidden	Displays, but does not print	Notes or comments you do not want printed
Small Caps	SMALL CAPS	Adds emphasis when case is not important
All Caps	ALL CAPS	Adds emphasis when case is not important
Color	Color Color Color	Adds interest

The menu equivalent is Format/Font/Font Style/Bold/Italic and the keyboard shortcuts are Ctrl + B for bold and Ctrl + I for italics.

You would like to change the itemized list to bold and italic.

If necessary, select the three numbered items.

Click: 

Clear the highlight.

Your screen should be similar to Figure 2-24.

Figure 2-24

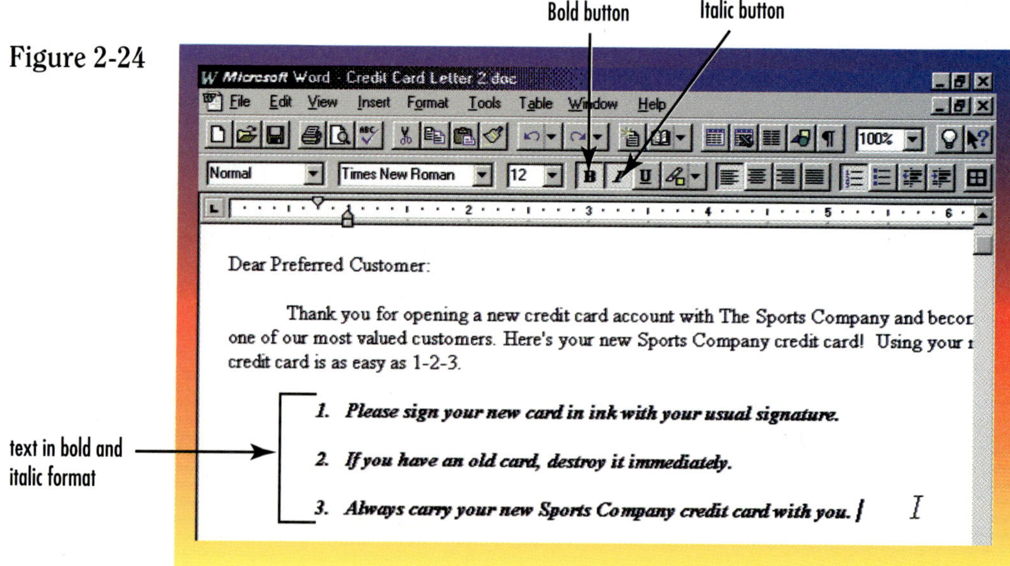

The three sentences appear in bold and italics.

Finally, you want to emphasize the information in the third paragraph about the 10 percent discount by underlining it.

Select the text "10% off the first purchase."

Click: U **Underline**

The menu equivalent is Format/Font/Underline/Single and the keyboard shortcut is Ctrl + U.

Clear the highlight.

The selected text appears underlined. However, you do not like how the underline looks. To clear any of the appearance settings, reselect the exact area of text and use the command again.

Remove the underline from the text.

You also could click Undo immediately to clear the underline.

Setting Paragraph Alignment

The final formatting change you want to make is to change the paragraph alignment.

Concept 9: Paragraph Alignment

Alignment is how text is positioned on a line between the margins or indents. There are four types of paragraph alignment: left, center, right, justified.

Alignment	Effect on Text
Left	Aligns text against the left margin of the page, leaving the right margin ragged. This is the most commonly used paragraph alignment type and therefore the default setting in all word processing software packages.
Center	Centers each line of text between left and right margins. Center alignment is used mostly for headings or centering graphics on a page.

Alignment	Effect on Text
Right	Aligns text against right margin, leaving left margin ragged. Use right alignment when you want text to line up on the outside of a page, such as a chapter title or a header.
Justified	Aligns text against right and left margins and evenly spaces out the letters. Newspapers commonly use justified alignment so the columns of text are even.

To add more style to your documents, mix the paragraph alignment settings.

Right

Left

Center

Justified

You want to change the alignment of the letter from the default of left-aligned to justified.

The commands to change paragraph alignment are under the Format/Paragraph menu. However, it is much faster to use the shortcuts shown below.

Alignment	Shortcut Keys	Button
Left	Ctrl + L	
Center	Ctrl + E	
Right	Ctrl + R	
Justified	Ctrl + J	

Select the entire letter.

The menu equivalent is Format/Paragraph/Indents and Spacing/Alignment/Justified.

Click: **Justify**

Clear the highlight and return to the top of the document.

To see the entire width of the document, you can change the zoom in Normal view.

The menu equivalent is View/Zoom/Page Width.

Click: 100% **Zoom Control**
Select: **Page Width**

Your screen should be similar to Figure 2-25.

Figure 2-25

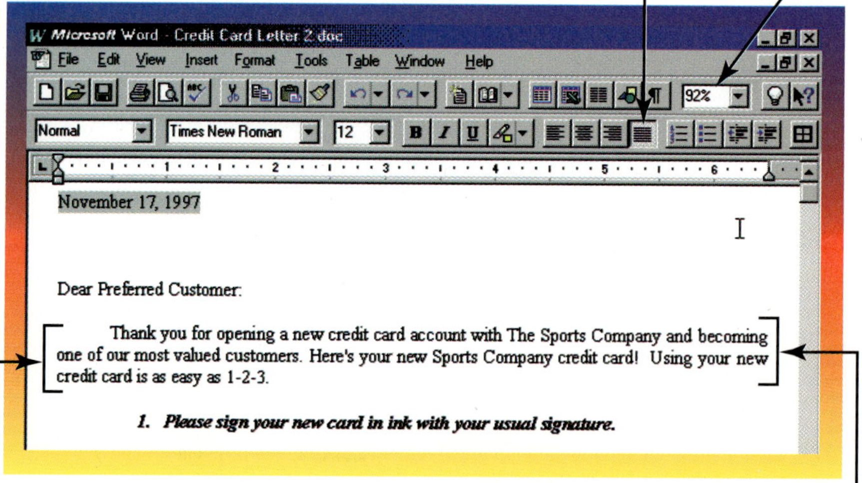

Scroll through the letter to see the changes in the alignment of text on the right margin.

All full lines now end even with the right margin. To do this, Word inserts extra spaces between words to push the text to the right margins. These are called **soft spaces** and are adjusted automatically whenever additions and deletions are made to the text.

Next, you want the date to be aligned flush against the right margin.

Move to: **the date field**

Click:  **Align Right**

The menu equivalent is Format/Paragraph/Indents and Spacing/Alignment/Right.

Your screen should be similar to Figure 2-26.

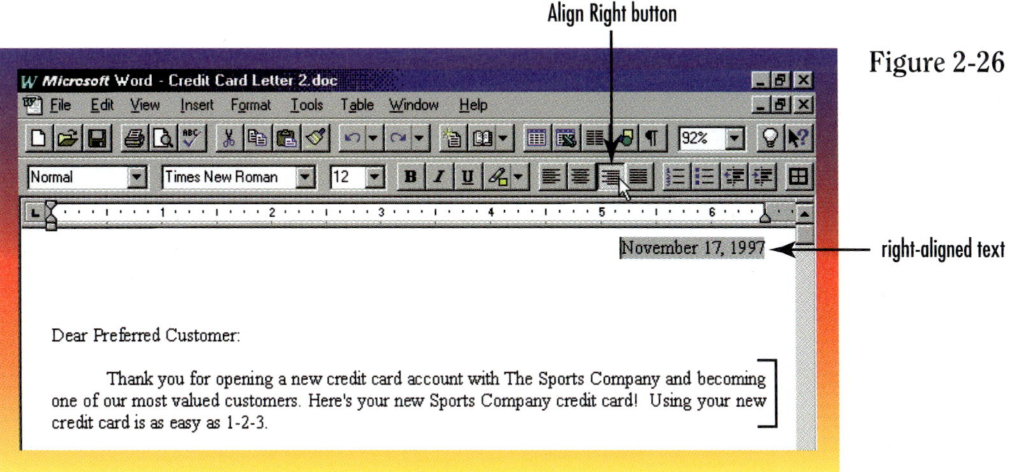

Figure 2-26

The date has moved so that it ends flush with the right margin.

The alignment settings can also be specified before typing in new text. As you type, it is aligned according to your selection until the alignment setting is changed to another setting.

Return the zoom percent to 100 percent. Replace Student Name with your name in the closing.

Saving, Previewing, and Printing

You would like to save the edited version of the credit card letter as Credit Card Letter 3. This will allow the original file, Credit Card Letter 2, to remain unchanged in case you want to repeat the lab for practice.

Use the Save As command to save the file on your data disk as Credit Card Letter 3.

Finally, before printing the letter, preview the letter.

Your screen should be similar to Figure 2-27.

Figure 2-27

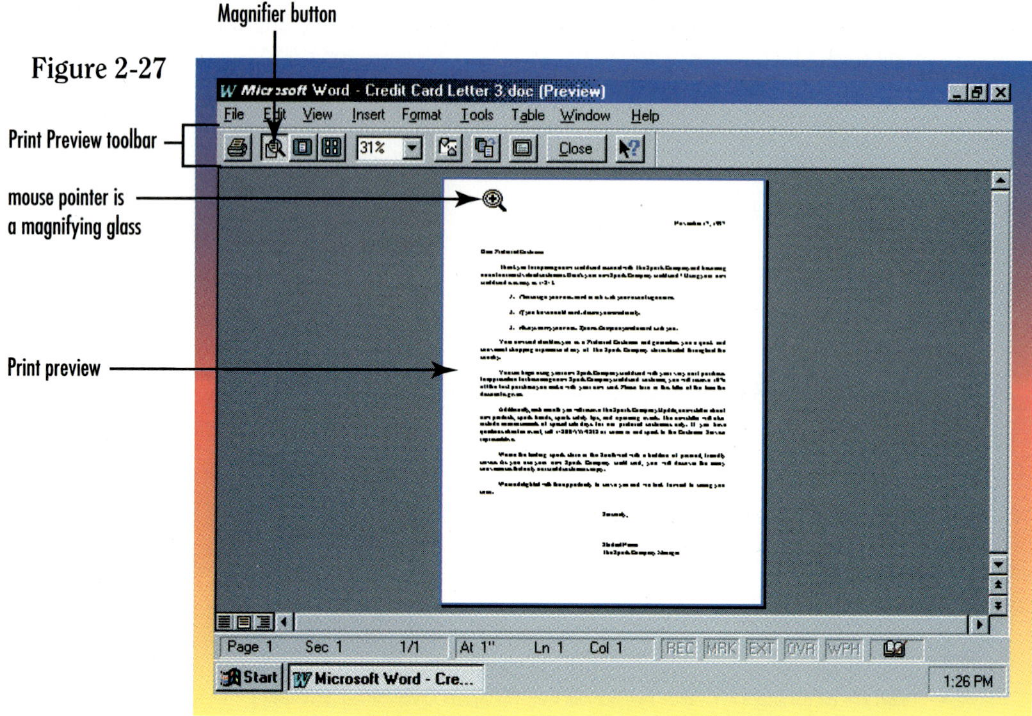

Now that you can see the entire letter, you decide that the date would look better at the 3.25-inch tab position.

While in Preview, you can edit and format text. Notice that the mouse pointer is a magnifying glass when it is positioned on text in the window. This indicates that when you click on a document the screen will toggle between the whole page view you currently see and 100% magnification.

To edit the date in the Preview window, point to the date and click the mouse button.

The text is displayed in the size it will appear when printed (100% zoom). Then, to switch between zooming the document and editing it,

Click: Magnifier

The mouse pointer changes to an I-beam and the insertion point is displayed. Now you can edit the document as in Normal view.

If necessary, move the insertion point to the beginning of the date.

First, you need to return the date to left-aligned.

Because the Formatting toolbar is not displayed, you will use the keyboard shortcut, Ctrl + L, to left-align the date.

Press: Ctrl + L

Then, to move the date to the 3.25-inch position,

Display the ruler. Move the upper indent marker to the 3.25-inch position. Hide the ruler again.

To switch back to zooming the document and restore it to the original preview size,

View Ruler turns on/off the display of the rulers.

100% Zoom Control button can also be used to specify the magnification.

Click:  **Magnifier**

Click: **the document**

To print a copy of the letter from the Preview window using the default print settings,

Make sure your printer is on and ready to print.

Click: **Print**

If you need to specify a different printer, you will need to close Print Preview and use the Print command on the File menu.

Your letter should be printing.

Close the Print Preview window. If necessary, change the view to Normal and the zoom percentage to 100 percent.

If you are ready to exit the Word program,

Choose: **File/Exit**

In response to the dialog boxes to save the files,

Choose: **Yes**

LAB REVIEW

Key Terms

active window (WP65)
alignment (WP93)
case-sensitive (WP72)
drag and drop (WP74)
field (WP77)
field code (WP77)
field result (WP77)
soft spaces (WP95)
Spelling tool (WP63)
Thesaurus (WP75)

Command Summary

Command	Shortcut Keys	Button	Action
File/Page Setup			Changes layout of page including margins, paper size, and paper source
Edit/Cut	Ctrl + X		Cuts selected text and copies it to Clipboard
Edit/Copy	Ctrl + C		Copies selected text to Clipboard
Edit/Paste	Ctrl + V		Pastes text from Clipboard
Edit/Select All	Ctrl + A		Selects all text
Edit/Find	Ctrl + F		Locates specified text
Edit/Replace	Ctrl + H		Locates and replaces specified text
View/Normal			Displays document in Normal view
View/Outline			Displays structure of document as an outline
View/Page Layout			Displays the document as it will appear when printed
View/Master Document			Shows several documents organized into a master document
View/Full Screen			Shows the document without Word's toolbars, menus, scroll bars, and other screen elements
View/Zoom		100%	Changes onscreen character size
View/Zoom/Whole Page			Displays entire page on screen
Insert/Date and Time			Inserts current date or time, maintained by computer system, in selected format
Format/Font/Font Style/Italic	Ctrl + I	*I*	Makes selected text italic
Format/Font/Font Style/Bold	Ctrl + B	**B**	Makes selected text bold
Format/Font/Underline/Single	Ctrl + U	U	Underlines selected text
Format/Paragraph/Indents and Spacing/ Special/First Line			Indents first line of a paragraph from the right margin
Format/Paragraph/Indents and Spacing/ Alignment/Left	Ctrl + L		Aligns text to left margin
Format/Paragraph/Indents and Spacing/ Alignment/Centered	Ctrl + E		Centers text between left and right margins
Format/Paragraph/Indents and Spacing/ Alignment/Right	Ctrl + R		Aligns text to right margin

Command	Shortcut Keys	Button	Action
Format/Paragraph/Indents and Spacing/ Alignment/Justified	Ctrl + J		Aligns text equally between left and right margins
Format/Bullets and Numbering			Inserts and removes bullets or numbers from selection
Tools/Spelling	F7		Starts the Spelling tool
Tools/Thesaurus	⇧Shift + F7		Starts the Thesaurus tool
Window/Arrange All			Displays all open documents in windows without overlapping
Window/#<filename>			Makes selected window active

Matching

1. justify	_____	**a.**	suggests synonyms and antonyms
2. date field	_____	**b.**	allows you to select the entire document
3. Edit/Select All	_____	**c.**	shortcut for bold command
4. margins	_____	**d.**	displays open document windows without overlapping
5. Ctrl + B	_____	**e.**	text that has even left and right margins
6.	_____	**f.**	white space between printed text and edge of paper
7. Window/Arrange All	_____	**g.**	removes text from the document and stores it in the Clipboard
8. Thesaurus	_____	**h.**	quickly locates specified text
9.	_____	**i.**	creates bulleted list
10. Find	_____	**j.**	a code that instructs Word to insert the current date in the document using the selected format whenever the document is printed

Fill-In Questions

1. Complete the following statements by filling in the blanks with the correct terms.

a. The white space between the text and the edge of the paper is the _______________ .

b. Use a _______________ list to convey a sequence of events.

c. The _____________ text format is used to indicate words to be deleted.

d. The ______________ and _______________ views show how text will appear on the printed page.

e. Use the _______________ to find synonyms for common words.

f. When text aligns evenly against the right and left margins, it is _________________ .

Discussion Questions

1. What is the purpose of formatting a document? What criteria would you suggest for a professional document?
2. Discuss how multiple windows can be used. When would it be appropriate to have multiple windows open?
3. Discuss the different ways information can be moved within a document. When would it be appropriate to use either method?
4. Discuss the different document views. When would it be appropriate to switch to a different view?
5. Discuss the problems that can be associated with finding and replacing text. What can you do to avoid some of these problems?

Hands-On Practice Exercises

Step by Step

Rating System

☆ Easy
☆☆ Moderate
☆☆☆ Difficult

1. To complete this exercise, you must have first completed Practice Exercise 2 in Lab 1. Open the file MOUSE TERMS 1 on your data disk.

- **a.** Bold and italicize the terms ("Point," "Click," "Double-click," etc.).
- **b.** Find all occurrences of the word "thing" and replace them with the word "object".
- **c.** Use the Thesaurus to find synonyms for the words "often" and "several" in the last sentence of the "Click" paragraph. Then, use the Thesaurus to find a synonym for "location" in the "Drag and Drop" paragraph.
- **d.** Set the paragraph alignment to justified, and center and bold the title. Change all margins to 1.5".
- **e.** Bullet the five terms and their definitions.
- **f.** Save the document as MOUSE TERMS 2. Print the document.

You will complete this exercise as Practice Exercise 1 in Lab 3.

2. You have been accepted at Metropolitan Community College, and have received a letter from the Director of Admissions informing you of the orientation that you will be required to attend. You will create that letter in this exercise.

- **a.** Before you type the letter (shown below), change all margins to 1.5", and set the alignment to justified. Type the letter as shown except that you will use the Date and Time command to insert the date, and substitute information that pertains to you in the bracketed areas.

Metropolitan Community College
123 Metropolitan Blvd.
Anytown, USA

[Current Date]

[Student's Name]
[Street Address]
[City, State Zip Code]

Dear [Student's Name]:

Congratulations on your acceptance into the [Student's Major] program at Metropolitan Community College

Orientation for new students will be held next Friday morning from 9:00 - Noon. It is imperative that you attend this session prior to your enrollment at Metropolitan Community College.

Student leaders from the [Student's Major] program will be there to give you a guided tour of the Metropolitan Community College campus with an emphasis on your course of study.

We will initially meet in the Student Center where you will be introduced to the [Student's Major] program coordinator. Light refreshments will be served at this time while you become acquainted with others in your major field as well as faculty

members in attendance.

After the orientation ends at 12:00, you are encouraged to join us for a luncheon in the cafeteria.

Once again, [Student's Name], congratulations on your acceptance, and we hope to see you next Friday.

If you are unable to attend, please call me at 1-800-555-1MCC.

Sincerely,

Joseph K. College
Director of Admissions

JKC/xxx

b. Add documentation to the file. Save the document as ACCEPTANCE LETTER. Print the letter.

c. Search for all occurrences of Metropolitan Community College. Replace all but the first occurrence (in the address) with M.C.C.

d. Italicize and bold the word "imperative" in the second paragraph. Then, use the Thesaurus to replace the word with an appropriate synonym.

e. Reverse the order of the third and fourth paragraphs.

f. Center and bold the return address. Right-align the date.

g. Indent the three closing lines to the 3" position on the ruler.

h. Save the document again with the same name. Print the letter.

You will complete this exercise as Practice Exercise 2 in Lab 4.

3. In this problem you will continue creating Grandma Gertie's cookie recipes cookbook. To complete this exercise, you must have completed Practice Exercise 5 in Lab 1. Open the file POTATO CHIP COOKIES from your data disk.

a. Bold the name of the cookie at the top of the document. Bold and italicize the headings "Ingredients:" and "Directions:".

b. Indent the instructions from "2 sticks of butter" to "Confectioner's sugar" 0.5" from the left. Bullet the directions from "Cream the butter. . ." to "Bake in 350 degree oven. . . ." Indent the bulleted directions 0.5" from the left.

c. Save the file using the same name. Do not close the document.

d. Open the file MORE RECIPES on your data disk. Display both document windows in the text area. Copy the POTATO CHIP COOKIES file to the end of the MORE RECIPES file. Close the POTATO CHIP COOKIES file. Maximize the document window.

e. Center and bold the title at the top of the document. Italicize the note at the top of the document, and justify that paragraph only.

f. The Cut-Out Sugar Cookies have their "Ingredients:" and "Directions:" sections mixed up. Reverse the order of these two sections. "Makes about 5 dozen 2" cookies" should be the last line in the recipe.

g. Bold the names of the first two cookies. Bold and italicize the headings "Ingredients:" and "Directions:" for the first two cookies.

h. Indent the instructions for the first two cookies 0.5" from the left. Bullet the directions for the first two cookies, and indent the bulleted directions 0.5" from the left. Do not be concerned that the recipes are split between pages. You will learn to keep text together on a page in the next lab.

i. Document the file. Save the document as UPDATED COOKIE RECIPES. Print the document.

You will complete this exercise as Practice Exercise 5 in Lab 3.

4. To complete this exercise, you must have completed Practice Exercise 6 in Lab 1. Open the file B&B AD from your data disk.

a. Bold and center the first three lines. Italicize the two lines that contain the host's phone number and name.

b. Bullet the lines from "Number of Rooms" to "Social Drinking", and indent to the 1" position on the ruler.

c. Reverse the order of the third and fourth paragraphs.

d. Set the alignment of the five paragraphs to justified, and change all margins to 1.3".

e. Search for all occurrences of "Poconos" and replace them with "Pocono Mountains".

f. Use the Thesaurus to find synonyms for "rustic" and "numerous" in the first paragraph and "breathtaking" in the second paragraph.

g. Save the document as B&B AD PART 2. Print the ad.

You will complete this exercise as Practice Exercise 4 in Lab 3.

On Your Own

5. Many people create lists of things they need to do each day or each week. In this problem you will create a list of things you need to do for the week.

Create a numbered "to do" list of all the things you have to do this week (or all the things you would *like* to do this week) in either order of importance or chronological order.

Add a title that includes your name and the current date. Use the formatting techniques you have learned to improve the appearance of the list.

Document the file. Save the document as TO DO LIST. Print the document.

6. In this exercise, you will modify a document containing tips on how to prepare for a job interview.

Open the file PREPARING FOR THE INTERVIEW on your data disk. Center and bold the title. Bold the heading "Helpful Tips."

Bullet the four Helpful Tips from "Know the exact place and time of the interview" to "Dress for success." Indent the bulleted list one tab stop.

Italicize and bold the first sentence in each of the four tips. In the second tip, emphasize the sentence "Failure to do homework can be the kiss of death." In the last tip, emphasize the text "only one" in the 7th sentence. In the same section, emphasize the last sentence "Call attention to what you say, not what you wear." Italicize the reference "CPC Annual 1990-91 Edition" below the list of tips.

Justify all lines below the title. Increase the margins to 1.5" all around.

Insert your name and the current date below the document. Document the file. Save the document as INTERVIEW TIPS. Print the document.

7. In this exercise, you will format a document that tells how to redisplay screen elements that have, for one reason or another, disappeared!

Open the file CAPTURING SCREEN ELEMENTS. This document tells how to hide and display toolbars and how to return the document from full screen view to the last view you used. Spell-check the document.

Enter the following text in a new document window:

> **The Ruler**
>
> **The Ruler Bar is usually displayed below the toolbars. You can use the Ruler Bar to conveniently set margins or tabs with a click of the mouse. If the Ruler Bar is not displayed, here's how to get it back.**
>
> **Open the View menu. The Ruler command is just below toolbars. Clicking a checked Ruler turns it off, and clicking an unchecked Ruler turns it on.**

Enter your name and the current date below the last paragraph. Save the document as THE RULER. Print the document.

Copy the ruler information (excluding your name and the date) into the CAPTURING SCREEN ELEMENTS file just before the "Toolbars" section. Adjust spacing as needed.

Add appropriate text formatting to emphasize the title "Capturing Screen Elements At Large" and the headings "The Ruler," "Toolbars," and "Help! All I Have Is This Big White Screen!" In the line "Choose: View/Toolbars," bold and underline the "V" in "View" and the "T" in "Toolbars."

Move "The Ruler" section below the "Toolbars" section. Adjust spacing as needed.

Change the alignment to justified for the document, and center the title.

Locate all occurrences of "Ruler Bar" and replace them with "Ruler."

Adjust margins until the document just fits on one page. What settings did you use?

Indent the three lines of instruction ("Choose: View/Toolbars," "Choose: OK when you are finished," and "Press: Esc!") to the 0.5" mark on the ruler.

Document the file and save it as CAPTURING SCREEN ELEMENTS 2. Print the document.

2 Formatting a Document

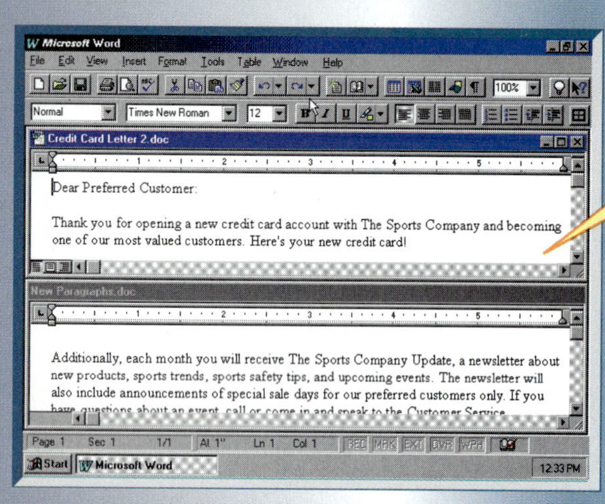

Multiple Document Windows

Opening multiple document windows lets you switch easily between documents to cut, copy, and paste, as well as to see reference information in other documents.

Thesaurus

A thesaurus is a reference tool that contains synonyms, antonyms, and related words for commonly used words. Use the Thesaurus to add interest and variety to your writing.

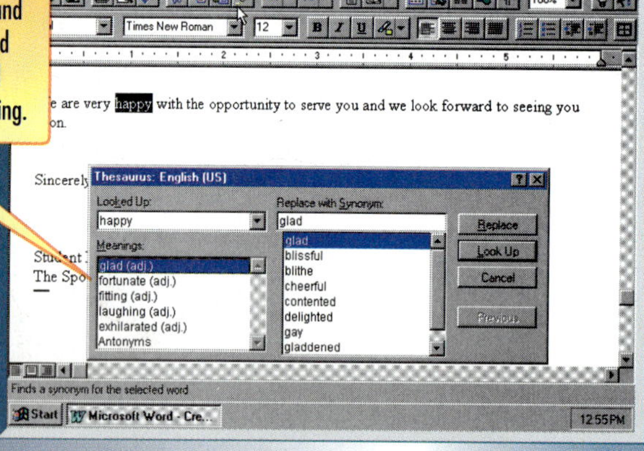

Document Views

There are six different ways that you can view a document. Each view offers different features for creating and editing your documents.

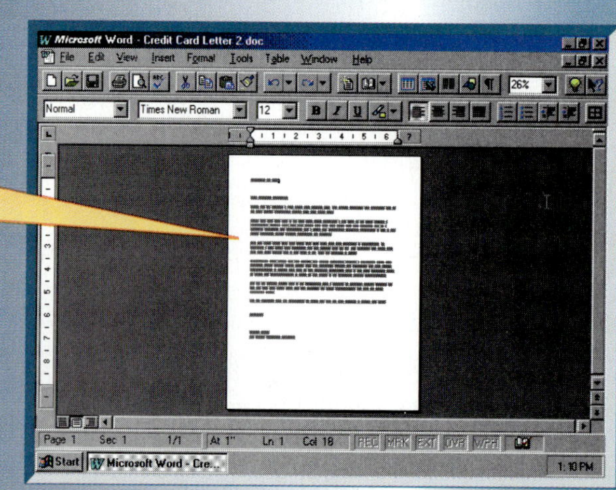

Find and Replace

To make editing easier, you can use the Find and Replace feature to find a word in a document and automatically replace it with another word.

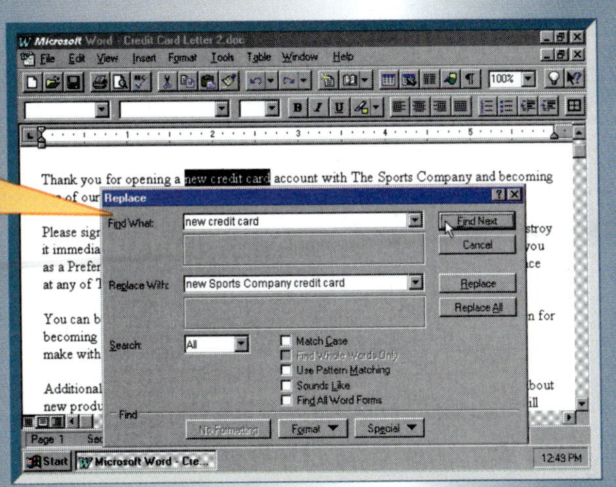

Concepts

- Multiple Document Windows
- Find and Replace
- Thesaurus
- Margins
- Document Views
- Indents
- Text Formats
- Bulleted and Numbered Lists
- Paragraph Alignment

Margins

The margin is the distance from the text to the edge of the paper. Specifying different margin settings for a document changes the appearance of the document on the printed page.

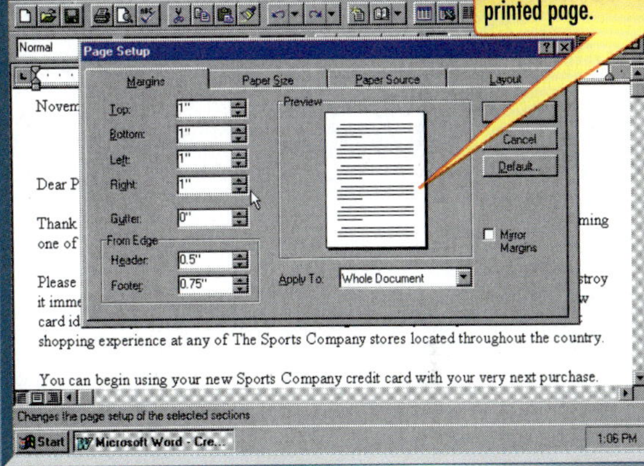

Indents

To help your reader find information quickly, you can indent paragraphs of similar content. Indenting paragraphs sets them off from the rest of the document.

Bulleted and Numbered Lists

Use bulleted or numbered lists to organize information and make the message clear and easy to read.

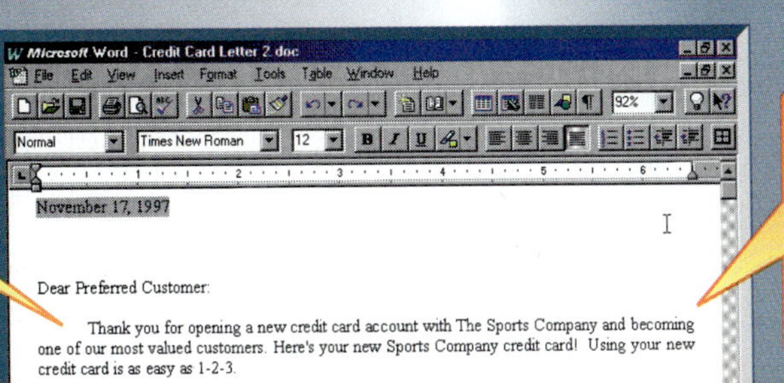

Paragraph Alignment

To give your documents more visual interest, you can change the alignment of paragraphs. Alignment is how text is positioned on a line between the margins or indents.

Text Formats

Different text formats can be applied to selections to add emphasis or interest to a document.

Creating Reports and Newsletters

3

You have seen how a word processor makes it easy to create professional letters and memos. These two types of correspondence are perhaps the commonest forms of written communications and the easiest to produce. Next, you will see how a word processor excels in the production of more complicated documents such as reports and newsletters.

COMPETENCIES

After completing this lab you will know how to:

1. Create a page break.
2. Change fonts and type sizes.
3. Apply heading styles.
4. Create a table of contents.
5. Create and edit footnotes.
6. Number pages.
7. Keep lines together.
8. Use WordArt.
9. Set tabs.
10. Add border lines.
11. Create newspaper columns.
12. Use hyphenation.
13. Add pictures.
14. Add a box and shading.
15. Add a drop cap.

As with all forms of correspondence, report and newsletter documents are both used to convey information. But each serves a different purpose. In a report, your focus should be on presentation and organization so the reader can find information quickly. In a newsletter, the information must be easy to read and, most importantly, be visually appealing. In this lab, you will use some of the desktop publishing tools in Word 7.0 to create a report and a newsletter.

Concept Overview

The following concepts will be introduced in this lab:

1. Fonts Different fonts are used to add interest to your document and provide visual cues to help find information quickly.

2. Style Applying different predesigned styles is a fast way to add professional-appearing formatting to your document.

3. Heading Styles Heading styles are designed to identify different levels of headings in a document. Heading styles include combinations of fonts, type sizes, bold, and italics.

4. Footnotes and Endnotes Footnotes are source references or text offering additional explanation that is placed at the bottom of a page. Endnotes are also source references or long comments that typically appear at the end of a document.

5. WordArt WordArt is a supplementary application included with the Word program. It allows you to enhance your documents by changing the shape of text, adding 3-D effects, and changing the alignment of text on a line.

6. Tabs A tab is a predefined stopping point along a line to which text will indent when you press Tab. As with other default settings, you can change the location of tabs in the document.

7. Graphics Graphics are non-text elements such as charts, drawings, and pictures that you can add to a document.

CASE STUDY

The Southwest Regional Manager is very pleased with your work so far, and has asked you to help with the development and design of the first monthly newsletter. Specifically, you have been asked to develop several topics to be used as articles in the newsletter, and to propose a sample newsletter design.

Your final sample newsletter will look like the one shown here.

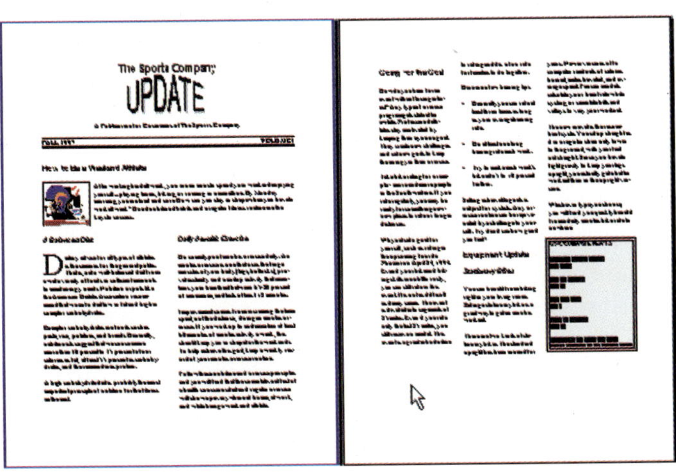

Part 1

Creating a Page Break

You have already researched several topics for the newsletter and would like to present the information to the manager before creating a final copy to use in the newsletter.

Load Word 7.0. Open the file Newsletter Research. If necessary, maximize the document window and switch to Normal view.

The first page of the document is a memo you have started to the manager.

Enter your name at the tab stop following "FROM:".

Next, you will enter the current date.

Move to: **the tab stop following "DATE:"**
Choose: **Insert/Date and Time**

From the Available Formats list, select the fourth format (Month Day, Year).

This time you do not want the date inserted as a field.

If necessary, clear the Update Automatically (Insert as Field) option box.

Choose: **OK**

The system date is displayed in the document at the insertion point. It is not a field, and will not update automatically when the document is opened on a later date.

The text for the first topic currently begins on the same page, below the text for the memo. You want the memo to be on a page by itself. To begin page 2 with the first line of the text,

The keyboard shortcut is Ctrl + ↵Enter.

Move to: **"H" in "Health and Fitness"**
Choose: **Insert/Break/OK**

Your screen should be similar to Figure 3-1.

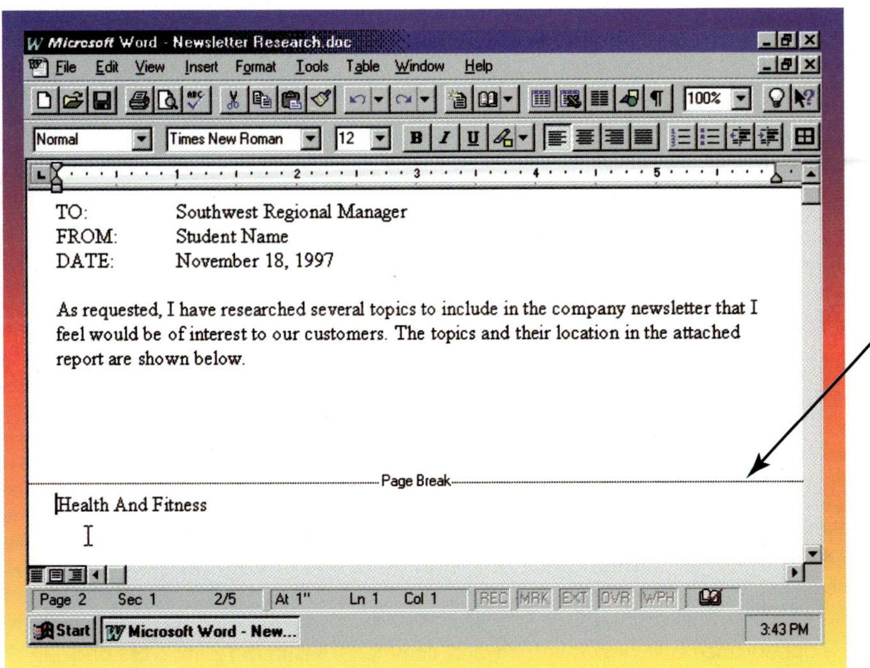

Figure 3-1

manual page break

A dotted line appears on the line above the insertion point, and the words "Page Break" appear in the middle of the line. The dotted line indicates that you have entered a manual page break at that position. A **manual page break** instructs Word to begin a new page at that location regardless of the amount of text on the previous page. All automatic page breaks following the insertion of a manual page break are immediately adjusted.

> To remove a manual page break, move to the beginning of the line that follows the page break and press ←Backspace.

Changing Fonts and Type Size

Next you want to add to the memo a table of contents that lists the topics and their page numbers. The table of contents will be displayed several lines below the text of the memo. First you will enter a heading for the table of contents.

Move to: **two lines below the memo (page 1, line 9)**

To center the heading on this line,

Click:  **Center**

> The menu equivalent is Format/Paragraph/Alignment/Centered or Ctrl + E.

The insertion point moves to the middle of the line. As you type the text, it will be centered on the line.

Type: **Table of Contents**

To make the table of contents heading stand out from the listing that will be displayed below it, you will change the character font and size.

Concept 1: Fonts

A **font**, also commonly referred to as a **typeface**, is a set of characters with a specific design. The designs have names such as Roman and Courier. Using fonts as a design element can add interest to your document and give readers visual cues to help them find information quickly.

There are two basic types of fonts, serif and sans serif. **Serif fonts** have a flair at the base of each letter that visually leads the reader to the next letter. Two common serif fonts are Roman or Times New Roman. Serif fonts generally are used in paragraphs. **Sans serif fonts** do not have a flair at the base of each letter. Arial and Helvetica are names of two common sans serif fonts. Because sans serif fonts have a clean look, they are often used for headers in documents. It is good practice to use only two types of fonts in a document, one for text and one for headers. Too many styles can make your document look cluttered and unprofessional.

Each font has one or more sizes. Size is the height and width of the character and is commonly measured in **points**, abbreviated "pt." One point equals about 1/72 of an inch, and text in most documents is 10 pt or 12 pt. Some fonts, such as Courier New, are **monospaced**, which means that each character takes up the same amount of space. Most fonts are **proportional**, which means that some letters, such as *m* or *w*, take up more space than other letters, such as *i* or *t*. Arial and Times New Roman are proportional fonts. Most fonts are **scalable**, which means they can be printed in almost any point size, depending on the capabilities of your printer. Nonscalable fonts are assigned a single point size.

In addition, as you have learned earlier, different styles, such as bold and italics, can be applied to a font to enhance the appearance of a document. Several common fonts in different sizes and styles are shown in the following table.

Font Name	Font Type	Font Size	Font Style (Bold)
Arial	Sans serif (proportional)	This is 10 pt. This is 16 pt.	**Bold 10 pt.** **Bold 16 pt.**
Courier New	Serif (monospaced)	This is 10 pt. This is 16 pt.	**Bold 10 pt.** **Bold 16 pt.**
Times New Roman	Serif (proportional)	This is 10 pt. This is 16 pt.	Bold 10 pt. **Bold 16 pt.**

To change the font, type size, or style before typing the text, use the command and then type. All text will appear in the specified font setting until another font setting is selected. To change a font setting for existing text, select the text you want to change and then use the command. Only the selected text appears in the new font setting.

You would like the heading to be in a different font and a larger type size than the text.

To do this, select the Table of Contents heading.

Choose: **Format/Font**

If necessary, select the Font tab.

The Font dialog box on your screen should be similar to Figure 3-2.

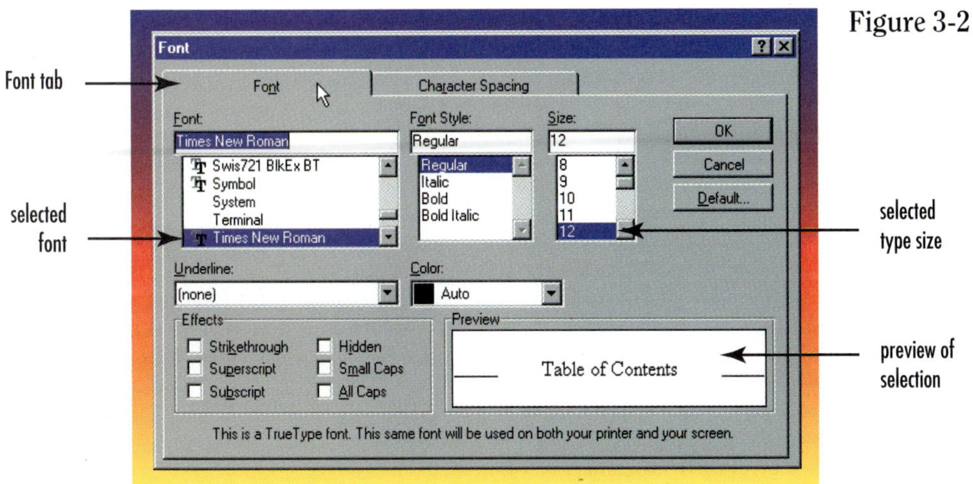

Figure 3-2

The Font list box displays the fonts supported by your active printer. The Word preset font, Times New Roman, is the currently selected font.

Notice the symbols next to many of the font names. The symbol indicates that the font is a True Type font. These fonts are scalable fonts that are automatically installed when you install Windows. They appear onscreen exactly as they will appear when printed. The symbol indicates that the font is a printer font. These are fonts that are available on your printer. A printer font must have a corresponding screen font in order for it to appear onscreen as it will appear on the printed page. If you choose a printer font that does not have a corresponding screen font, your screen image will not exactly match your printed output. Word will use a font onscreen that is as close in appearance to your selected font as possible.

To change the font to True Type Arial from the Font list,

Select: Arial

The Preview box displays how the selected text will appear in the selected font. As you can see, it is a sans serif font and is appropriate for a heading. Next, to enlarge the type size to 14, from the Size list box,

Select: 14

Again the Preview box reflects the selected settings. Finally, you want to bold the selection. From the Font Style list box,

Choose: Bold/OK

The selected text is displayed in the Arial font, in 14 pt. type size, and bold (see Figure 3-3). The Formatting toolbar displays the current font and size setting for the text at the location of the insertion point in the Font and Font Size buttons.

The keyboard shortcut is Ctrl + ⇧Shift + A, or use ⇧Shift + F3 to cycle text between uppercase, lowercase, and sentence case (capitalizes first word of sentences).

You also decide to change the heading to all uppercase characters. Rather than retype the text, you can quickly convert the selection to uppercase characters. To do this,

Choose: **Format/Change Case/UPPERCASE/OK**

Clear the highlight.

Your screen should be similar to Figure 3-3.

Figure 3-3

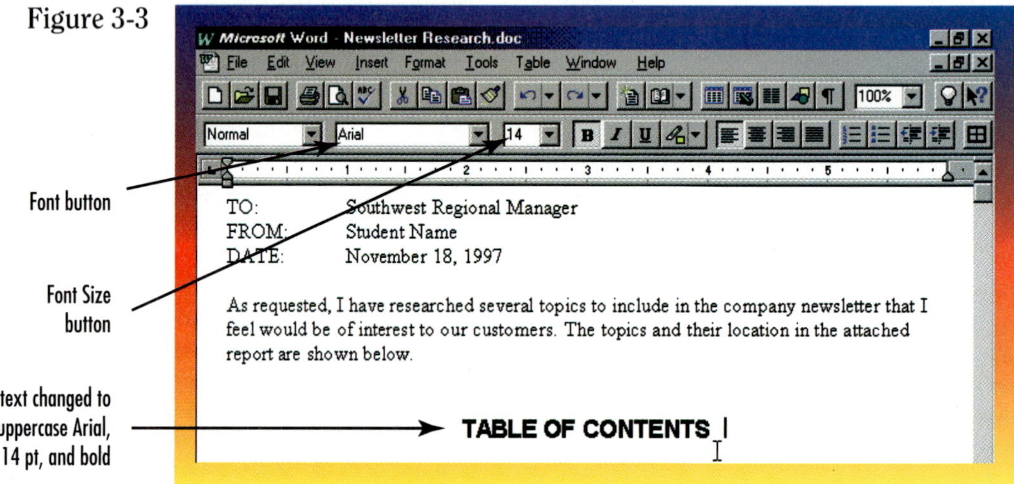

Applying Heading Styles

Next you will create a table of contents for the memo. When completed, the table of contents will look like the one shown here.

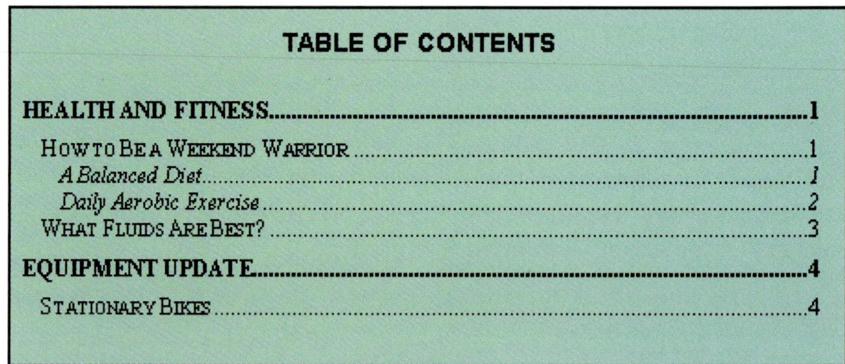

TABLE OF CONTENTS

A table of contents can be generated automatically by Word from text within the document. Before you can do this, each heading that you want included in the table of contents list must have a heading style applied to it.

Concept 2: Style

A **style** is a group of formats that are assigned a name. Word includes 75 predefined styles, or you can create your own custom styles. Styles can be applied to characters or paragraphs. **Character styles** consist of a combination of any character formats in the Fonts dialog box that affect selected text. The default character style for the Normal document sets the font to Times New Roman, 10 point. **Paragraph styles** are a combination of any character formats and paragraph formats that affect all text in a paragraph. A paragraph style can include all the font settings that apply to characters as well as tab settings, indents, and line settings that apply to paragraphs. The default paragraph style of Normal includes such settings as the left indent to 0, single line spacing, and left alignment. Among the many styles you can apply are styles to format headings, table of contents, listings, annotations, and footnotes.

This document contains three levels of headings that need to be identified with three different heading styles.

Concept 3: Heading Styles

A **heading style** is a style that is designed to identify different levels of headings in a document. Heading styles include combinations of fonts, type sizes, bold, and italics. The nine different heading styles and the formats associated with each are shown below:

Heading 1: Arial 14pt bold

Heading 2: Arial 12pt. bold, italic

Heading 3: Arial 12pt

Heading 4: Arial 12pt bold

Heading 5: Arial 11pt

Heading 6: Times New Roman 11pt italic

Heading 7: Arial 10pt

Heading 8: Arial 10pt italic

Heading 9: Arial 9pt bold, italic

The most important heading should be assigned a Heading 1 style. This style is the largest size and most prominent style. The next most important heading should be assigned the Heading 2 style, and so forth. Headings give your reader another visual cue about how the information is grouped in your document.

The first-level heading is the topic category. "Health and Fitness" at the beginning of page 2 is the first topic category heading.

To assign this heading a Heading 1 style, move to anywhere in the heading "Health and Fitness."

Choose: **Format/Style**

The Style dialog box is displayed. If the Styles list box does not display the list of styles as in Figure 3-4,

Choose: **List/All Styles**

The Style dialog box on your screen should be similar to Figure 3-4.

Figure 3-4

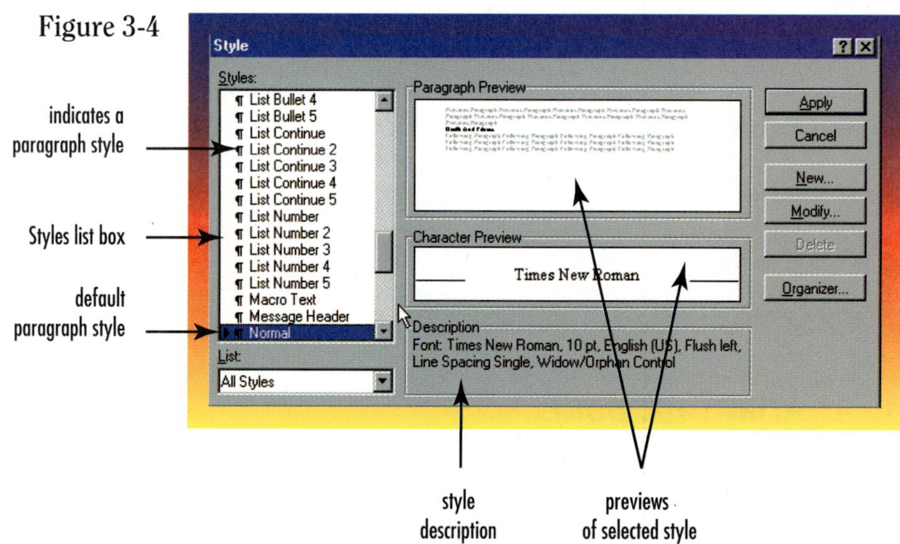

The Style list box displays the names of all the preset styles that are included in the Word program. The default style, Normal, is highlighted. Notice the ¶ symbol preceding the style. This indicates it is a paragraph style. A character style is preceded with the letter *a*. The format settings included in the selected style are displayed in the Description box. To apply the Heading 1 style to the text,

Select: ¶ **Heading 1**

The Description box now displays the format settings associated with the Heading 1 style. The two preview areas show examples of how the selected style will appear. To use this style,

Choose: **Apply**

Your screen should be similar to Figure 3-5.

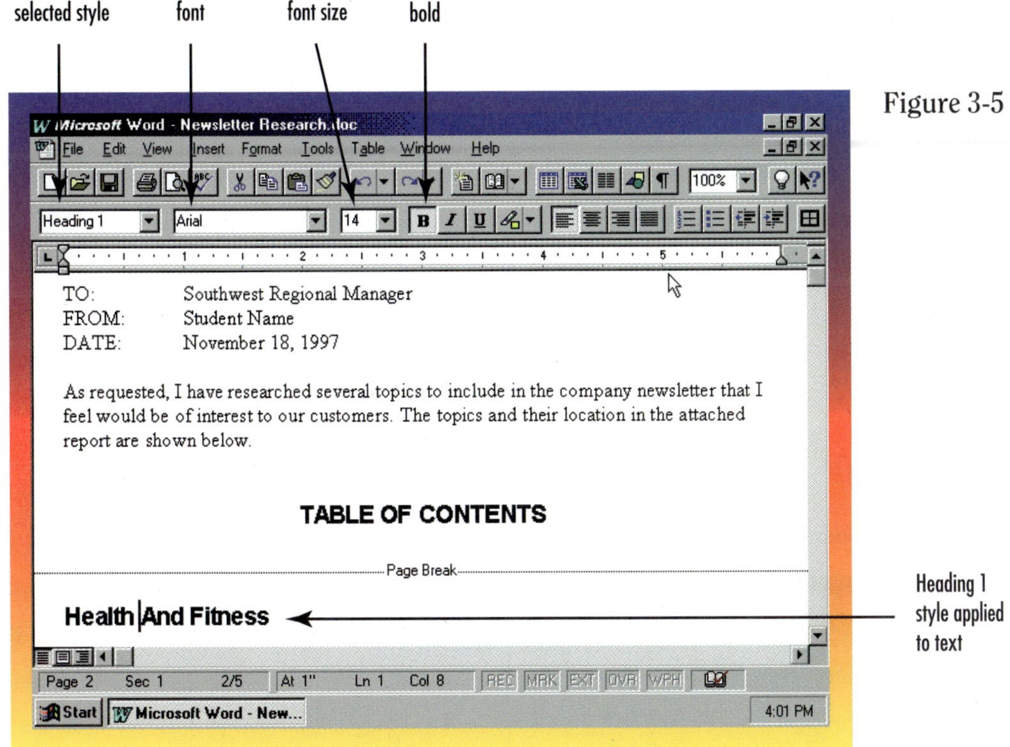

Figure 3-5

Notice that the Style box in the Formatting toolbar displays Heading 1 for the text the insertion point is on. This heading style formats the text to Arial, 14 pt., and bold. The Heading 1 style is applied to the entire paragraph that the insertion point is on.

You can check the style of a particular paragraph or character by clicking  and pointing to the text.

The second topic heading is "Equipment Update" on page 4.

Move the insertion point to anywhere in this head.

To quickly apply the same format style that you just used,

Word 7.0 will apply Heading 1 style automatically to text as you type if you end a sentence without punctuation and press ←Enter twice.

Choose: **Edit/Repeat Style**

The keyboard shortcut is Ctrl + Y.

This command repeats your last action and the topic heading is formatted using the Heading 1 style.

The next heading to be formatted is the article title, "How to Be a Weekend Warrior," on page 2.

Move the insertion point to anywhere in this heading.

The article title is a subheading below the topic heading. Because it is one level lower than the heading above it, the Heading 2 style will be used. To apply the Heading 2 style to this text,

Open the Style drop-down list box.

Select: **Heading 2**

The menu equivalent is Format/Style/Styles/Heading 2/Apply.

Your screen should be similar to Figure 3-6.

Figure 3-6

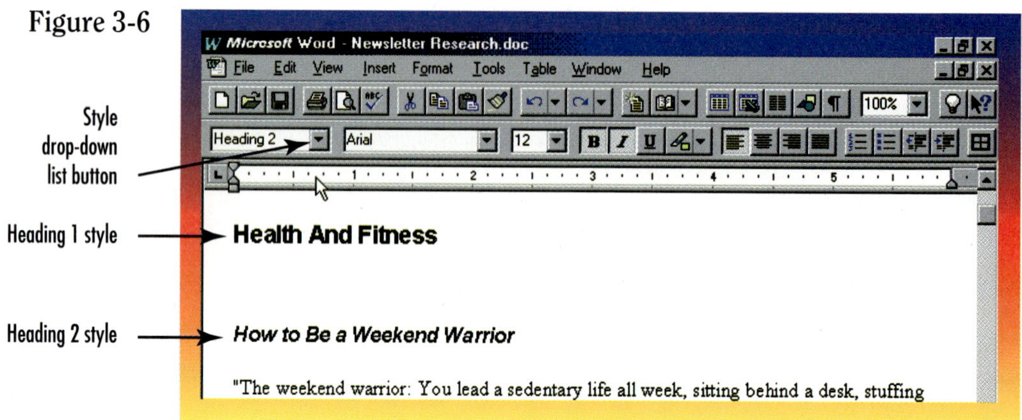

The Heading 2 style formats the text to Arial, 12 pt., bold, and italic.

Apply the following heading styles to the remaining headings in the document:

Heading	Page #	Style
A Balanced Diet	2	Heading 3
Daily Aerobic Exercise	3	Heading 3
What Fluids Are Best?	3	Heading 2
Stationary Bikes	4	Heading 2

If you accidentally apply the wrong heading style, reselect the text and select the correct style. To return the style to the default, select Normal.

When you are done, return to the top of the document.

Creating the Table of Contents

Once heading styles are assigned to all the headings you want included in the table of contents, you can create the table of contents. You want the list of topics to be displayed several lines below the heading TABLE OF CONTENTS on the memo page. To place the insertion point where you want the table of contents to begin,

Move to: **second blank line below the Table of Contents heading (page 1, line 11)**

To create the table of contents,

Choose: **Insert/Index and Tables**

If necessary, select the Table of Contents tab.

The Index and Tables dialog box on your screen should be similar to Figure 3-7.

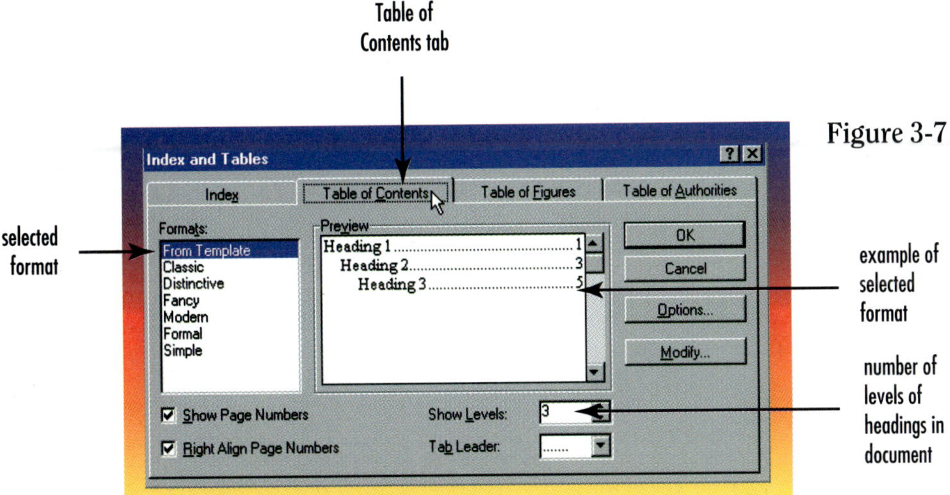

Figure 3-7

First you need to select the format or design of the table of contents that you want Word to create. The Formats list box displays the names of the available formats, and the Preview box displays an example of the selected format, From Template. This format option allows you to create your own table of contents and save it as a template by modifying the existing format.

Highlight each format option to preview the different table of contents formats.

You decide the Formal format is the most appropriate one for this table of contents. This style will display the page numbers flush with the right margin, and with a series of dots called **tab leaders** between the heading and the page number.

Select: **Formal**

The Show Levels text box shows that Word has located three levels of headings that have been applied to the document. The number of levels of headings you assigned controls the number of levels that will be displayed in the table of contents. To complete the command and create the table of contents,

Choose: **OK**

After a few moments, the table of contents is displayed.

Your screen should be similar to Figure 3-8.

Figure 3-8

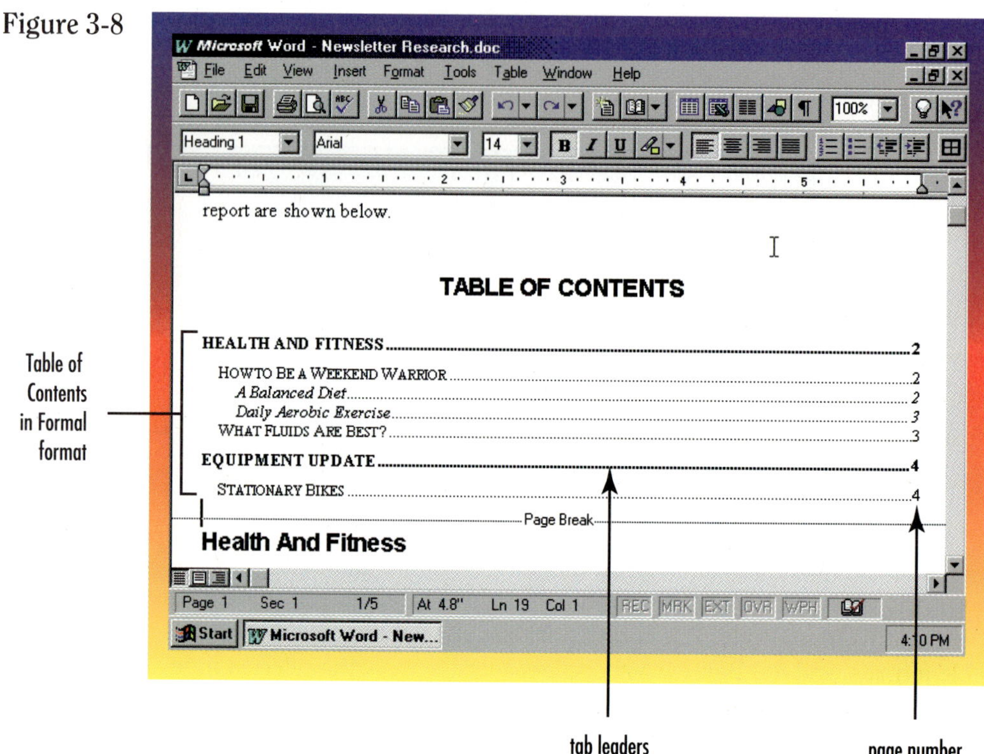

The table of contents is generated from the text to which you applied the three levels of headings. The headings that were assigned a Heading 1 style are aligned with the left margin. Level 2 and 3 headings are indented below the level 1 and level 2 headings as appropriate. The page numbers are displayed flush with the right margin. Tab leaders separate the heads from the page numbers.

Move to anywhere in the table of contents.

The entire table of contents is shaded, indicating that the table of contents is a field.

The text in the table of contents uses the default font size of 10 pts.

To make the text the same size as the text in the rest of the document, select the entire table of contents and set the type size to 12 pts.

> Because the table of contents is a field, if you add or remove headings, you can update the table of contents using the Update Field command on the Shortcut menu or F9.

Creating Footnotes

Next you need to add several footnotes to the document.

Concept 4: Footnotes and Endnotes

Footnotes are source references or text offering additional explanation that is placed at the bottom of a page. **Endnotes** are also source references or long comments that typically appear at the end of a document. You can have both footnotes and endnotes in the same document.

Footnotes and endnotes consist of two parts; the reference mark and the note text. The **reference mark** is commonly a superscript number that appears in the document text at the end of the material being referenced. The **note text** for a footnote appears at the bottom of the page on which the reference mark appears. The footnote text is separated from the document text with a horizontal line called the **note separator**. Endnote text appears as a listing at the end of the document.

The Footnote command on the Insert menu will automatically number and place footnotes and endnotes in a document. The first reference that needs to be footnoted is the quotation in the first paragraph on page 2. Before using the Footnote command, the insertion point must be positioned where the footnote number is to be displayed.

You can double-click on the table of contents page number to move to that page in the document.

The keyboard shortcut to insert a footnote using the default setting is Alt + Ctrl + F.

Move to: end of the quote on page 2 (after the quotation marks)
Choose: Insert/Footnote

In the Footnote and Endnote dialog box, you specify whether you want to create footnotes or endnotes and the type of reference mark you want to appear in the document: a numbered mark or a custom mark. A custom mark can be any nonnumeric character, such as an asterisk, that you enter in the text box. You want to create numbered footnotes, so the default settings of Footnote and AutoNumber are acceptable.

Choose: OK

Your screen should be similar to Figure 3-9.

Figure 3-9

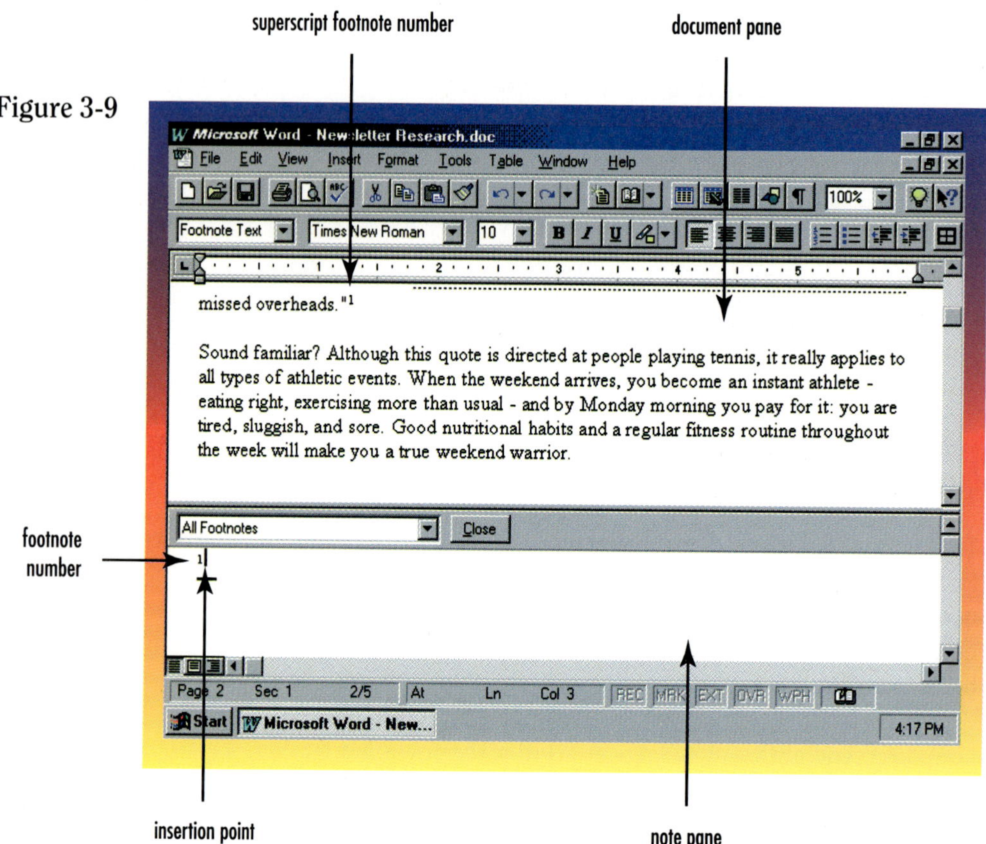

The workspace is divided into two panes. The upper or **document pane** displays the document. The footnote number, 1, appears as a superscript in the document at the location of the insertion point. The lower or **note pane** displays the note text. The note pane also displays the footnote number 1 and the insertion point. This is where you enter the text for the footnote.

To enter a space after the number and before the text of the footnote,

Press: Spacebar

When you enter a footnote, you can use the same menus, commands, and features as you would in the document window. Any commands that are not available are dimmed.

If the word "Flunkie" is identified as misspelled, choose Ignore All from the Spelling Shortcut menu.

Type: **Julie Anthony, "Are You a Nutrition Flunkie?" Tennis, May 1992, p. 89.** (Do not press ←Enter.)

The note pane on your screen should be similar to Figure 3-10.

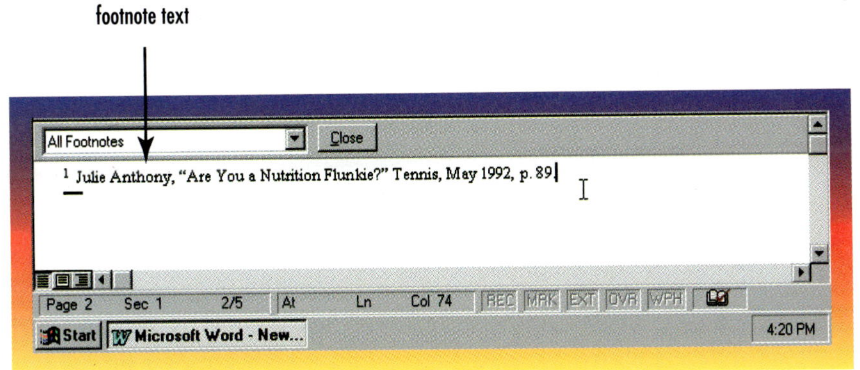

Figure 3-10

The text for the first footnote is complete. However, the magazine title needs to be italicized.

Select the magazine name and italicize it.

The second footnote will provide the source for a quote located at the top of page 3. To move to the document pane to position the insertion point,

Click: **the document pane**

You can also press F6 to switch panes.

The document pane is active. The active pane contains the insertion point. The status bar reflects your location in the active pane.

Move to: **end of quote on page 3 following the word "maximum"**

To insert a second footnote,

Choose: **Insert/Footnote/OK**

The footnote number 2 is entered at the insertion point location. The note pane is active again, so you can enter the text for the second footnote. To do this,

Press: Spacebar

Type: **Covert Bailey, The New Fit or Fat (Boston: Houghton Mifflin Company), p. 161.**

If necessary, choose Ignore All for all names that are identified as misspelled words as they occur when you enter the note text.

This footnote reference is to a book.

Italicize the book title.

Now you realize that you forgot to enter a footnote earlier in the text, on page 2.

Switch to the document window and move to the end of paragraph 3 on page 2 (following the word "protein").

To delete a footnote or endnote, highlight the reference marker and press Delete. The reference marker and associated note text are removed, and the following footnotes are renumbered.

The insertion point should be positioned following the period after the word "protein" on the last line of the third paragraph.

A footnote or endnote can be copied or moved by selecting the marker and using cut or copy and paste. You also can use drop and drag to copy or move a note.

Insert a footnote as this location.

Notice that this footnote is number 2 in the document and a blank footnote line has been entered in the footnote pane for the footnote text. Word automatically adjusted the footnote numbers when the new footnote was inserted.

Press: Spacebar

Type: **Doug Henderson, "Nutrition and the Athlete," FDA Consumer, May 1987, p. 18.**

You also can hide and display the footnote pane any time by using the View/Footnote command or by double-clicking on a footnote reference marker.

Italicize the name of the journal.

Now you are finished entering footnotes. All three footnotes are displayed in the footnote pane. The footnotes will appear at the bottom of the page on which they were referenced. When you are done, to close the Footnote pane,

Click: 

Click Page Layout or choose View/Page Layout.

If the zoom percent is too small, the footnote numbers do not display correctly.

To see how the footnotes will appear at the bottom of the page when the document is printed, change the view to Page Layout. Set the zoom percent to 75%. If necessary, scroll to the bottom of page 2 to see the footnotes.

This view displays all the document elements, including footnotes, as they will appear on the printed page.

Your screen should be similar to Figure 3-11.

Figure 3-11

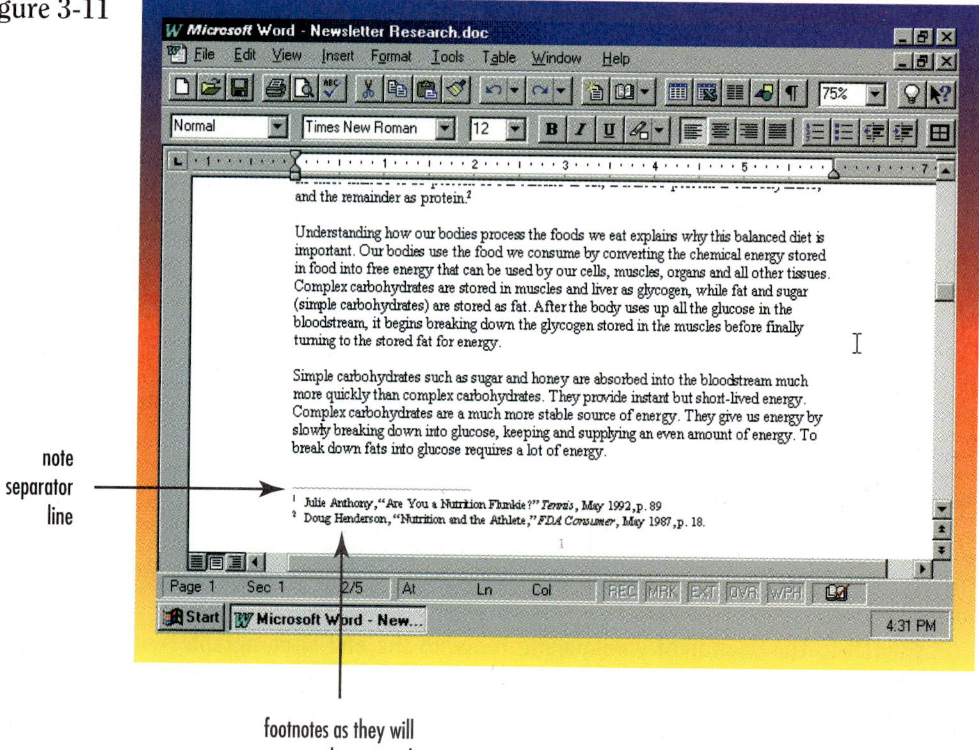

The footnotes are displayed at the bottom of the page, separated from the text by the note separator line. The bottom margin is 1 inch. Footnotes are placed immediately above the bottom margin.

Scroll to the bottom of the next page to see the third footnote.

While looking at the footnote, you see that you forgot to enter the publication date for the third footnote. While in Page Layout view, you can edit and format text just as in Normal view. To add the date before the page number of the footnote,

Move to: **between "y" of "Company" and the parenthesis**
Type: **, 1991**

If you see any other errors, correct them.

Numbering Pages

Next you want to add page numbers to the document. Although page numbers are displayed in the status line, in Page Layout view you can see that they do not automatically appear on the document. The Page Numbering command on the Insert menu is used to display page numbers in a document.

Move to: **anywhere in the document text area (not in the footnote area)**
Choose: **Insert/Page Numbers**

In the Page Numbers dialog box (see Figure 3-12), you select the position and alignment of the page numbers. You want the page numbers displayed centered at the bottom of the page. By default Word places the page numbers right aligned at the bottom of the page in the footer.

To change the alignment of the page numbers, open the Alignment drop-down list box.

Select: **Center**

The Page Numbers dialog box on your screen should be similar to Figure 3-12.

Figure 3-12

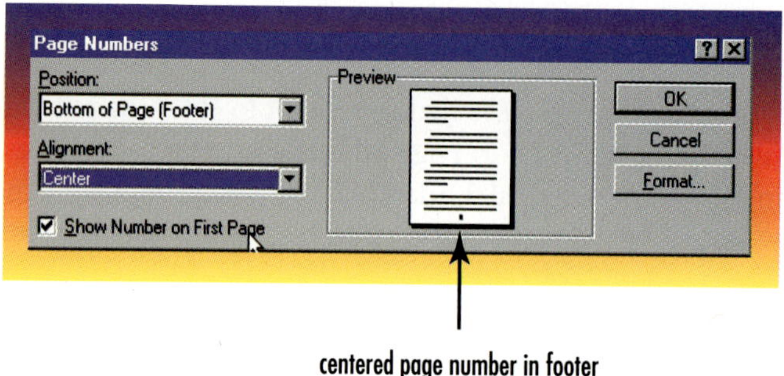

centered page number in footer

Now the Preview box shows how this selection will appear. You also do not want the page number to be printed on the memo page. You can turn off the page numbering for the first page by clearing the Show Number on First Page option box. To do this,

Choose: **Show Numbers on First Page**

Clearing this option, however, does not alter the page numbering sequence of the document. You want to change the numbering sequence of the document so that the first page of the report is page 1. To make this change,

Choose: **Format**

The Page Number Format dialog box is used to change the format of page numbers, include chapter numbers, and change the page numbering sequence. To reset the page number sequence,

Choose: **Start At**

In the Start At text box,

Type: **0**

The first page of the document, containing the memo, is now page 0, the second page is page 1, the third page is page 2, and so on.

Choose: **OK**
Choose: **OK**

Your screen should be similar to Figure 3-13.

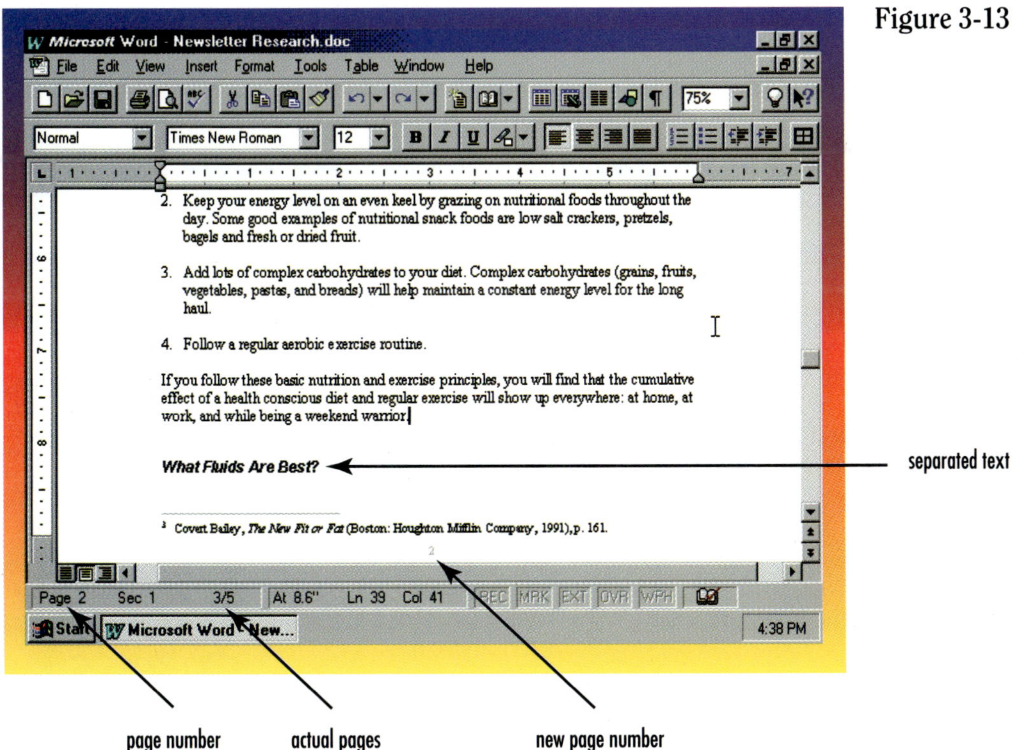

Figure 3-13

The page number 2 appears at the bottom center of the current page (page 3) below the footnote.

Keeping Lines Together

As you continue to check the document, you see a problem at the bottom of page 2. The heading "What Fluids Are Best?" is displayed on the last line of the page. You want to keep this heading and the text in the following paragraph together on a page.

If necessary, scroll the document so you can see the bottom of page 2 and the top of page 3.

Your document may have a different line spacing than is described here, depending on your selected printer and monitor. Continue with this section even if your spacing is satisfactory, because with further editing, the lines may become separated.

Text that should remain together on one page, such as a table or a long quote, is often divided over two pages because Word automatically calculates the length of each page and begins a new page whenever needed without discrimination about where it falls in the text. To control where a page ends, you could simply enter a manual page break to make Word begin a new page. However, if you continue to edit the document by adding and deleting text that affects the length of the document, the location of the manual page break may no longer be appropriate. Then you would need to delete the manual page break code and reenter it at the new location. This can be very time-consuming.

The Keep with Next command can be used to keep selected text together on a page. Before using this command, the text must be selected.

Select the heading "What Fluids Are Best?" and the following blank line.

Choose: **Format/Paragraph**

If necessary, select the Text Flow tab.

The four pagination options are described in the following table.

Option	Effect
Widow/Orphan Control	Prevents Word from printing the last line of a paragraph by itself at the top of a page (widow) or the first line of a paragraph by itself at the bottom of a page (orphan).
Keep Lines Together	Prevents a page break within a paragraph.
Keep with Next	Prevents a page break between a paragraph and the following paragraph.
Page Break Before	Inserts a page break before a paragraph.

Widow/Orphan control is on by default. To keep the selected text together with the following text,

Choose: **Keep with Next/OK**

Clear the highlight.

Your screen should be similar to Figure 3-14.

Figure 3-14

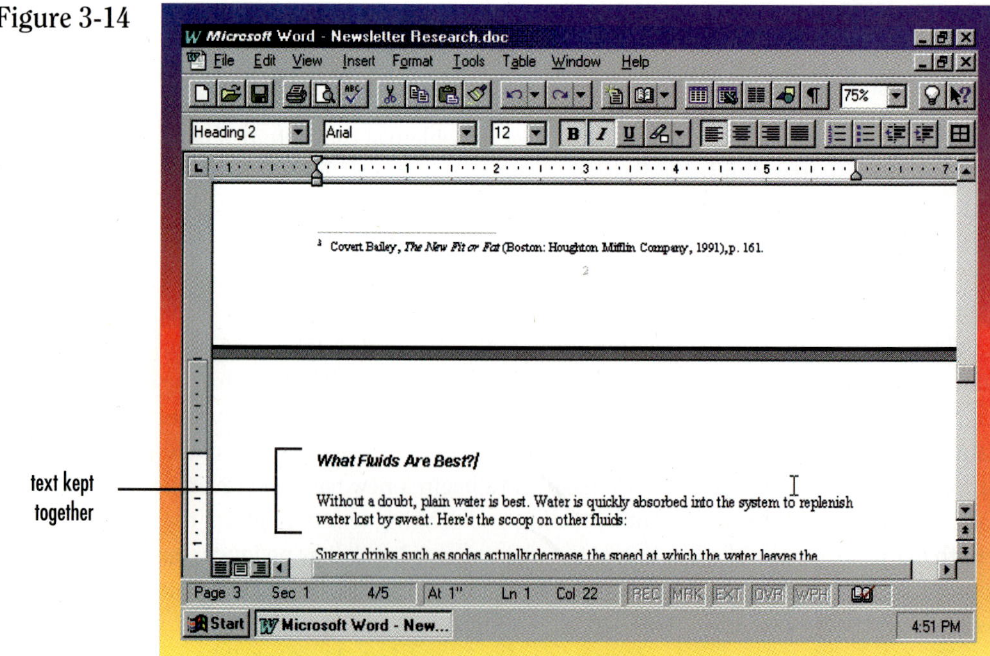

In order to keep the selected text together, all the selected text has moved to the top of page 4.

Scroll the document to the bottom of page 3.

You notice that another text flow problem occurs at this location.

Select the two headings "Equipment Update" and "Stationary Bikes" and the blank line following them. Use the **E**dit/**R**epeat Paragraph Formatting command to keep the text together.

Clear the highlight.

You are now ready to print the document.

If necessary, select the appropriate printer for your computer system and prepare the printer for printing.

Your text will be reformatted to the capabilities of your printer. Word will pick the closest available fonts to the ones selected in the document.

Preview, then print the entire document. Use the Save As command on the File menu to save the edited document as Newsletter Topics. Close the file.

Note: If you are ending your lab session now, exit Word. When you begin Part 2, load Word and continue the lab exercises.

Part 2

Using WordArt

You presented your suggested articles to your manager, who found the topics interesting. The manager suggested, however, that several of the articles were too long and that it would be better not to include any information that requires footnotes. You have revised the articles and saved the revision in a file called Newsletter Articles. Now you are ready to create a sample newsletter using the revised articles.

Open the file Newsletter Articles.

Following your manager's suggestions, you shortened several of the articles and removed any text that required footnotes. You also added a brief article on how to train for an upcoming biking event and a list of several future event dates.

Scroll through the text to view the contents of the articles. When you are done, return to the top of the document.

The first thing you want to do is to create a headline for the newsletter. The headline will display the name of the newsletter, "The Sports Company Update," and issue identification information such as the date of publication and volume number. The headline is shown here.

You will create the headline in a new file so that it can be saved and used for any newsletter issue. To display a new blank document window,

Click: New

The headline will be centered on the page and include different fonts, type sizes, and styles. To enter the first line of the newsletter title,

Click: Center
Type: The Sports Company
Press: ←Enter

Next you want to change the title to a different font type, a larger size, and bold.

Select the text and set the font to Arial, size to 18, and bold.

The rest of the newsletter name, UPDATE, will be on the next line.

Move to the next line.

You will use the Word WordArt feature to enter this line of text.

Concept 5: WordArt

WordArt is a supplementary application included with the Word program. It allows you to enhance your documents by changing the shape of text, adding 3-D effects, and changing the alignment of text on a line. The text that is added to the document is an **embedded object** that can be edited, sized, or moved to any location in the document. An embedded object is created using another application, called the **server,** and inserted into the document. It can be edited by activating the object that opens the server application for use.

Use WordArt to add a special touch to your documents. Its use should be limited to headlines in a newsletter or to a single element in a flyer. You want the WordArt to capture the reader's attention. Here are some examples of WordArt.

Sale
Lasts
Through
Sunday!

Roberto's
Coffee House

To open the WordArt dialog box,

Choose: Insert/Object

If necessary, select the Create New tab. Select Microsoft WordArt 2.0 from the Object Type list box.

Choose: OK

Your screen should be similar to Figure 3-15.

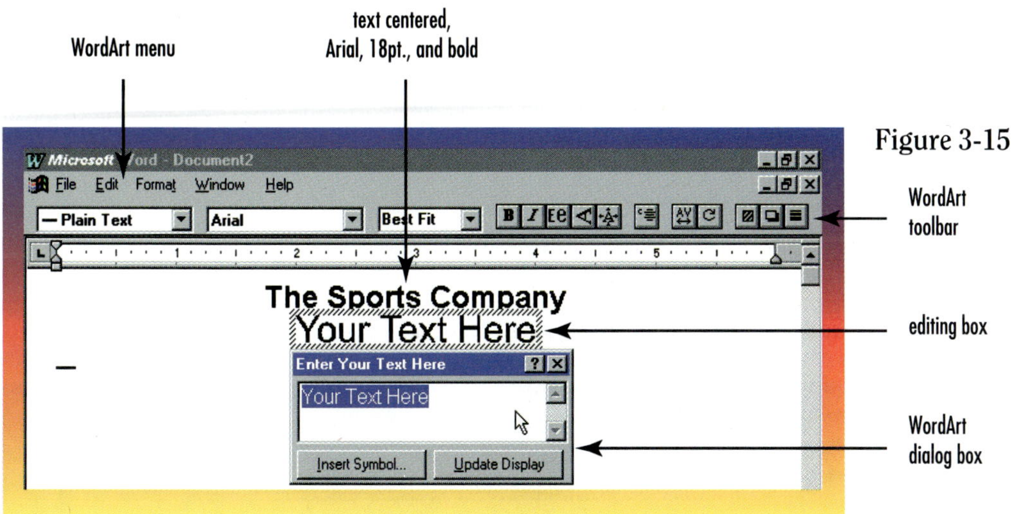

Figure 3-15

The WordArt "Enter Your Text Here" dialog box is displayed. The sample text "Your Text Here" is highlighted in the text box and appears in an editing box at the location of the insertion point. To change the sample text to UPDATE,

Type: UPDATE

To see how the word will look in the document,

Choose: Update Display

Now the word you entered in the editing box is displayed in the default WordArt shape and size.

Close the dialog box.

The text is still surrounded by the editing box, which indicates that the WordArt object is active and can be modified. Whenever a WordArt object is activated, the WordArt menu and toolbar are displayed in place of the Word menu and toolbars. The menu and toolbar contain commands that can be used to modify the WordArt. The WordArt toolbar buttons are identified below.

WordArt is the server application.

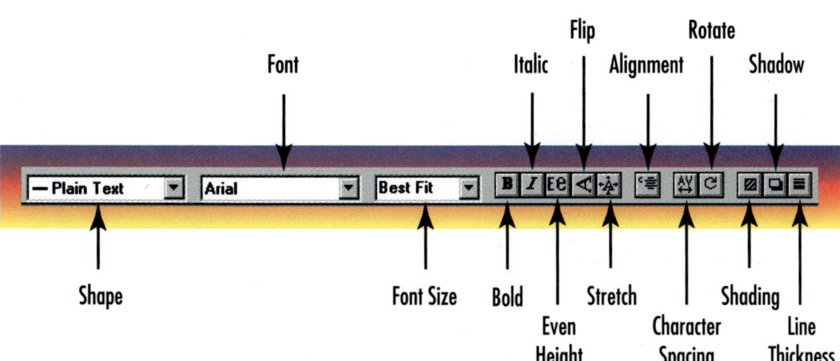

Now you can use the WordArt application to change the appearance of the WordArt text. First you will change the shape of the text. The toolbar Shape button shows that the default shape is Plain text. To select another shape,

Click:  **Shape**

A palette of 36 shape buttons is displayed. You would like to change the shape of the text to Inflate (Top).

Choose: **(fifth column, fifth shape)**

Your screen should be similar to Figure 3-16.

Figure 3-16

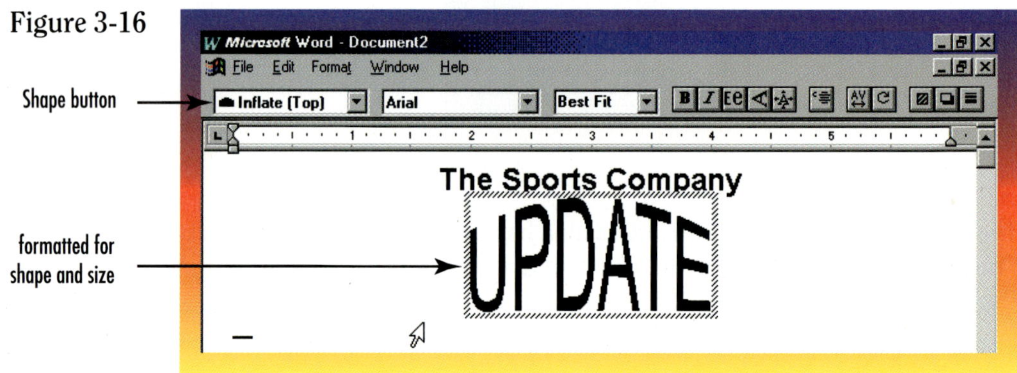

Notice that the size of the WordArt text is larger now. This is because WordArt automatically adjusts the size of the art to the selected shape.

Next you want to add a shadow to the WordArt characters.

Click: **Shadow**

The Shadow dialog box displays the shadow options you can use.

Click: **(second button from the left)**
Choose: **OK**

Your screen should be similar to Figure 3-17.

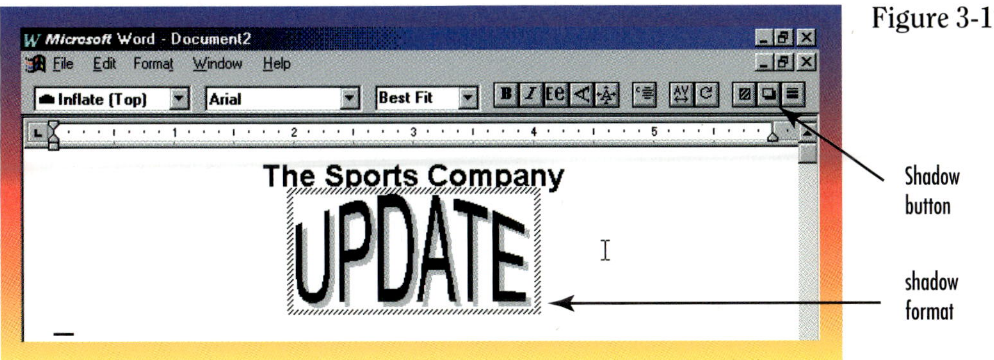

Figure 3-17

To place the WordArt object in the Word document,

Click: **anywhere outside the graphic**

The WordArt object is no longer activated, and the WordArt application is closed. The Word menu and toolbar are displayed again. The object is surrounded by a border and eight boxes, called **handles**. This indicates the object is selected and can be moved or sized as you would a window.

> You can select the object again by clicking it or activate it by double-clicking it.

Clear the selection.

If necessary, move the insertion point to the right of the WordArt.

The next line in the newsletter title will be in a smaller type size, two lines below the main title. To move the insertion point below the WordArt,

Press: ←Enter **(2 times)**

To enter the line of text,

Type: **A Publication for Customers of The Sports Company**

Change the size to 12 points and bold the text. Insert two blank lines below this line of text.

Setting Tabs

Finally, the issue identification information needs to be entered. It will not be centered.

> Reminder: Click  Left or press Ctrl + L.

Return the alignment to left.

The newsletter date is entered on the left end of the line and the volume number on the right end of the line.

Type: **FALL 1997**

The volume information will be displayed on the right end of the same line. To align the text with the right margin, you will set a right tab stop at the 6-inch position.

Concept 6: Tabs

A **tab** is a predefined stopping point along a line to which text will indent when you press Tab. Each tab stopping point on the ruler is called a **tab stop**. The tab stops are visible on the ruler as light vertical lines below the numbers. Each time you press Tab, the text on that line will advance to the next tab stop. The default tab setting is a left tab stop at every half-inch.

As with other default settings, you can change the location of tabs in the document. When setting new tabs, the new tab settings affect the current paragraph or selected paragraphs. When you insert custom tab stops, all default tab stops to the left of the custom tab stop are deleted.

Five types of tab settings control how characters are positioned or aligned with a tab stop. The five tab types, the alignment tab mark that appears on the ruler, and the effects on the text are explained in the following table.

Alignment	Tab Mark	How It Affects Text	Example
Left	∟	Extends text to right from tab stop	|left
Center	⊥	Aligns text centered on tab	cen|ter
Right	┘	Extends text to left from tab stop	right|
Decimal	⊥.	Aligns text with decimal point	35|78
Bar	|	Draws a vertical line through text at the tab stop	|

Tabs are useful for aligning text or numeric data vertically in columns. Using tabs ensures that the text will indent to the same set location. Setting custom tab stops instead of pressing Tab or Spacebar repeatedly is a more professional way to format a document, and it's faster and more accurate. It also makes editing easier because you can change a tab setting for several paragraphs at once.

To add a tab stop setting, click the tab alignment selector box on the left end of the ruler. A different alignment mark is displayed as you click in the box. When the tab mark is the alignment you want, you can click on the ruler position to place the selected tab type as a tab stop.

Click the tab alignment selector box until the right tab icon (┘) appears.

To place this tab marker at the 6-inch position on the ruler,

> You may need to click to the left of the 6-inch position on the ruler and then drag the tab marker to the 6-inch position.

Click: 6.0

> The menu equivalent is Format/Tabs/6/Right.

A right tab mark is displayed at the 6-inch position on the ruler. All default tabs to the left of the new tab setting are cleared. To see how the tab setting works,

Press: Tab
Type: VOLUME I

As you type, the last character is right-aligned to the left side of the tab stop (see Figure 2-18).

Press: ←Enter

Creating Border Lines

Next, you want the issue identification information to be displayed between two horizontal lines. Lines can be added to any side of a paragraph or object using the Borders toolbar. The paragraph or object must be selected first.

Move to anywhere within the issue identification text.

Open the Borders toolbar.

By default, a thin single line style is selected for borders. To increase the weight of the line, from the Line Style drop-down list box,

Reminder: Click Borders to open and close the Borders toolbar.

Select: 1 ½ pt

To add a top border line above the selected text,

Click: Top Border

The menu equivalent is Format/Borders and Shading/Border

A horizontal line extending between the margins appears above the text.

You want the lower border line to be even heavier.

Set the line style to 3 pt.

Click: Bottom Border

You also can create border lines automatically as you type. To create a single line, press - three times and press ←Enter. To create a double line, press = three times and press ←Enter.

Your screen should be similar to Figure 3-18.

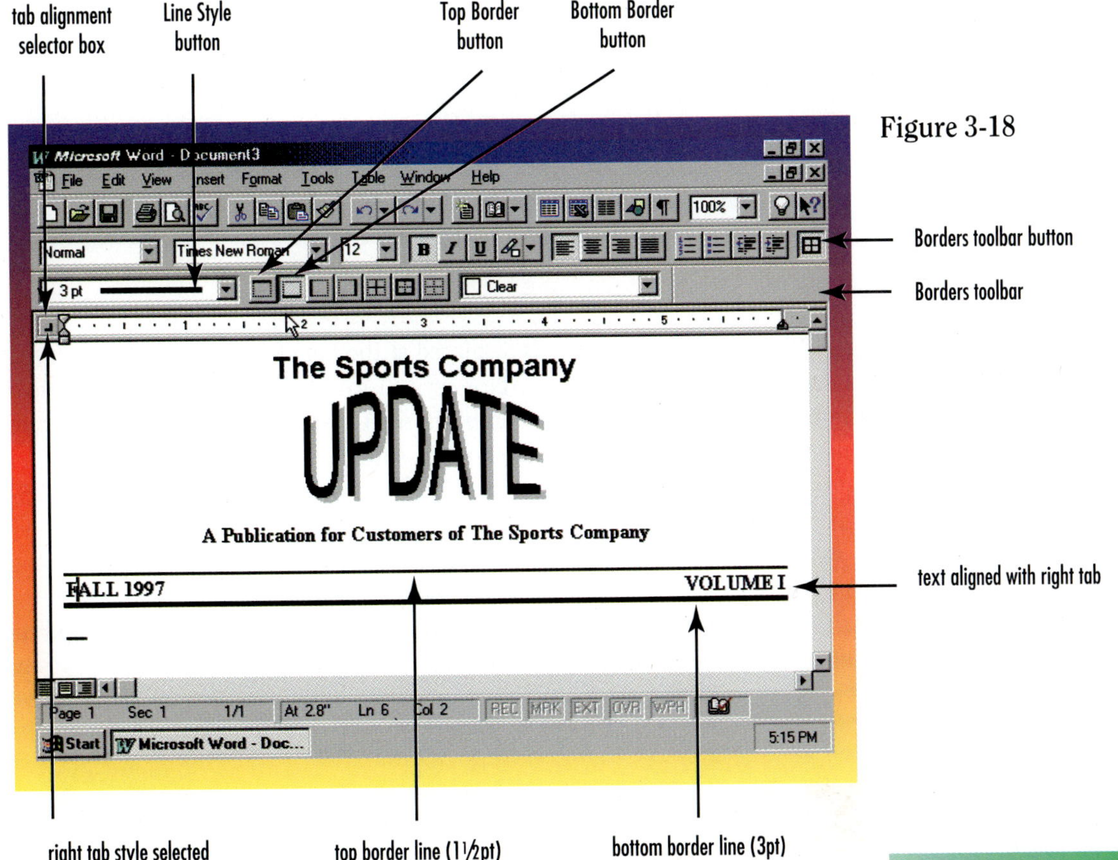

Figure 3-18

Close the Borders toolbar.

The newsletter headline is now complete and can be used with any newsletter.

Save the newsletter headline as Newsletter Headline.

Now you are ready to copy the headline for the newsletter into the file containing the newsletter text.

Use the Select All command to select the entire file. Use the Copy command to copy the selected text to the Clipboard.

Make the Newsletter Articles window active. If necessary, move the insertion point to the top of the file (Ctrl + Home). Paste the text from the Clipboard to this location in the file.

Your screen should be similar to Figure 3-19.

Figure 3-19

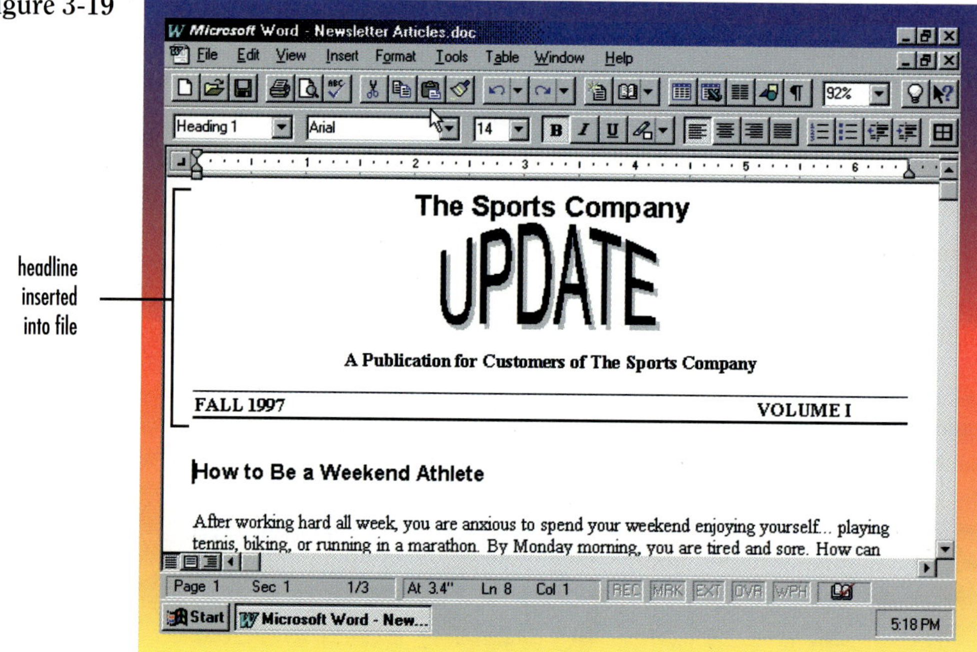

The newsletter headline is displayed at the top of the document. However, because this document has margins set at 1 inch, the volume issue identification number is no longer flush with the right margin. To fix this, the right tab marker needs to be moved to the same position as the right margin.

Move to the issue identification line. Drag the right tab marker to the 6.5-inch position on the ruler.

Notice that the border lines automatically lengthened to accommodate the increased page width and they do not need adjustment.

The heading "How to Be a Weekend Athlete" should be separated by one blank line from the bottom border line.

If it's not, insert or delete blank lines above it to position it there.

Creating Newspaper Columns

You want the articles in the newsletter to be displayed in newspaper column format. **Newspaper columns** display text so that it flows from the bottom of one column to the top of the next column. The Columns command on the Format menu lets you easily set the text format of a document to columns. As with many Word commands, the text must be selected before the command is used. You want the column format to begin with the heading "A Balanced Diet" and end before the section heading "Going for the Goal."

Select this text.

To create newspaper columns,

Choose: Format/Columns

The Columns dialog box on your screen should be similar to Figure 3-20.

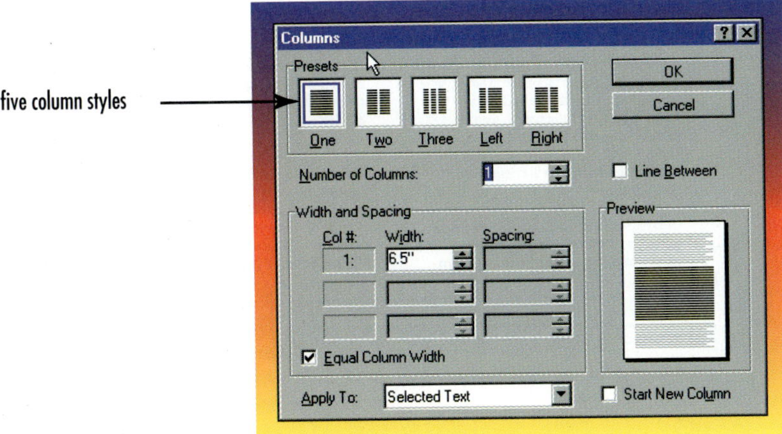

Figure 3-20

The dialog box displays five preset column styles. The default style is one column the full width of the page. You want the newsletter to have two columns of text on the first page. From the Presets area,

Select: Two

The Number of Columns text box now displays 2. If none of the preset styles was appropriate, you could enter a number in the Number of Columns text box. Based on the number of columns you specify, Word automatically calculates the left and right margins for the columns. Using the default setting, the two columns will be 3 inches wide, separated by 0.5 inch. The columns are equally sized.

The Preview box shows how text will appear on the page using the specified column settings.

Choose: OK

To see the text in column layout, the view must be Page Layout.

Switch to Page Layout view and set the zoom to 75 percent. Move to the article title at the beginning of the two-column section.

Your screen should be similar to Figure 3-21.

0.5-inch space between columns

Figure 3-21

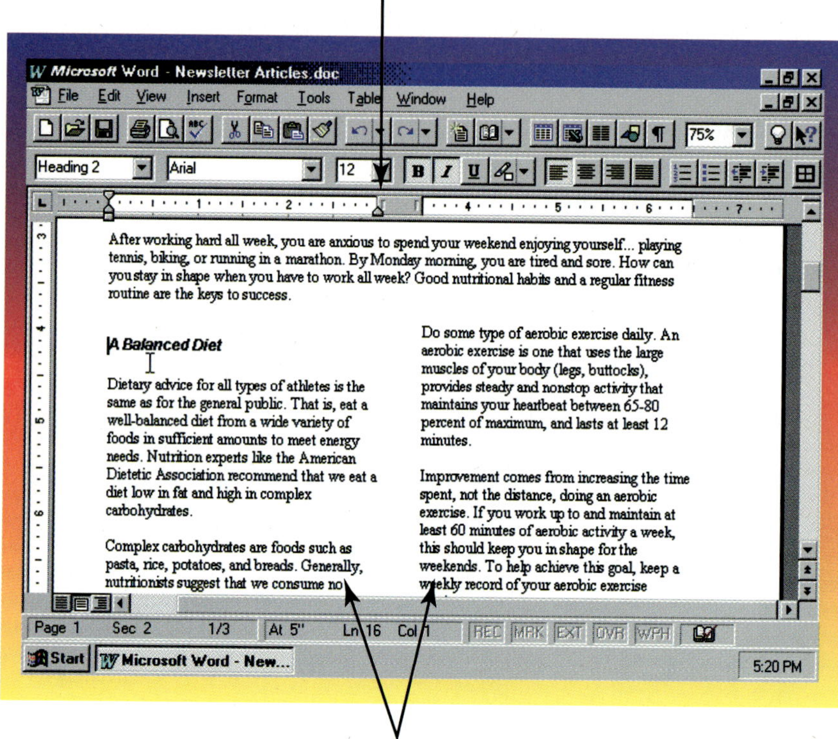

two-column format in Page Layout view

Do not be concerned if the text in your columns wraps differently than Figure 3-21. This is a function of the selected printer on your system.

The text is displayed as two even-sized newspaper columns, with 0.5 inch of space between. The text at the bottom of the first column continues at the top of the second column.

You would like the second page of the newsletter to be in three-column format.

Select the text from the article heading "Going for the Goal" to the end of the last sentence of the document.

The Columns button on the Standard toolbar can also be used to set columns. It allows you to specify up to six columns using the default column definitions.

Click: Columns

The drop-down menu displays four sample columns. To specify the number of columns, drag from left to right until the number of columns you want appears highlighted. As soon as you release the mouse button, the columns are created.

> The menu equivalent is **F**o**rmat/**C**olumns/**N**umber of Columns/3.**

Drag to select 3 columns. Move to the article title at the top of page 2.

Your screen should be similar to Figure 3-22.

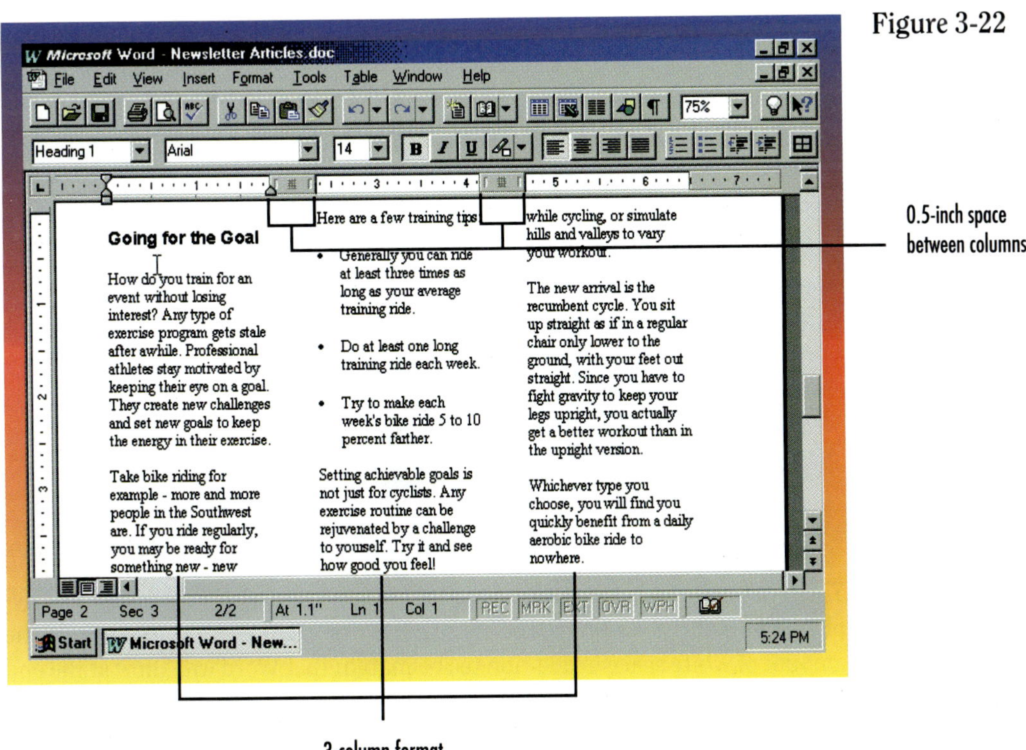

Figure 3-22

The text that was selected is displayed as three columns. By default, the width between the columns is set to 0.5 inch. This setting was appropriate for two columns, but seems too wide for three columns. To reduce the space between columns to 0.3 inch,

Choose: **F**o**rmat/**C**olumns**

In the Width and Spacing section of the dialog box, set the spacing to 0.3 for both Column 1 and Column 2.

> You can also drag the column divider in the ruler to adjust the spacing between columns.

Choose: **OK**

The columns are reformatted to the new spacing setting.

Using Hyphenation

Now that the layout is in columns, you notice that many of the lines have very uneven right margins, especially in the three-column layout. On lines of text where there are several short words, the wrapping of text to the next line is not a problem. However, on lines that contain long words, the long word is wrapped to the next line, leaving a large gap on the previous line. Hyphenating a long word so that part of it stays at the end of a line will help solve this problem.

To hyphenate the document,

Choose: **Tools/Hyphenation**

The Hyphenation dialog box shown in Figure 3-23 is displayed on your screen.

Figure 3-23

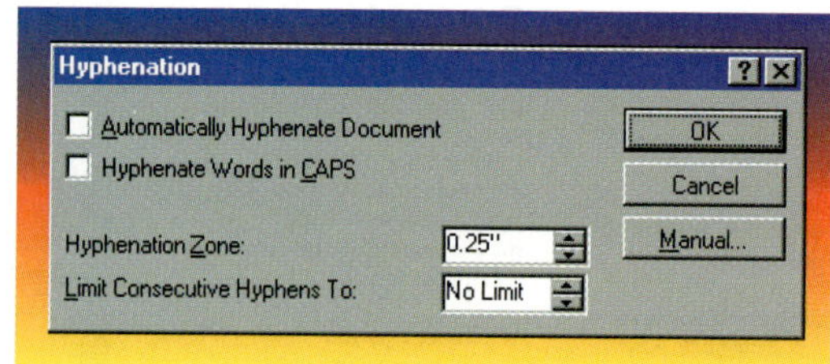

The Hyphenation dialog box displays the default hyphenation settings. The **hyphenation zone** is an unmarked space along the right margin. It controls the amount of white space in addition to the margin that Word will allow at the end of a line. Making the hyphenation zone narrower (a smaller number) reduces raggedness by hyphenating more words, while making the zone wider (a larger number) hyphenates fewer words. If the first word in a line is a word that can be hyphenated, Word inserts a special hyphen called an **optional hyphen** in the word and moves the first part of the word to the preceding line. The default setting looks satisfactory.

The Automatically Hyphenate Document option lets Word set hyphenation for the entire document. The Manual command button allows you to control the hyphenation of words. Manual will display each word that Word is considering hyphenating and how it would be hyphenated. Then you can accept the proposed hyphenation, change the hyphenation, or not hyphenate the word. It is fastest to allow Word to hyphenate the entire document. Word generally proposes accurate hyphenation. If you do not agree with how a word is hyphenated after it has been done, you can select the word and hyphenate it individually.

Choose: **Automatically Hyphenate Document/OK**

Your screen should be similar to Figure 3-24.

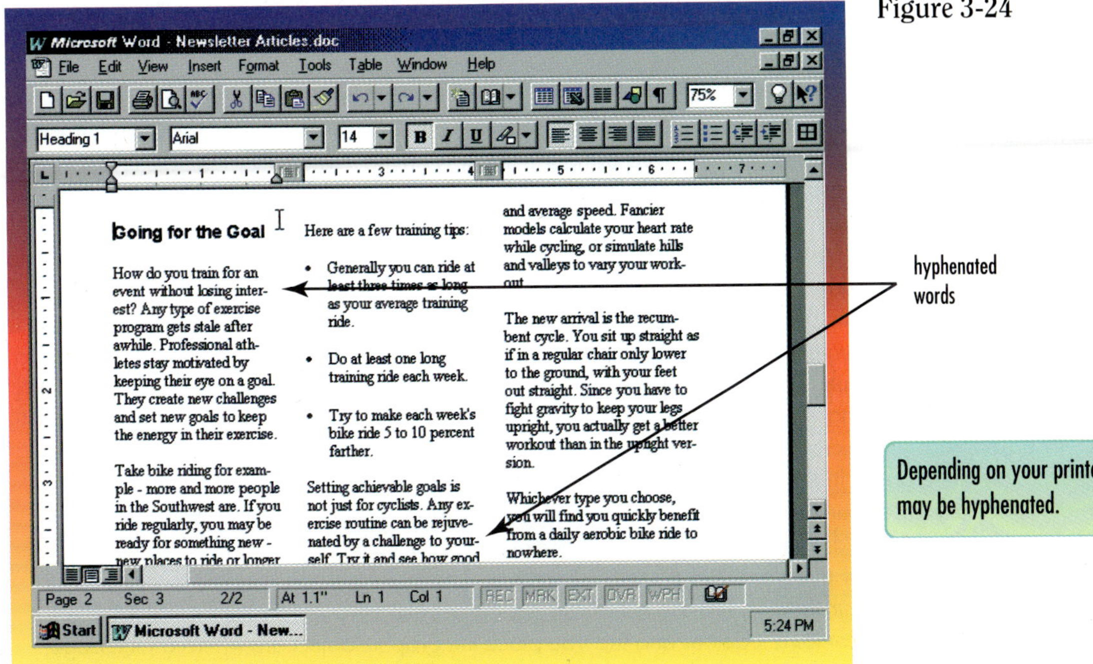

Figure 3-24

Depending on your printer, different words may be hyphenated.

Word has examined each line and determined where it is possible to hyphenate a word. Hyphenating the newsletter has made the column margins much less uneven.

If the text in three-column format now begins at the bottom of page 1, insert a hard page break before the heading "Going for the Goal."

To save the changes you have made to the document to this point, save the file as Fall 1997 Newsletter.

Adding Pictures

Next, you want to add to the newsletter a picture that will complement the subject of the first article. A picure is one of several different graphic objects that can be added to a Word document.

Concept 7: Graphics

Graphics is a term used to describe non-text elements, such as drawings and pictures, that can be added to a document. A graphic object can be a simple **drawing object** consisting of shapes such as lines and boxes that can be created using the Drawing toolbar. A **picture** is an illustration created by combining lines, arcs, circles, and other shapes. It is commonly created using a graphic application such as Paint. You can also draw a picture in Word using the features on the Drawing toolbar. Pictures created using other applications are stored as graphic files. They commonly have file extensions such as .WMF, .BMP, .TIF, .PCX, .WPG, .PIC, and .CGM. The file extension is used to identify the type of graphic and whether it is compatible with your software package.

A graphic can be added to a document by copying it to the Clipboard and then pasting a copy of it into the document. You can also add a graphic by importing the file into the document. Once a graphic file is inserted into a document, it is saved as part of the Word document file.

You can place a graphic object anywhere on a page, just as you would text. The graphic object can then be manipulated in many ways. For example, you can change its size by scaling the object (changing its proportions) or by cropping the image (cutting off any part of the picture). You can also change the location of the object in the document, align it with the margins, and add captions or a border. To create space around the graphic, you can add paragraph spacing before and after or apply line spacing. You can use borders and shading to add special effects.

If you want to anchor the graphic to a paragraph and yet move it freely on the page, you need to add a frame around the graphic. A **frame** is an invisible box or container for a graphic object. The frame keeps the items it contains together and lets you place the graphic object anywhere on the page, including the margins, and the text will flow around it.

Add graphics to your documents to help the reader understand concepts, to add interest, and to make your document stand out from others.

You would like the picture to appear on the left side of the first paragraph of the newsletter.

Move to: **The "A" of "After" at beginning of first paragraph of page 1**

To add a picture to the document,

Choose: **Insert/Picture**

You can also purchase clip art packages to add to your collection.

From the Insert Picture dialog box you select the name of the picture file you want to open, just as you would select a document file. You will add a clip art picture that is supplied with the Word program. **Clip art** is a term used to describe a collection of graphics that usually is bundled with a software application. The picture you will use is located in the Word Clip Art folder and is also included with your data files on your data disk.

Change the location to the drive containing your data disk.

Select: **Sports.wmf**

The Preview box displays the selected picture. To insert the picture in the document,

Choose: OK

Your screen should be similar to Figure 3-25.

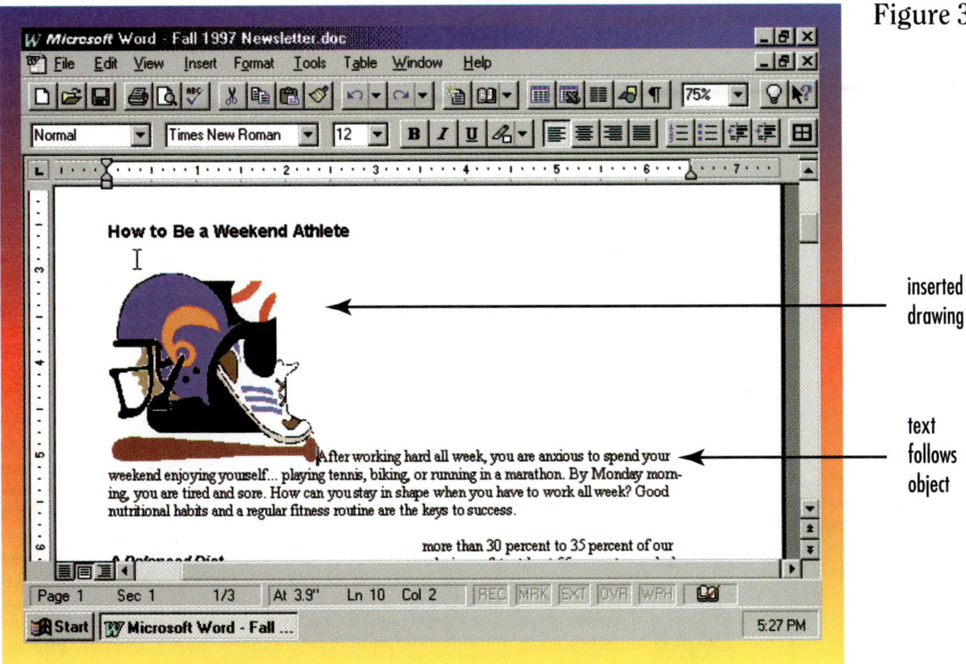

Figure 3-25

The picture of sporting equipment is inserted in the document at the insertion point; however, it is too large. In addition, the text follows the object, leaving a large blank area to its right. You want to make the picture smaller and have the text flow around it.

Select the picture.

> Click the picture or press Shift + ← to select it.

The object is selected and can be sized or moved on the page within the margins. Because you want the text to flow around the object, you need to enclose the object in a frame first. To do this,

Choose: Insert/Frame

The graphic is surrounded by a hashed border, indicating it is enclosed in a frame. The text in the paragraph now wraps alongside the picture rather than below it. The handles are used to size a selected object.

Point to the lower right corner handle.

> Some pictures include a lot of white space. If you press Shift when you click on a handle, the pointer changes to ⌗ and you can cut off or crop parts of the picture.

The mouse pointer changes to a two-headed diagonal arrow(↘), just as it does when sizing a window. When you resize a graphic, if you drag a corner handle the graphic keeps its original proportions.

Drag the mouse to reduce the size of the picture until the paragraph is all displayed next to the picture. (See Figure 3-26 for size reference.)

Deselect the object.

> The menu equivalent is Format/Picture. The options in the Picture dialog box let you set the size, width, and scaling of the object.

The frame and handles are no longer displayed.

Adding a Box

You also feel the graphic would look better if it were enclosed in a box.

To do this, select the graphic.

To add a box around the graphic,

Open the Borders toolbar. Select 1 1/2 pt as the line style.

Click: **Outside Border**

> The menu equivalent is Format/Borders and Shading/Box.

Deselect the object.

Your screen should be similar to Figure 3-26.

Figure 3-26

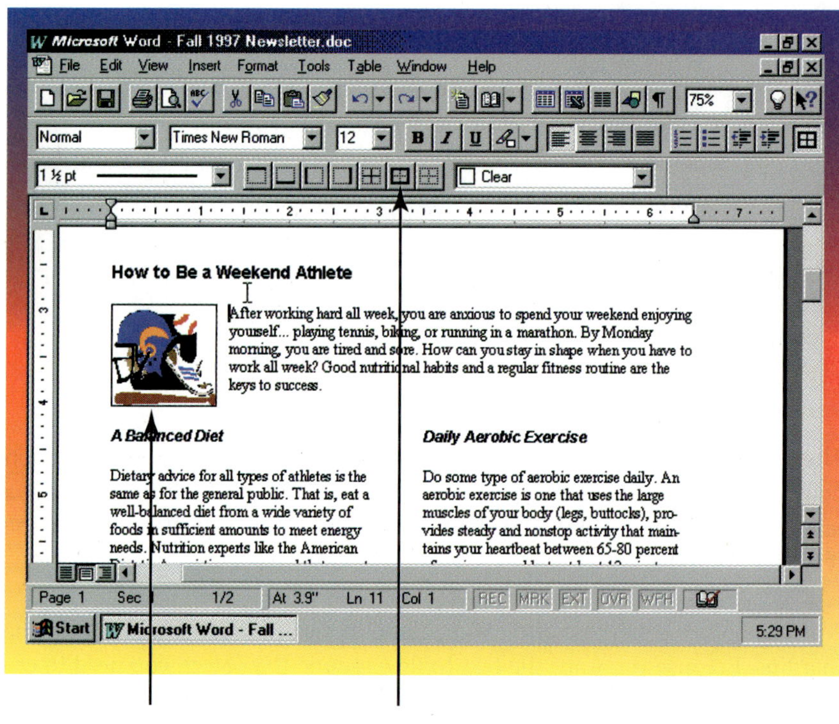

You like the addition of the box to the picture and think the list of upcoming events would stand out better if it were enclosed in a box too.

To see the list of upcoming events, move to the end of the third column on page 2.

First you want to make the font smaller and bold the items in the upcoming events list. To make these changes,

Move to: "C" of "Celebrity"

Select the text to the end of the column. Change the font size to 10 pt. and bold the text. Clear the highlight.

Next, you need to select the text to enclose in a box.

Select the heading "UPCOMING EVENTS" and text to the end of column 3.

To add a box with a double-line style, from the Line Style drop-down list box,

Select: ¾ pt ══════

Click: Outside Border

Adding Shading

Next, you want to add shading behind the text in the box. From the Shading drop-down list box you can select the degree of shading or pattern you want to appear behind a selection.

Open the Shading drop-down list box.

Select: 10 percent

> The menu equivalent is Format/Borders and Shading/Shading/10%.

Clear the highlight.

Your screen should be similar to Figure 3-27.

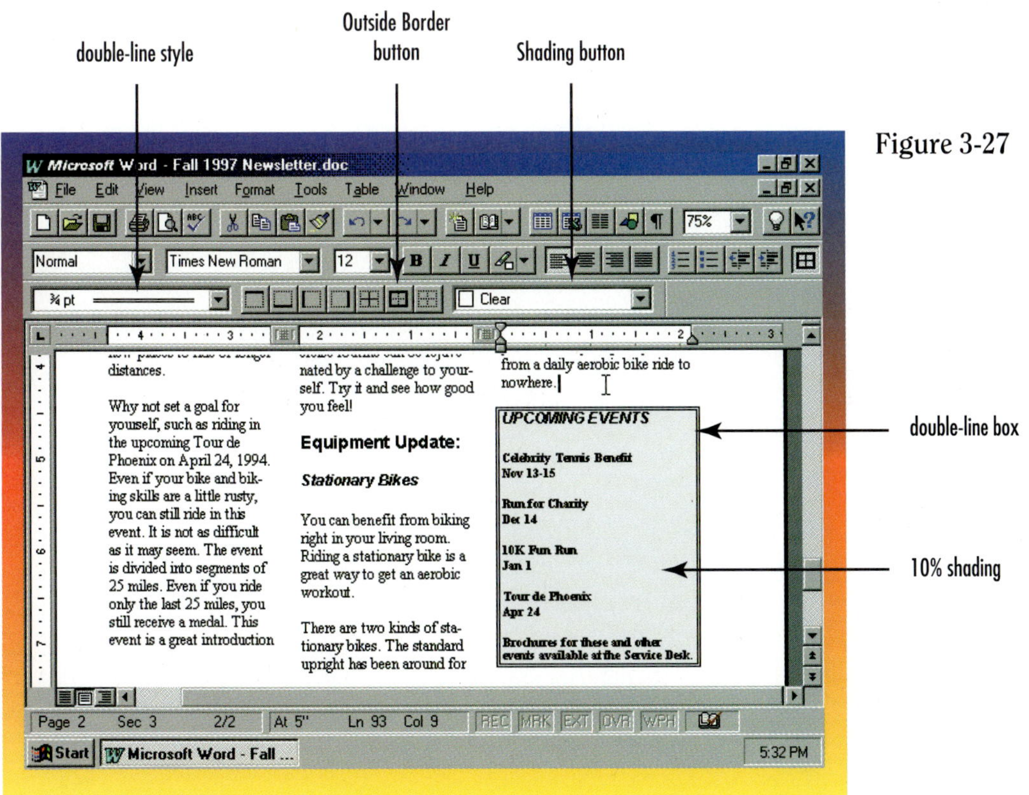

Figure 3-27

The selection is displayed surrounded by a double-line box and with the background shading you specified.

Close the Borders toolbar.

Adding a Drop Cap

Finally, you would also like to make the first letter (on the first page where the columns start) a drop cap. A **drop cap** is a special effect that is applied to a letter. It is used most often with the first character in a paragraph. The letter appears as a large, uppercase character with the top part of the letter even with the line and the rest of the letter extending into the paragraph below it. The character is changed to a graphic object in a frame and the text wraps to the side of the object. To create a drop cap,

Select: **"D" in "Dietary" (first letter on the first page where the columns start)**

Choose: **Format/Drop Cap/Dropped/OK**

The "D" in "Dietary" is now enlarged. This effect emphasizes the beginning of the paragraph and makes the columns appear more like those in a magazine.

The last adjustment you want to make is to check how the headings appear on the pages. You want the Daily Aerobic Exercise heading to appear at the top of the second column on the first page.

If necessary, insert blank lines above the heading to force it to scroll to the next column.

Preview the newsletter. Set the Print Preview window to display two pages by selecting View/Zoom/Many Pages or by clicking Multiple Pages and then selecting 1x2 pages.

Your screen should be similar to Figure 3-28.

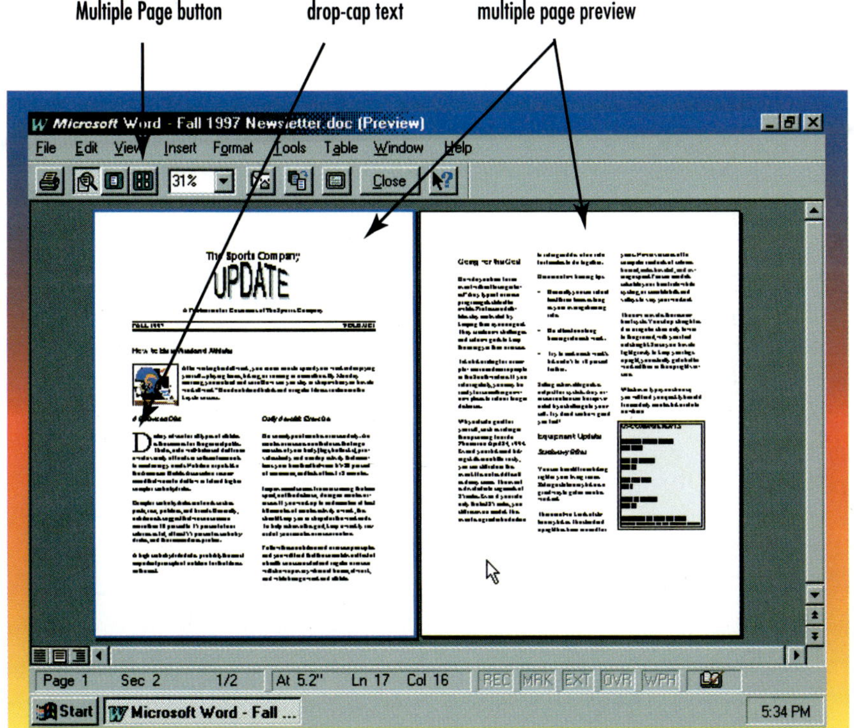

Figure 3-28

Close the Preview window.

Move to the bottom of page 2 and enter your name. Save the formatted newsletter.

If your instructor wants you to print the newsletter:

- Select the appropriate printer for your computer system and prepare the printer for printing if necessary. The text is reformatted to the font and graphic capabilities of your printer.
- Scroll through the document to see the changes that were made. Adjust the text wherever necessary to produce a newsletter as similar as possible to the one you created in this lab. Preview, then print the newsletter. Resave the document.

Set the Page Layout view zoom back to 100% and the view back to Normal. Close all the open files. Exit Word.

LAB REVIEW

Key Terms

character styles (WP113)
clip art (WP140)
drawing object (WP140)
document pane (WP120)
drop cap (WP144)
embedded object (WP128)
endnotes (WP119)
font (WP110)
footnotes (WP119)
frame (WP140)
graphics (WP140)
handles (WP131)
heading style (WP113)
hyphenation zone (WP138)
manual page break (WP109)
monospaced (WP110)
newspaper columns (WP135)
note pane (WP120)
note separator (WP119)
note text (WP119)
optional hyphen (WP138)
paragraph styles (WP113)
picture (WP140)
points (WP110)
proportional (WP110)
reference mark (WP119)
sans serif fonts (WP110)
scalable (WP110)
serif fonts (WP110)
server (WP128)
style (WP113)
tab (WP132)
tab leaders (WP117)
tab stop (WP132)
typeface (WP110)
WordArt (WP128)

Command Summary

Command	Shortcut	Button	Action
Edit/Repeat	Ctrl + Y		Repeats last action
View/Footnote			Hides or displays the footnote pane
Insert/Break	Ctrl + ←Enter		Inserts manual page break
Insert/Page Numbers			Specifies page number location
Insert /Footnote	Alt + Ctrl + F		Inserts a footnote reference at insertion point
Insert/Index and Tables			Inserts an index or table, such as a table of contents
Insert/Frame			Inserts a frame around selected object
Insert/Picture			Inserts a picture from a graphics file
Insert/Object			Inserts objects
Format/Font			Changes appearance of characters
Format/Tabs			Sets type and position of tab stops
Format/Borders and Shading			Adds borders and shadings to selection
			Adds box border
			Adds top border
			Adds bottom border
Format/Columns			Specifies number, spacing, and size of columns
Format/Change Case/ UPPERCASE	Ctrl + ⇧Shift + A		Changes selection to uppercase

Command	Shortcut	Button	Action
Format/Drop Cap/Dropped			Changes character to a drop cap
Format/Style			Applies, creates, or modifies styles
Format/Picture			Changes the picture scaling, size, and cropping information
Tools/Hyphenation			Specifies hyphenation settings

Matching

1. Ctrl + Y	______	**a.** fonts that can be printed in almost any point size
2. tab leaders	______	**b.** right tab marker
3. frame	______	**c.** shortcut command to repeat last action
4. note pane	______	**d.** dots that separate table of contents headings from page numbers
5. scalable	______	**e.** source references displayed at the bottom of a page
6. WordArt	______	**f.** an invisible box surrounding a graphic object
7. ┘	______	**g.** non-text element that adds visual interest to a document
8. footnotes	______	**h.** lower division of workspace that displays footnote text
9. graphics	______	**i.** instructs Word to begin a new page at that location regardless of the amount of text on the previous page
10. manual page break	______	**j.** a supplementary application used to add special effects to text

Discussion Questions

1. Discuss the differences between serif and sans serif fonts. When would it be appropriate to combine font styles? How does a font's point size affect the display of characters?

2. Discuss the differences between footnotes and endnotes. Why is it necessary to add notes to a document?

3. Discuss the four text flow options that affect pagination. Discuss why these features are important.

4. Discuss the types of graphic objects that can be added to a document. Why would you want to add objects to a document? What things should you consider before adding objects to documents?

5. How can newspaper columns enhance the look of a document? What types of documents are columns best suited for? How can the adjustment of widths, spacing, and hyphenation affect the layout?

Fill-In Questions

1. Complete the following statements by fillin in the blanks with the correct terms.

a. A ____________________ is a named group of formats.

b. A ________________________________ or ____________________ is a set of characters with a specific design.

c. Fonts are commonly measured in ____________________.

d. WordArt creates an ____________________ in the document.

e. A ____________________ tab stop extends text to the left from the tab stop.

f. Non-text elements such as drawings and pictures are called ____________________.

Hands-On Practice Exercises

Step by Step

Rating System

☆ Easy
☆☆ Moderate
☆☆☆ Difficult

1. To complete this exercise, you must have completed Practice Exercise 1 in Lab 2. Open the file MOUSE TERMS 2 from your disk.

Note: You can only complete step a if you have Wingdings in your font collection. If you do not have Wingdings, select and change the title to Arial 16 pt., and go to step b.

a. Wingdings are a set of icons that can be used to add fun and flair to your documents. A "Wingding" 7 is a keyboard; a "Wingding" 8 is a mouse. In this portion of the exercise, you will replace the word "Mouse" with a picture of a mouse. Remove the bold style from the title. Replace the word "Mouse" in the title with the number 8. Select the number 8, and change the font to Wingdings 18 pt. Change the font of the word "Terms" in the title to Arial 16 pt.

b. Add a 1 ½ pt. box around the five terms, and change the font size for the terms to 14 pt. Add shading behind the text in the box.

c. Save the file as COMPLETED MOUSE TERMS. Print the document.

2. In this exercise, you will create a letterhead for yourself using a WordArt image for your name.

a. Enter your name as a WordArt object. Apply a shape and a shadow to the image.

b. Increase the size of the object and center it between the margins.

c. Enter your address, centered, below your name. Change the font and size of the address.

d. Place the object 0.5 inch from the top of the page. Two lines below the address, enter a date that will update automatically when the letter is printed. Right align the date, and change its font to Times New Roman 12 pt.

e. Document the file. Save the letterhead as LETTERHEAD. Print the letterhead.

3. To complete this exercise, you must have completed Practice Exercise 3 in Lab 1. Open the file NO SMOKING MEMO on your data disk.

a. Apply the following setting changes to the entire document: Change the font to Arial 12 pt. Set a left-aligned tab at 0.75", and set the alignment to Justified. Change all margins to 1.5".

b. Insert three new lines at the top of the document. On the first line, create a centered WordArt title "Interoffice Memo." Apply a shape and a shadow to the WordArt image.

c. Go to the beginning of the first paragraph, and insert the picture NOSMOKE. If the picture is not in the default Clipart folder, it will be located on your data disk. Frame the picture, and size it until it fits perfectly to the left of the two paragraphs.

d. Save the file as REVISED NO SMOKING MEMO. Print the memo.

4. To complete this exercise, you must have completed Practice Exercise 4 in Lab 2. Open the file B&B AD PART 2.

a. Cut the name of the inn (Pocono Mountain Retreat) to the Clipboard. Insert a blank line at the top of the document, and move to that blank line. Create a WordArt object and paste (use Ctrl + U) the name of the inn into the Enter Your Text Here dialog box. Use one of the Arch Up shapes (first column, second or third row), and apply the second shadow on the third row (to the left of "More") to the image. Close WordArt.

b. Select the five paragraphs below the indented items, and increase the font size to 11 pt. Draw a drop-shadow box around the selected paragraphs.

c. Convert the first letter of the first paragraph to a Drop Cap.

d. Update the documentation to indicate that this is the final ad. Save the file as CAMERA READY B&B AD. Print the ad.

5. To complete this problem, you must have completed Practice Exercise 3 in Lab 2. Open the file UPDATED COOKIE RECIPES from your data disk.

a. Change the font to Times New Roman 12 pt. for the entire document. Then, change the title to a 14 pt. font of your choice.

b. Go to the beginning of the title line. Insert the picture COOKIE from your data disk. Select and frame the COOKIE picture. Reduce the size of the picture to 75 percent of full size. Go to the beginning of the title, and insert a blank line to center the text to the right of the cookie image. Go to the end of the title line and press ←Enter three times. Your insertion point should be centered, and the font should still be 14 pt. Change the font back to 12 pt. Times New Roman. Turn off bold.

c. Enter your name on the current line, and the current date on the next line. Make sure they are centered.

d. Insert three blank lines after the date. Increase the font to 16 pt. Type **Table of Contents**. Make sure the heading is centered. Insert two blank lines, and change the alignment to Left.

e. Draw a box around the note and add shading to the box.

f. Insert a hard page break at the beginning of each type of cookie so that each page will contain just one recipe. Insert page numbers that will print at the bottom center of each page, except the first page, and instruct the program to start at page 0.

g. Apply the Heading 1 style to the names of the cookies at the top of each recipe.

h. Use the Formal format to create a table of contents of the cookies on the second blank line below the Table of Contents heading. Increase the font size of the table of contents to 12 pt. Make sure there are two or three blank lines between the table of contents and the note.

i. Use ←Enter to move the table of contents (including the heading) down about five or six lines so it is in the center of the page. Use Print Preview as a guide. Use ←Enter to move the note to the bottom of the title page.

j. Next, you will insert three footnotes to add information to some of the recipes.

(1) Go to the Cut-Out Sugar Cookies recipe on page 1. Move to the end of the line that displays the ingredient "1 1/2 tsp. vanilla extract." Insert a footnote that reads "You can substitute pure anise extract for vanilla."

(2) Go to the Cut-Out Gingerbread People recipe on page 2. Move to the end of the line that displays the ingredient "1 tsp. allspice." Insert a footnote that reads "Add a bit more of each spice to give the cookies an extra kick."

(3) Go to the Peanut Butter Surprise recipe on page 4. Move to the end of the line that displays the ingredient "Double Peanut Butter Cookie recipe. . . ." Insert a footnote that reads "Use smooth peanut butter for this recipe."

k. Draw a box around each comment above the "Ingredients:" section for each cookie.

l. Remove your name and date from below the Potato Chip Cookie recipe. Save the file as COMPLETED COOKIE RECIPES. Print the document.

m. *Optional:* Open the file UPDATED COOKIE recipes, and modify the document using layouts of your own choice. Save the file with a new name, and print the document.

6. Open the file TOP 10 SCENIC DRIVES from your data disk. In this exercise you will create a document that uses many of the desktop publishing features you learned in this lab.

a. Insert two blank lines at the top of the document. Move to the first line and set the alignment to Center. Insert the picture AUTO on that line. If you cannot find the image AUTO in the default Clipart folder, it will be on your data disk. Size the picture to 75 percent of its original size.

b. Insert a page at the top of the document. Create a centered WordArt report title that displays "Top 10 Scenic Drives." Center your name and the current date three lines below the title, and use ←Enter to center the lines vertically on the page. Use Print Preview as a guide.

c. Create a drop cap as the first character in the first paragraph.

d. Add a footnote at the end of the first sentence of the third paragraph that reads: "This top 10 list was obtained from the Weissmann Travel Reports in the America Online Traveler's Corner."

e. Justify the first three paragraphs only.

f. Bold each of the numbered locations. Change the format to two columns for the 10 locations. Change the spacing between columns to 0.6" and check the Line Between box in the Columns dialog box to place a line between the columns of text. Hyphenate the document.

g. Insert the picture 1STPLACE at the beginning of the Rocky Mountains paragraph. If you cannot locate the picture in the Clipart folder, it will be on your data disk. Frame the picture and size it to fit to the left of the first five lines of the paragraph.

h. Number the pages, excluding the cover page, and start the page numbering at 0.

i. Make adjustments to the text as necessary. For example, you may have to insert or delete blank lines or use the Keep with Next command to keep headings with related text.

j. Document the file. Save the document as SCENIC DRIVES NEWSLETTER. Print the document.

k. *Optional:* Open the file TOP 10 SCENIC DRIVES and modify the document using layouts of your own choice. Save the file with a new name, and print the document.

On Your Own

7. Create a flier to announce an event (party, garage sale, bake sale, auction, and so on) or advertise something you have for sale (used car, used books, and so on), a service you are offering, or a service you need (baby sitting, tutoring, car pool, dog walking, and so on).

Integrate any or all of the following features into the flier:

Borders, shading, colors

Bullets and/or numbering

Indents

Different fonts in different sizes, colors, and styles

WordArt

Pictures (You can use the images from the Clipart directory or you can create your own with the Paint program)

Different alignment options

Anything else you can think of!

Document and save the file. Print the flier.

8. In this exercise, you will use Word to write a paper. The paper can be a paper you have written in the past. It must be a minimum of five pages. You must have demonstrated the following:

Title page

(1) The title of the paper must be centered and bold. Use WordArt to enhance the appearance of the title.

(2) The title should be in a font size two sizes larger than the default font for your printer.

(3) Center your name and the current date (using the Date command) near the bottom of the title page.

Table of contents

(1) The heading on this page should be centered and bold.

(2) The table of contents should show three main headings as Heading 1 styles. The structure of your report will determine the number of Heading 2 or Heading 3 styles.

(3) Use any of the Table of Contents formats you want.

Body of the paper

(1) There must be a minimum of three pages of text.

(2) There should be at least two levels of headings.

(3) Enter a minimum of four footnotes.

Report layout

(1) Display the page numbers on the top right corner of every page. Turn off the page number on the title page.

(2) Keep headings and text together as needed.

Preview and print the paper. Document and save the paper.

★★★

9. In this exercise, you will modify a document that tells how to write an effective resume and cover letter. Open the file HOW TO WRITE A RESUME on your data disk.

Justify the entire document. Center the report title, and apply a font of your choice in your choice of size. Center the name and date lines below the title. Enter the heading "Table of Contents" below the date. Make sure the heading is centered, and increase the point size. Insert a page break at the beginning of "The Resume" title line on page 1.

Replace the headings "The Resume" and "The Cover Letter" with WordArt titles that display the same text. Apply the same formatting (shape, shadow) to both WordArt titles.

Apply Heading 1 style to the following headings:

Overview of Resumes

Overview of Cover Letters

Apply Heading 2 to the following headings:

Basic Principles of Resume Construction

Organizing Your Resume

In the "Overview of Resumes" section, bullet and indent the five lines that tell a prospective employer "Who you are" to "What kind of job you would like." In the "Overview of Cover Letters" section, bullet and indent the four measures that are needed for the cover letter.

Number the eight "Basic Principles of Resume Construction" in the resume section and the four "abilities you have developed in school" at the end of the cover letter section.

In the "Organizing Your Resume" section, draw a box around the first paragraph. Use some of the formatting techniques you learned to attract attention to the heading "The Information Below Should Be Included" and resume headings at the beginning of each paragraph (Career Objective, Education, etc.). Arrange the paragraphs so they are in the following order: Name, Address, and Phone Number, Career Objective, Education, Work Experience, Activities, Honors and Awards, Special Skills, and References. Apply two default newspaper columns to only the eight paragraphs that describe the information that should be included in a resume. Add a line between the columns (see option in Columns dialog box). Left-align the columns of text only, and hyphenate the document.

Insert page numbers in any position you wish as long as you exclude the title page and start the page numbering at 0.

Insert the following information as a footnote below the first sentence of the "Overview of Resumes" on page 1:

This information was obtained from The Work Book by Barbara N. Price, Ph.D., Director or Career Planning and Placement, Luzerne County Community College, Nanticoke, PA.

The following pages should contain the following information:

Page 0: The report title, your name, the current date, and the table of contents.

Page 1: The "Overview," all eight "Basic Principles of Resume Construction," and the footnote.

Page 2: All of the "Organizing Your Resume" information

Page 3: All of "The Cover Letter" information.

If necessary, change margins and/or use hard page breaks or Keep with Next to reformat the text so it meets the above guidelines.

Create a table of contents on the cover page. Use any format you wish. Adjust the spacing and overall layout of the cover page any way you wish.

Document the file. Save the file as RESUME TIPS. Print the document.

Optional: Open the file HOW TO WRITE A RESUME, and modify the document using layouts of your own choice. Save the file with a new name, and print the document.

Creating Reports and Newsletters

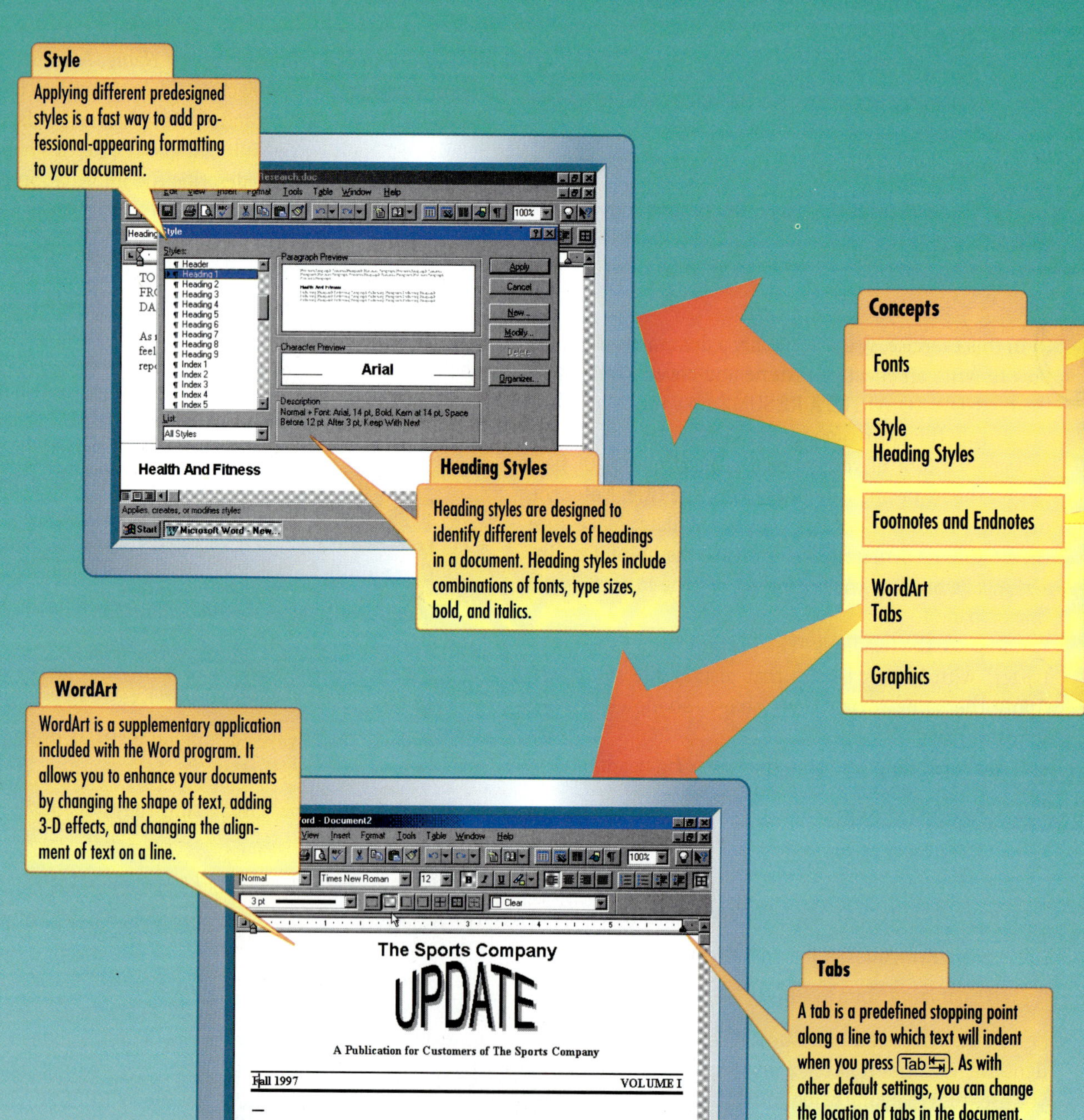

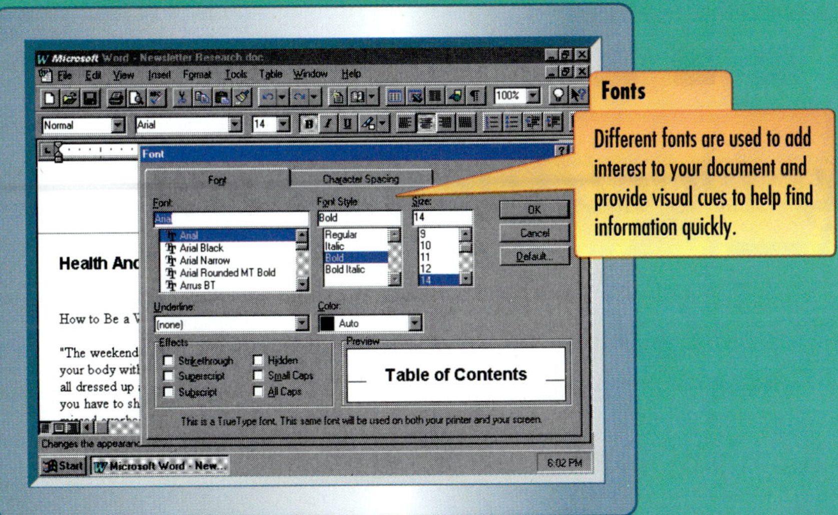
Fonts
Different fonts are used to add interest to your document and provide visual cues to help find information quickly.

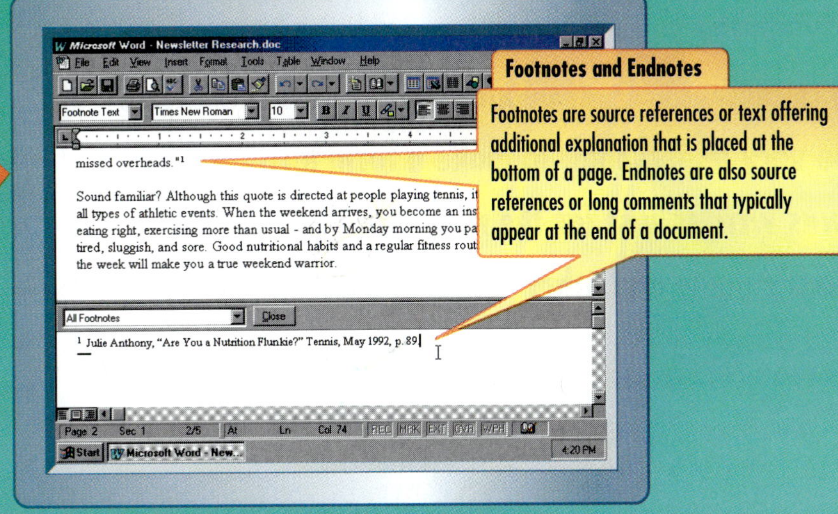
Footnotes and Endnotes
Footnotes are source references or text offering additional explanation that is placed at the bottom of a page. Endnotes are also source references or long comments that typically appear at the end of a document.

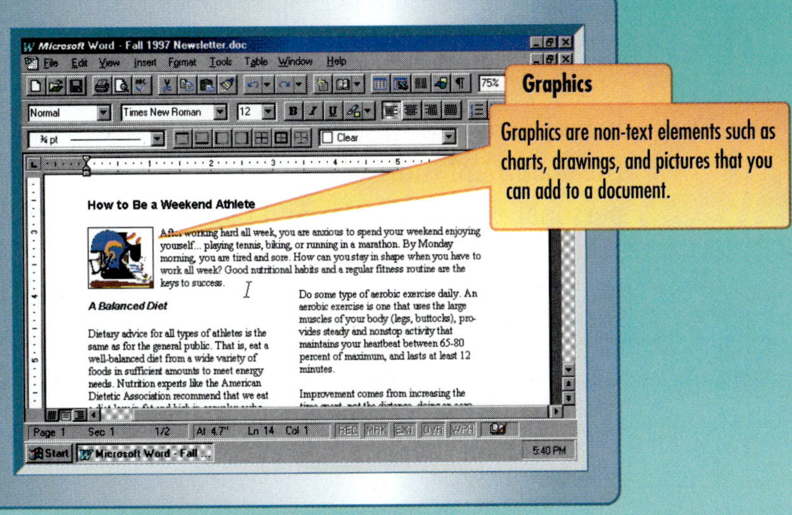
Graphics
Graphics are non-text elements such as charts, drawings, and pictures that you can add to a document.

Merging Documents and Creating Tables

4

Probably sometime in this past month you have received a form letter. Form letters are common business documents used when the same information needs to be communicated to many different people. However, form letters can be very impersonal. To make a form letter appear as if it was written just for the recipient, you can include the recipient's name and other personal information.

COMPETENCIES

After completing this lab, you will know how to:

1. Create the main document for merging.
2. Create the data source file.
3. Enter merge fields in the main document.
4. Perform the merge.
5. Use a template.
6. Create a table with the Table Wizard.
7. Enter text in a table.
8. Use formulas in a table.
9. Insert a row in a table.

You have probably also recently read information that was presented in a table. Tables are an effective way to present complicated data in an orderly format. You commonly see tables used to present numeric information. The table helps the reader compare data and eliminates a lot of text that makes the document more difficult to read. You will learn how to create a personalized form letter and tables using Word 7.0 in this lab.

Concept Overview

The following concepts will be introduced in this lab:

1. Mail Merge	The Mail Merge feature combines a list of data, typically names and addresses, that are contained in one file with a document, commonly a form letter, in another file to create a new document.
2. Field Names	Field names are used to label each data field in the data source.
3. Tables	A table displays information in rows, which run horizontally, and columns, which run vertically. The intersection of a row and column creates a cell in which you can enter data or other information.
4. Formulas and Functions	Formulas and functions are used to perform calculations.

CASE STUDY

You submitted the final copy of the credit card letter to the regional manager. The manager is very pleased with the content and form of the credit card letter, but would like it to be more personalized. It should include the first name of the preferred customer and an inside address. You will create a form letter using Word's Mail Merge feature to personalize each credit card letter.

As a second project, you have been asked to prepare a summary of gross sales for the four metropolitan stores. You will use Word to create a table of this data.

Part 1

The Merge Feature

Load Word 7.0.

To create the personalized letter to be sent to new credit card recipients, you will use the Mail Merge feature of Word.

Concept 1: Mail Merge

The **Mail Merge** feature combines a list of data, typically names and addresses, that is contained in one file with a document, commonly a form letter, in another file to create a new document. The names and addresses are entered (merged) into the form letter in the blank spaces provided. The result is a personalized form letter.

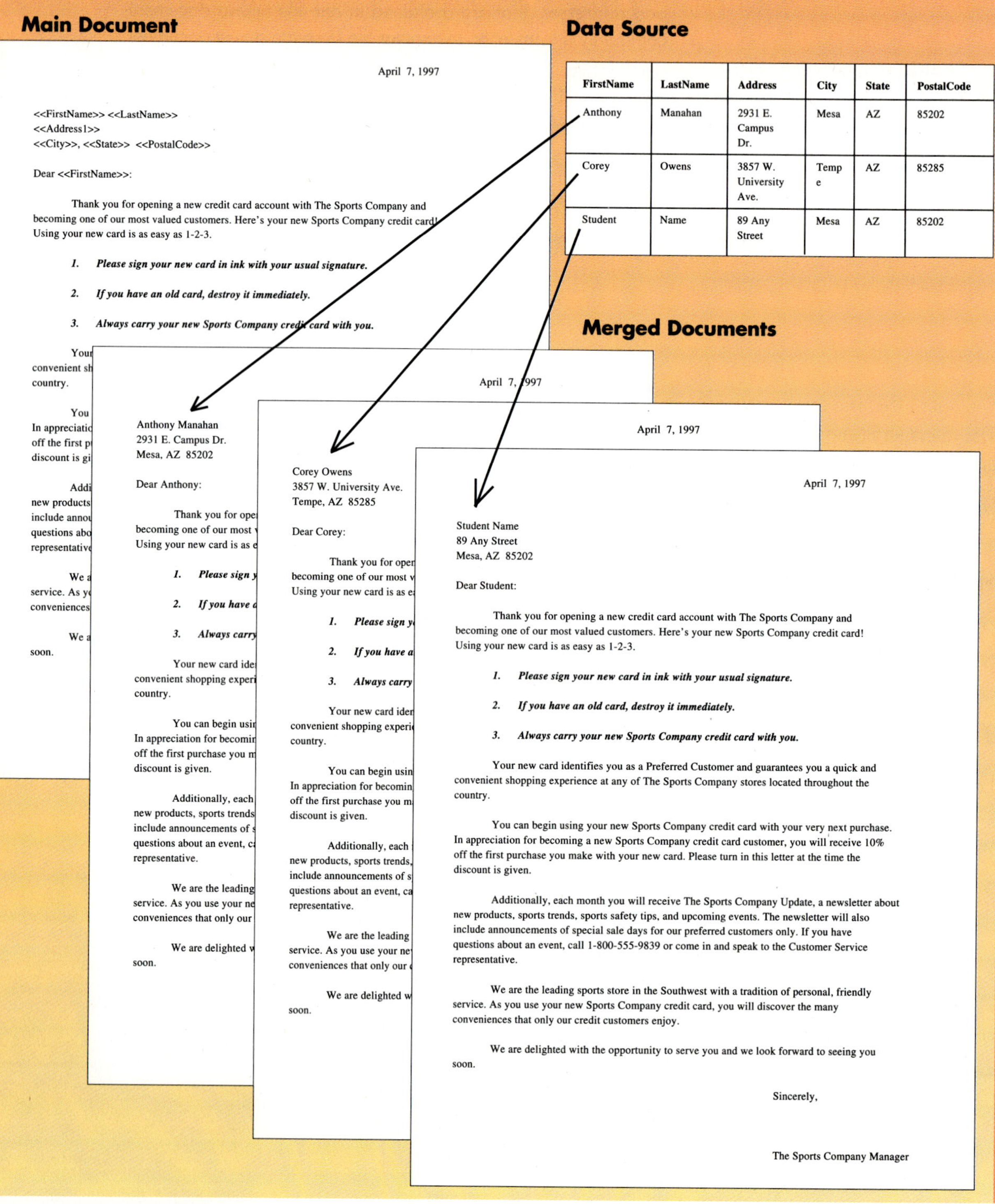

April 7, 1997

<<FirstName>> <<LastName>>
<<Address1>>
<<City>>, <<State>> <<PostalCode>>

Dear <<FirstName>>:

Thank you for opening a new credit card account with The Sports Company and becoming one of our most valued customers. Here's your new Sports Company credit card! Using your new card is as easy as 1-2-3.

1. ***Please sign your new card in ink with your usual signature.***
2. ***If you have an old card, destroy it immediately.***
3. ***Always carry your new Sports Company credit card with you.***

FirstName	LastName	Address	City	State	PostalCode
Anthony	Manahan	2931 E. Campus Dr.	Mesa	AZ	85202
Corey	Owens	3857 W. University Ave.	Temp e	AZ	85285
Student	Name	89 Any Street	Mesa	AZ	85202

April 7, 1997

Anthony Manahan
2931 E. Campus Dr.
Mesa, AZ 85202

Dear Anthony:

April 7, 1997

Corey Owens
3857 W. University Ave.
Tempe, AZ 85285

Dear Corey:

April 7, 1997

Student Name
89 Any Street
Mesa, AZ 85202

Dear Student:

Thank you for opening a new credit card account with The Sports Company and becoming one of our most valued customers. Here's your new Sports Company credit card! Using your new card is as easy as 1-2-3.

1. ***Please sign your new card in ink with your usual signature.***
2. ***If you have an old card, destroy it immediately.***
3. ***Always carry your new Sports Company credit card with you.***

Your new card identifies you as a Preferred Customer and guarantees you a quick and convenient shopping experience at any of The Sports Company stores located throughout the country.

You can begin using your new Sports Company credit card with your very next purchase. In appreciation for becoming a new Sports Company credit card customer, you will receive 10% off the first purchase you make with your new card. Please turn in this letter at the time the discount is given.

Additionally, each month you will receive The Sports Company Update, a newsletter about new products, sports trends, sports safety tips, and upcoming events. The newsletter will also include announcements of special sale days for our preferred customers only. If you have questions about an event, call 1-800-555-9839 or come in and speak to the Customer Service representative.

We are the leading sports store in the Southwest with a tradition of personal, friendly service. As you use your new Sports Company credit card, you will discover the many conveniences that only our credit customers enjoy.

We are delighted with the opportunity to serve you and we look forward to seeing you soon.

Sincerely,

The Sports Company Manager

Mail Merge usually requires the use of two files: a main document and a data source. The **main document** contains the basic form letter. It directs the merge process through the use of merge fields. A **merge field** is a field code that controls what information is used from the data source and where it is entered in the main document.

The **data source** contains the information needed to complete the letter in the main document. It can also be called an **address file** because it commonly contains name and address data. Each category of information in the data source is called a **data field**. For example, the customer's first name is a data field, the customer's last name is a data field, the street address is another data field, the city a fourth data field, and so on. All the data fields that are needed to complete the information for one person (or other entity) are called a **record**. Commonly, a database file created using a database application is used as the data source. However, the data source can also be created using Word.

The credit card letter will be modified to be the main document. You will create the data source using Word. It will contain the following fields of information for each record: first name, last name, street address, city, state, and postal code. When you perform the merge, Word takes the data field information from the data source and combines or merges it into the main document. The merge fields in the main document control what data fields are used from the data source and where they are entered in the main document.

Creating the Main Document

Open the file Credit Card Letter 4. If necessary, maximize the document window and switch to Normal view. Set the zoom to Page Width so that the entire document width is visible.

This is the same as the credit card letter you saved as Credit Card Letter 3 in Lab 2. Notice that the date in the letter on your screen is the same date the file was saved. When this letter is printed, the date will automatically be updated to print the current system date. This is because you entered a date field in the document. To manually update the date displayed on your screen,

Move to: **Date field**
Press: F9 **Update field**

The Update Field command is also on the Shortcut menu.

To begin the Mail Merge,

Choose: **Tools/Mail Merge**

The Mail Merge Helper dialog box on your screen should be similar to Figure 4-1.

Figure 4-1

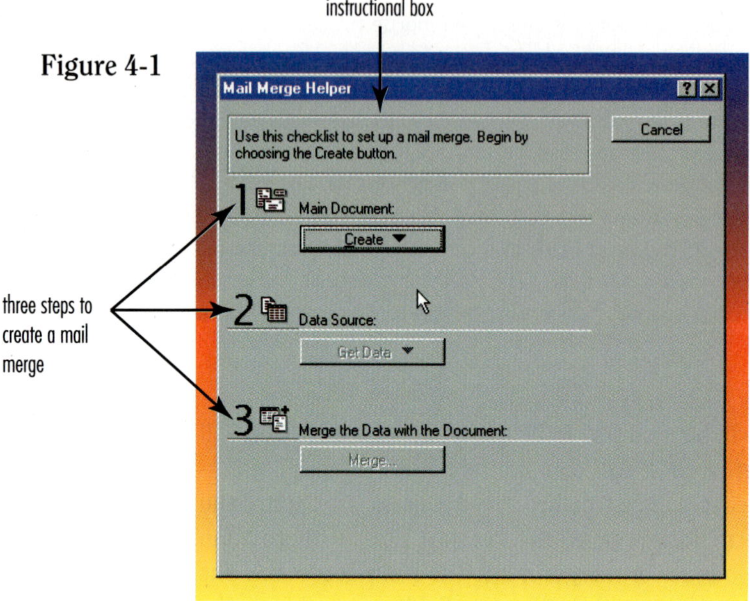

This dialog box is designed to take you step by step through the process of creating a merge. The three steps are:

Steps 1 and 2 can be performed in either order.

1. Create a main document.
2. Create a data source.
3. Perform the merge.

As the instructional box at the top of the dialog box indicates, the first step is to create or edit the main document.

Choose: **Create**

You can use Mail Merge to create form letters, mailing labels, envelopes, or a catalog (providing information such as a parts list). You want to use Mail Merge to create a form letter.

Choose: **Form Letters**

The main document can be an existing document like the credit card letter, or a new document. To use the credit letter in the active window as the main document,

Choose: **Active Window**

The dialog box on your screen should be similar to Figure 4-2.

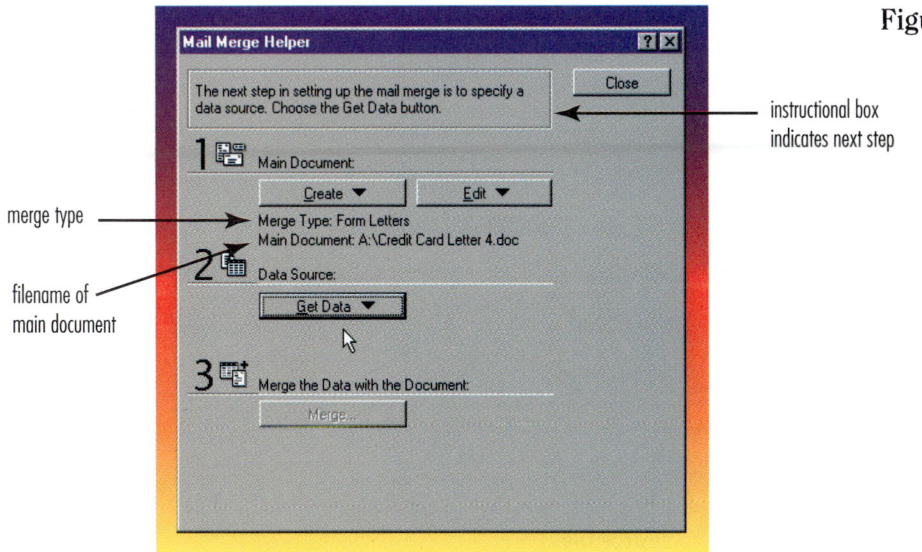

Figure 4-2

The dialog box shows the type of merge and name of the file that will be used as the main document, along with a second button, Edit.

Creating the Data Source

The instructional box now indicates that the next step is to create the data source file, which will contain preferred customers' names and addresses so they can be entered into the main document. To create this file,

Select: Get Data

Again, you can use an existing file or create a new file. You need to create the data source file.

Choose: Create Data Source

Your screen should display the Create Data Source dialog box shown in Figure 4-3.

Figure 4-3

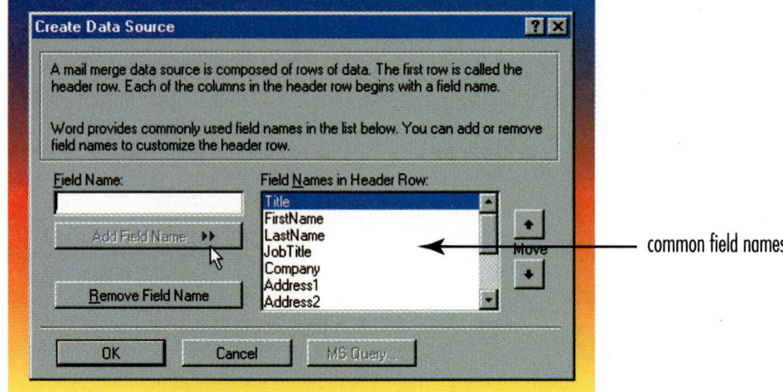

In this dialog box, you specify the field names for the data that will be entered in the data source file.

Concept 2: Field Names

Field names are used to label each data field in the data source. A field name can contain only letters, numbers, or the underscore character. It can be a maximum of 40 characters and cannot contain spaces. The first character of a field name must be a letter. Field names should be descriptive of the contents of the data field.

The dialog box lists commonly used form letter field names in the Field Names in Header Row list box. You can remove from thethe fields list that you do not need in your letter, or you can add additional fields to the list by typing them in the Field Name text box. In this case, you will remove from the list the fields that you do not want to use in the credit letter. The first field you do not need is Title. It is the selected field. To remove it,

If you accidentally remove a field you need, type the name in the Field Name text box and choose Add Field Name. Then adjust the order using the Move buttons.

Choose: **Remove Field Name**

The Title field name is deleted from the Field Names in Header Row list box. The next field you do not need is JobTitle. To remove the field,

Select: **JobTitle**
Choose: **Remove Field Name**

In the same manner, remove the following field names: Company, Address2, Country, HomePhone, and WorkPhone.

The dialog box on your screen should be similar to Figure 4-4.

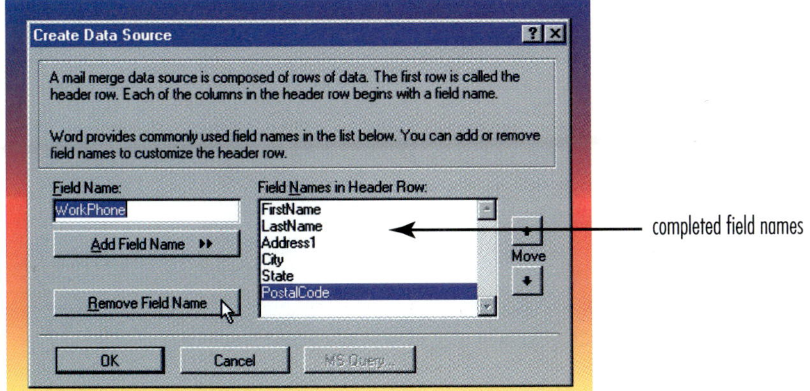

Figure 4-4

The list now reflects only those fields you will include in the data source.

The Move buttons to the right of the list let you rearrange the order of fields. However, the order is acceptable for this file. To indicate that you have completed defining the field names,

Choose: **OK**

In the Save As dialog box, you enter the name you want to assign to the data source file.

Save the file as Credit Data Source on your data disk.

The informational dialog box shown in Figure 4-5 is displayed.

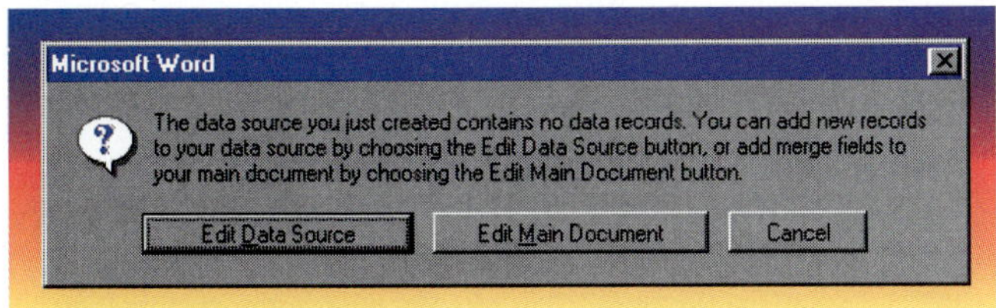

Figure 4-5

Now that you have created the main and source documents, you need to add the record information to the data source file and edit the main document to include the merge fields. You will add data to the data source file first.

Choose: **Edit Data Source**

Your screen should display the blank Data Form dialog box shown in Figure 4-6.

Figure 4-6

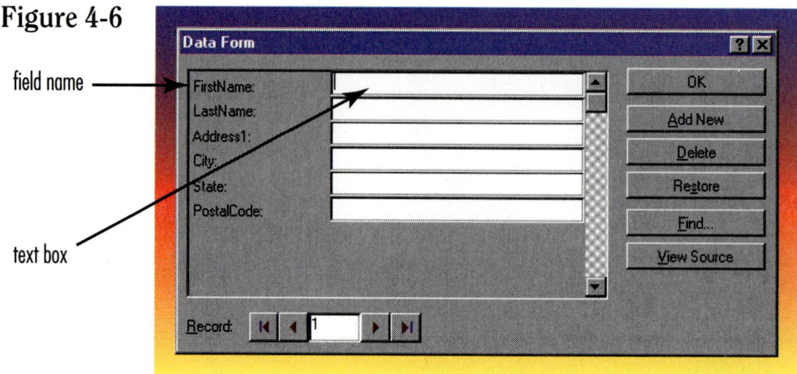

The Data Form dialog box displays the field names and a text box to be used to enter the data for each record. To enter the data for the first field of the first record, the customer's first name,

Type: **Anthony**

The data must be entered exactly as you want it to appear in the letter. If you do not have the information needed to complete a field, you can leave it blank. To move to the next field,

You can also click on the text box to move to the next field.

Press: Tab

To enter the next field of data,

Type: **Manahan**
Press: ←Enter

Enter the information for the remaining four fields for this record using the following information:

Address1:	**2931 E. Campus Dr.**
City:	**Mesa**
State:	**AZ**
PostalCode:	**85202**

The dialog box on your screen should be similar to Figure 4-7.

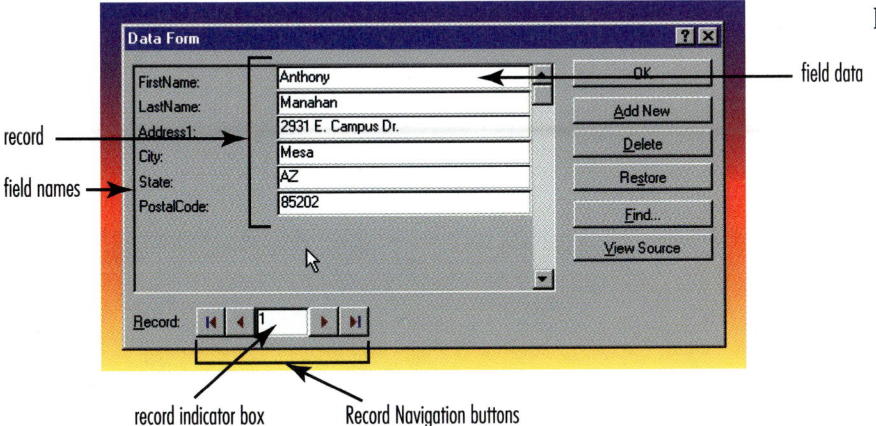

Figure 4-7

The information needed for the main document's inside address and salutation is complete for the first record.

If you see any errors in the field data, move back to the entry and edit it.

To add this record to the data source file and display a new blank data form,

Choose: Add New

Notice that the record indicator shows that the current data form will be used to hold the data for the second record.

Enter the field data for the second record using the following information:

FirstName:	**Corey**
LastName:	**Owens**
Address1:	**3857 W. University Ave.**
City:	**Tempe**
State:	**AZ**
PostalCode:	**85285**

To complete the record and create a third record,

Choose: Add New

Enter your name and address as the third record in the data source.

The number of records you enter into the data source is limited only by your disk space. At any time, you can add more records using the Data Form as you just did.

Move to each of the records and verify the data you entered. If necessary, correct any errors.

⇧Shift + Tab ⇆ will move to the previous field.

The Record Navigation buttons are used to move to the first ⏮, last ⏭, previous ◀, or next ▶ record, or you can type a number in the Record box.

You can also view multiple records at once in the window. To see the three records,

Choose: **View Source**

Your screen should be similar to Figure 4-8.

Figure 4-8

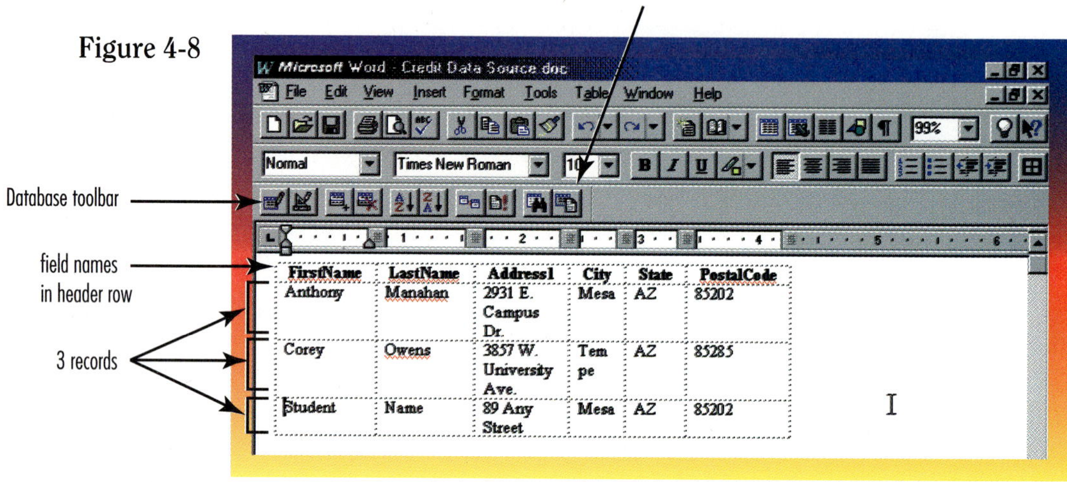

The data source is displayed in a document window in table form. The field names are displayed as the top row of the table, and each record is displayed as a row. In addition, the Database toolbar is displayed.

Choose Ignore All for all identified misspelled words as they occur.

If necessary, move the Database toolbar below the Formatting toolbar. Display the ToolTip for each button and read the description in the status bar.

Now that the data source contains records, save the file again.

To return to the main document,

The menu equivalent is Window/1 Credit Card Letter 4 or Ctrl + F6.

Click:  **Mail Merge Main Document**

The main document is displayed in the window along with the Mail Merge toolbar shown below.

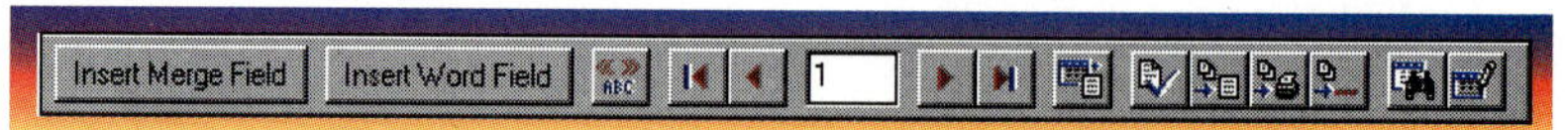

Display the ToolTip for each button and read the description in the Status bar.

Entering Merge Fields in the Main Document

How will Word know where to enter the customer's name and other source data in the main document? Word uses merge fields to do this. Merge fields direct the program to accept information from the data source at the specified location in the main document. To prepare the credit card letter to accept the fields of information from the data source, you need to add merge fields to the letter.

The credit card letter needs to be modified to allow entry of the name and address information for each preferred customer from the data source. The inside address will hold the following three lines of information:

FirstName LastName
Address1
City, State PostalCode

The first line of the inside address, which will hold the preferred customer's full name, will be entered as line 5 of the credit card letter.

Move to: **blank line above salutation**

A merge field needs to be entered in the main document for each field of data you want copied from the data source. The location of the merge field indicates where to enter the field data. The insertion point is positioned on the line where the preferred customer's name will appear as the first line of the inside address. To enter the fields into the main document,

Click: 

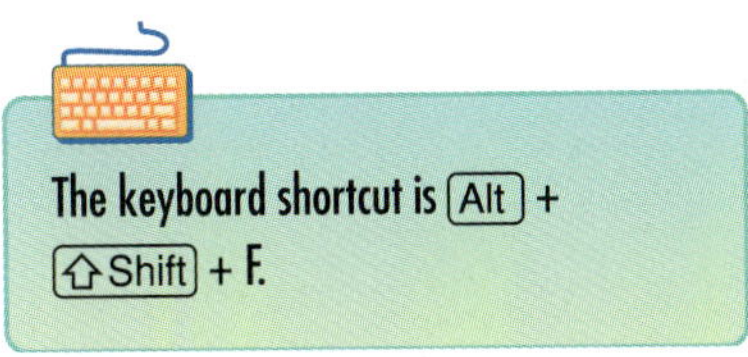

A drop-down list of field names from the data source file is displayed. To insert the First Name merge field at the location of the insertion point,

You cannot type a merge field directly into a document. However, you can move, copy, and format merge fields.

Select: **FirstName**

Your screen should be similar to Figure 4-9.

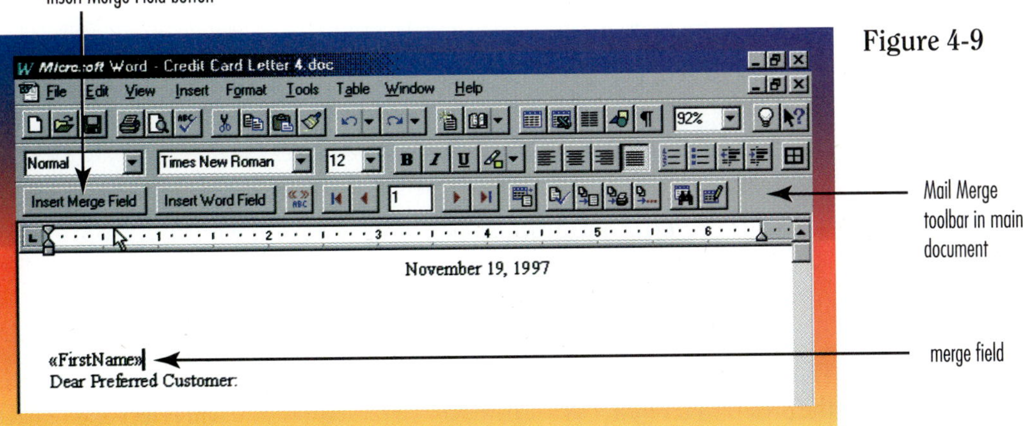

Figure 4-9

The merge field, {{FirstName}}, is displayed at the insertion point location in the main document. It is a field code that instructs Word to insert the information

The field code for this merge field is {MERGEFIELD FirstName}.

from the first name data field (from the data source) at this location in the main document when the merge is performed.

The next merge field that needs to be entered is the preferred customer's last name. To enter a blank space between the first name and the last name,

Press: Spacebar

To enter the last name merge field,

Click: Insert Merge Field
Choose: **LastName**

The next line of the inside address will contain the street address. To create and move to the next line,

Press: ←Enter

Insert the Address1 merge field at this location.

The next line of the inside address will display three fields: City, State, and PostalCode.

Press: ←Enter

Insert the City merge field at this location.

To separate the City field from the next field with a comma and a space,

Type: ,
Press: Spacebar

The State field will be entered on the same line as the City field.

Insert the State merge field at this location.

To separate the State field from the next field, PostalCode,

Press: Spacebar **(2 times)**

Insert the PostalCode merge field at this location.

To enter a blank line between the inside address and the salutation,

Press: ←Enter

The last field of information that needs to be entered in the main document is the preferred customer's first name in the salutation. You will select and replace the words "Preferred Customer" with the FirstName merge field.

Select the text "Preferred Customer" (do not include the :).

A merge field can be used more than one time in the main document. For example, the FirstName merge field can be used again in the letter without assigning it a new field name.

Insert the FirstName merge field at this location.

Your screen should be similar to Figure 4-10.

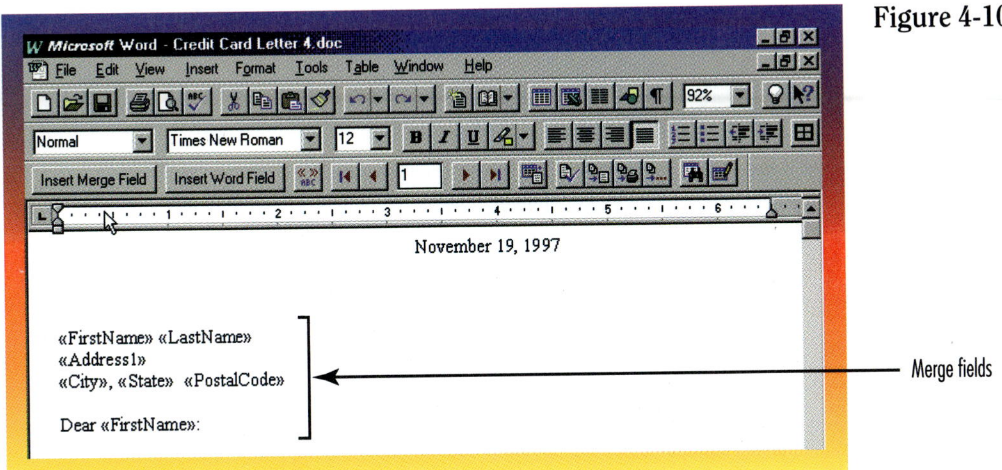

Figure 4-10

The merge field replaces the selected text. You have completed entering all the merge fields that are needed to personalize the credit card letter.

To see how the form letter will appear with the merged data,

Click: View Merged Data

The data in the first record of the data source is displayed in place of the merge fields. To redisplay the merge fields,

Click: View Merged Data

Next, you need to check that the entire letter still fits on a single page.

Preview the letter.

If your letter is longer than one page,

Click: Shrink to Fit

Close the Print Preview window.

Once all the merge fields that are needed in the main document are correctly entered, the file needs to be saved.

Save the main document as Credit Main Document.

Performing the Merge

Now that you have created the main document and data source documents, you are ready to combine them to create the new personalized credit card letter. During this process, a third file is created. The original main document and data source file are not altered or affected in any way. The third file is the result of merging the main document with the data source file.

The menu equivalent is Tools/Mail Merge.

Click: 

Your screen should display the Mail Merge Helper dialog box shown in Figure 4-11.

Figure 4-11

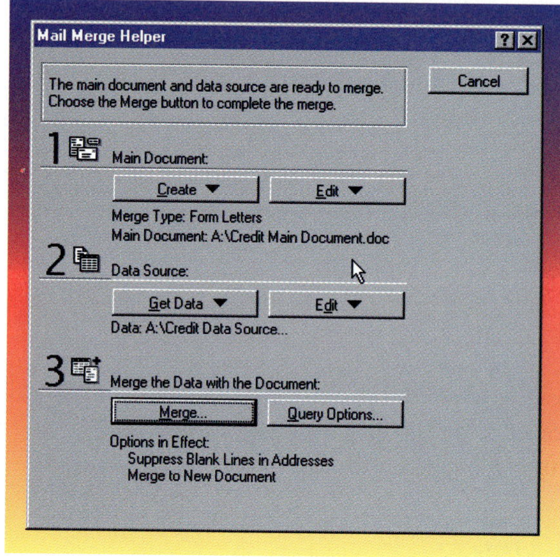

The dialog box now displays the names of both the main document and the data source file. To start the merge,

You could also click Merge to go directly to the Merge dialog box.

Choose: Merge

From the Merge dialog box you can merge to a new document or to the printer. You can also select specific records to merge. To merge all the records in the data source to a new document,

Choose: Merge

The information from the data source is merged with the main document. At the completion of the merge, the file containing the three merge letters is displayed. It has a default file name of Form Letters1.

Your screen should be similar to Figure 4-12.

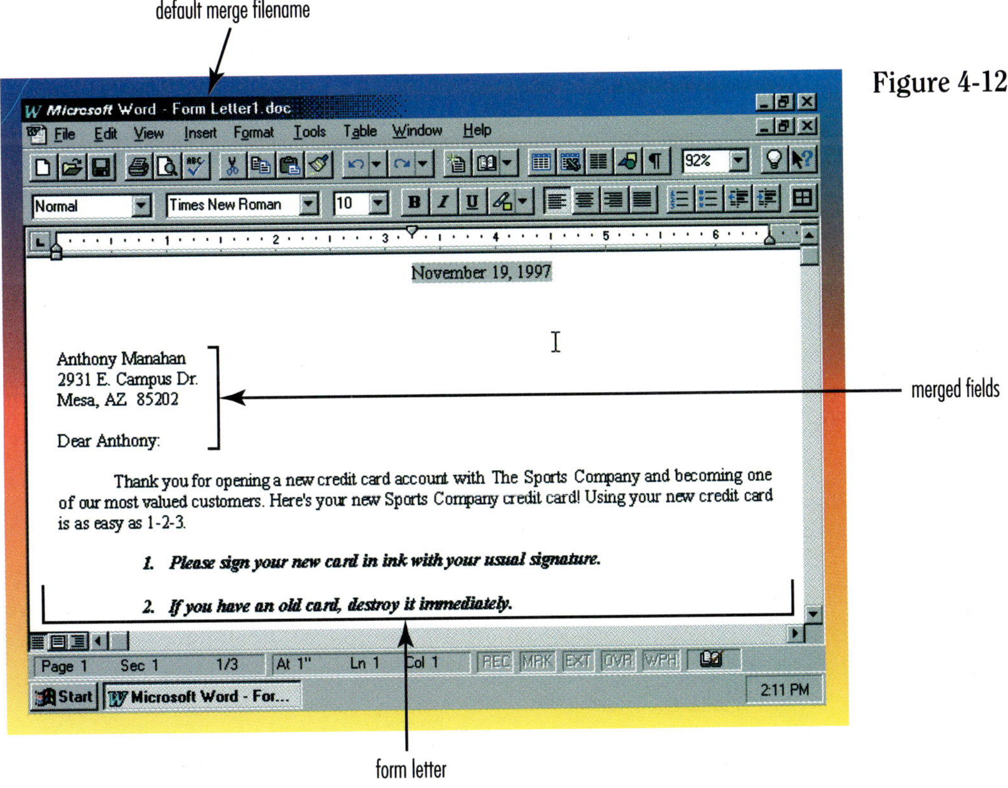

Figure 4-12

The data from the first record of the data source file has been entered into the main document at the location of the merge fields.

To see the letter using the data for the second record,

Press: Ctrl + Alt + Page Down

Finally, to see the letter containing your name and address information,

Press: Ctrl + Alt + Page Down

Now each time you need to send credit card letters, all you need to do is to edit the preferred customer data source file and issue the Merge command. Because the Date field was used, the date will automatically reflect the date the letter is printed.

Save the merged document of three personalized credit card letters as Credit Merge Document to your data disk. Print only the letter containing your name and address information. Close all document windows, saving the files as necessary.

Part 2

Using a Template

Refer to Lab 1 for information on templates.

Your next project is to prepare a summary of gross sales for the four metropolitan area stores for the past three years. You want to include the data in a brief memo to the regional office manager. You would like to create the memo using one of the predesigned document templates included with Word.

The templates are designed to help you create professional-looking business documents such as letters, faxes, memos, reports, brochures, press releases, manuals, newsletters, resumes, invoices, purchase orders, and weekly time sheets. Using the templates gives you an excellent starting point to creating these documents. Once created, you can change different elements to give the document your own personal style.

To open a template file,

Choose: **File/New**

The keyboard shortcut, Ctrl + N, and the New button will open a new document based on the Normal template.

The New tab dialog box categorizes the templates into related groups. You have been using the Normal template (Blank Document) for all the documents you have created so far. You would like to use one of the predesigned memo templates to create the memo.

Open the Memos tab.

Word has several memo templates and a Memo Wizard that guides you step by step through creating a memo.

Select each template icon to preview the format in the Preview area of the dialog box.

You will use the Professional memo template to create your memo.

Select: Professional Memo.dot

Choose: **OK**

Type the percent value in the Zoom Control button text box.

The memo template is displayed in Page Layout view.

If necessary, zoom the document to 85%.

Your screen should be similar to Figure 4-13.

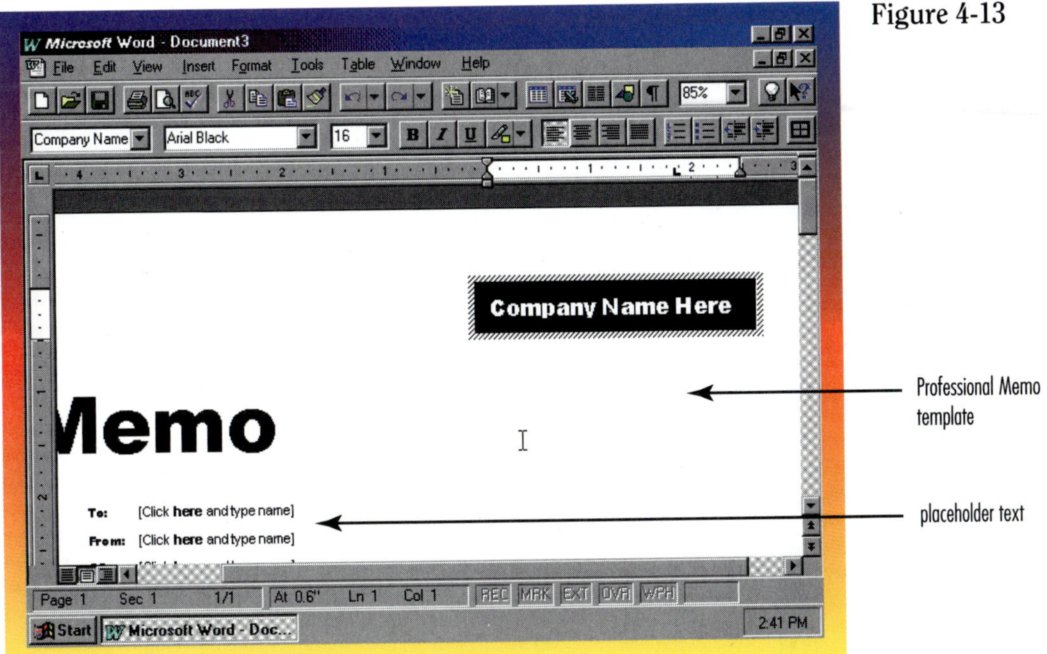

Figure 4-13

At the top of the memo a box displays Company Name Here, and the insertion point is in the box. You need to replace the text in the box with the company name.

Select: **Company Name Here**
Type: **The Sports Company**

Choose Ignore All for all identified misspelled words as they occur.

The next area in the memo template you need to modify is the memo header, which includes the name of the recipient, sender's name, a carbon copy (CC) recipient, the date, and a subject line.

Scroll the window to see the entire memo header.

Notice that the date is the current system date. The text in brackets is called **placeholder text** and tells you what information to enter. To replace the placeholder text, click on it to select it and type in the information you want to include in your document. This is called the **click-and-type** feature and is found in most templates. You can delete any items you do not want from the memo template. To replace the placeholder following the TO: in the memo header,

Select: **[Click here and type name]**
Type: **Ramon Martinez**

Notice that the Style button displays Message Head as the built-in style; this sets the font to Arial and 10 pt.

In a similar manner, enter your name after FROM:.

You plan to send a "carbon copy" or duplicate copy to Donna Blackcloud, the sales coordinator.

Replace the CC: placeholder text with **Donna Blackcloud**.

To enter the subject of the memo, replace the RE: placeholder text with **Sales Comparison**.

Your screen should be similar to Figure 4-14.

Figure 4-14

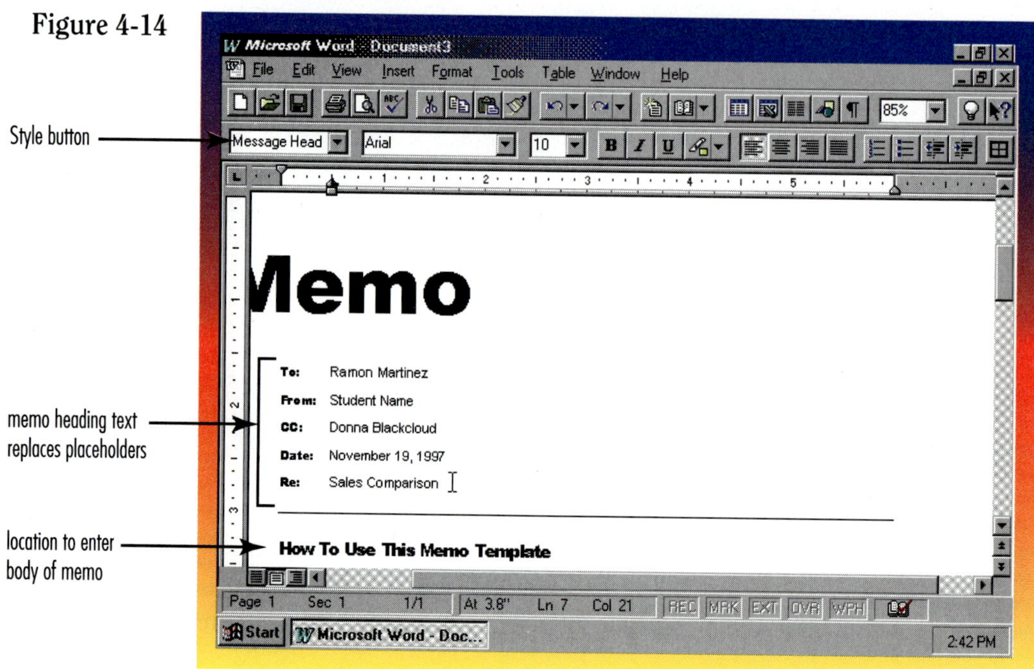

Next you want to enter the body of the memo. The memo template also includes instructions on how to use the template in the body of the memo.

Scroll the window to see the two paragraphs of template instructions.

To enter your memo text, you select the template instructions and then enter you own memo text.

Select the instructions on how to use the memo template.

Enter the text shown below.

> **As requested, the data comparing sales for the years 1994 through 1996 for the four metropolitan stores in the Southwest region is shown below.**

Press: ←Enter **(2 times)**

Your screen should be similar to Figure 4-15.

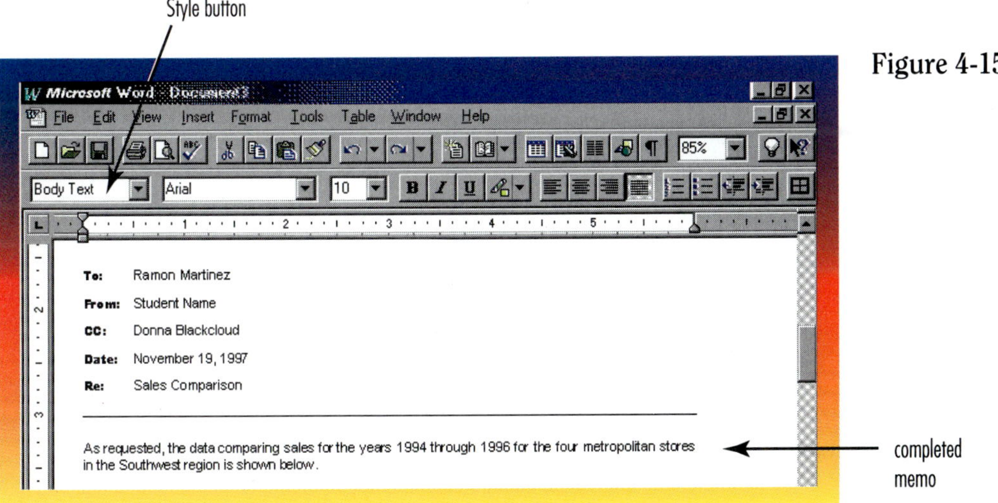

Figure 4-15

Notice that the Style button shows the style as Body Text and the font as Arial 10 pt.

Creating a Table

Next you want to enter the sales data as a table.

Concept 3: Tables

A **table** displays information in **rows**, which run horizontally, and **columns**, which run vertically. The intersection of a row and column creates a **cell** in which you can enter data or other information.

Cells in a table are identified first by a letter and number, called a **table reference**. Columns are lettered from left to right beginning with a letter A, and rows are numbered from top to bottom beginning with the number 1. The table reference of the top left-most cell is A1 because it is in the first column (A) and first row (1) of the table. The second cell in the second column is cell B2. The fourth cell in column 3 is C4.

Cell A1			
	Cell B2		
		Cell C4	

Tables are a very effective method for presenting information. The table layout organizes the information for the reader and greatly reduces the number of words they have to read to interpret the data. Use tables whenever you can to make your documents easier to read.

The table you want to create will display the data for the three years in the columns. The rows will display the data for the four stores and a total. Your completed table will be similar to Figure 4-16.

Figure 4-16

ANNUAL SALES			
	1994	1995	1996
Store 48	749300	778800	789900
Store 55	544900	589800	592800
Store 57	620700	633800	631700
Store 62	578900	569400	565300
Total	2493800	2571800	2579700

You will use the Table Wizard to create the table. Table Wizard is an interactive program that guides you through the steps for creating a table. To use the Table Wizard,

Choose: **Table/Insert Table/Wizard**

Your screen should display the Table Wizard dialog box shown in Figure 4-17.

Figure 4-17

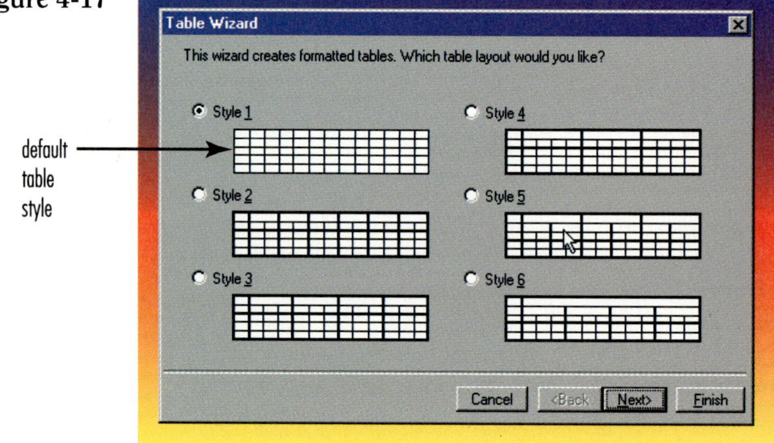

The first step in Table Wizard is to select the table layout. The Style 1 layout creates a basic tabular layout and is appropriate for this table. It is the default style. To confirm the style and go to the next step,

Choose: 

The dialog box shown in Figure 4-18 now asks you to define the column headings by specifying the type of information they will contain.

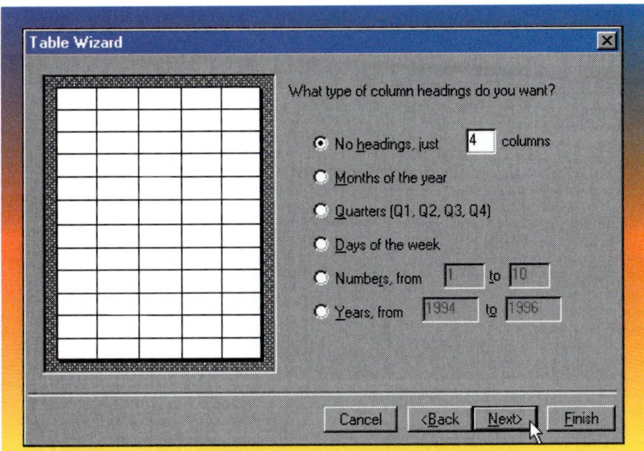

Figure 4-18

You want the years 1994 through 1996 displayed as the column headings. To do this, in the Years, From text box,

Type: 1994

Then, in the Years To text box,

Type: 1996

Choose: Next

If your dialog box already displays the correct years, skip to the next step.

The next Table Wizard dialog box shown in Figure 4-19 is used to refine the appearance of the column headings.

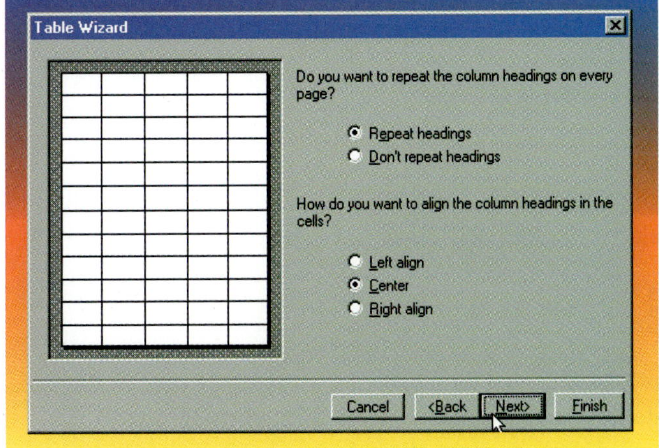

Figure 4-19

This dialog box asks you if you want headings displayed on every page and how you want the headings aligned. The default settings of repeat headings and center are acceptable for this table.

If necessary, select Repeat headings and Center.

Choose: 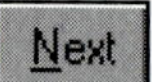

Now the Table Wizard dialog box, shown in Figure 4-20, asks you to specify the row headings.

Figure 4-20

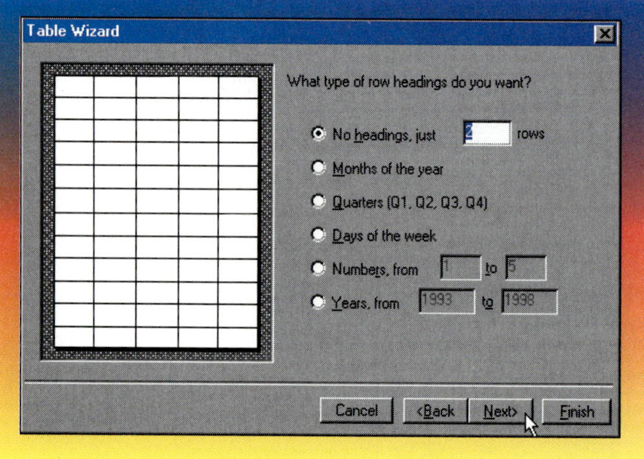

You will enter the store numbers and a Total label as row headings. You cannot enter actual labels in the wizard, so to hold space for the row labels, you will use numbers as placeholders. To do this, in the Numbers, From text box,

If your dialog box already displays the correct numbers skip to the next step.

Type: 1

Press: Tab

In the Numbers To text box,

Type: 5

Choose: 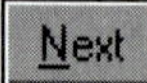

In this dialog box you are asked to specify the alignment of the row headings.

If necessary, select Left align.

Choose: Next

The next dialog box asks you what kind of data is going to be used in the table. Your table will contain the sales figures for 1994 through 1996.

If necessary, select Numbers: right-aligned.

Choose: 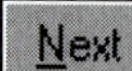

Next you are asked to specify how you want the table printed. **Portrait** prints across the width of the page, and **landscape** prints across the length of the page.

If necessary, select Portrait.

You have given the Table Wizard all the information it needs to create the table.

Choose: 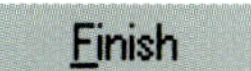

The Table AutoFormat dialog box on your screen should be similar to Figure 4-21.

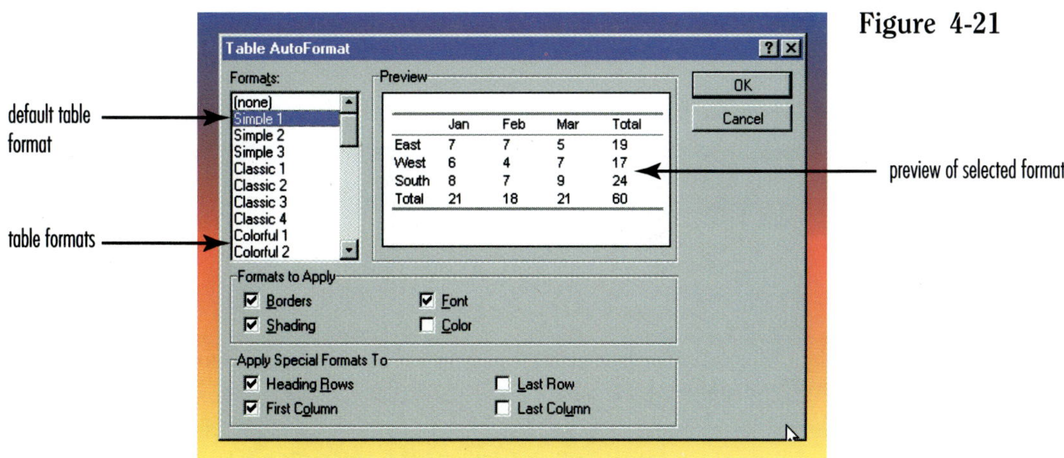

Figure 4-21

Before displaying the table, Word lets you format the table by choosing a predesigned table layout from the Table AutoFormat dialog box. The Formats list box displays the names of the different table formats, and the Preview box shows how the selected format will appear.

Select several table format names and look at the layout in the Preview box.

You think the Grid 8 format would be appropriate for the data in the sales table. To format the table using this layout,

Select: **Grid 8**
Choose: **OK**

Your screen should be similar to Figure 4-22.

Figure 4-22

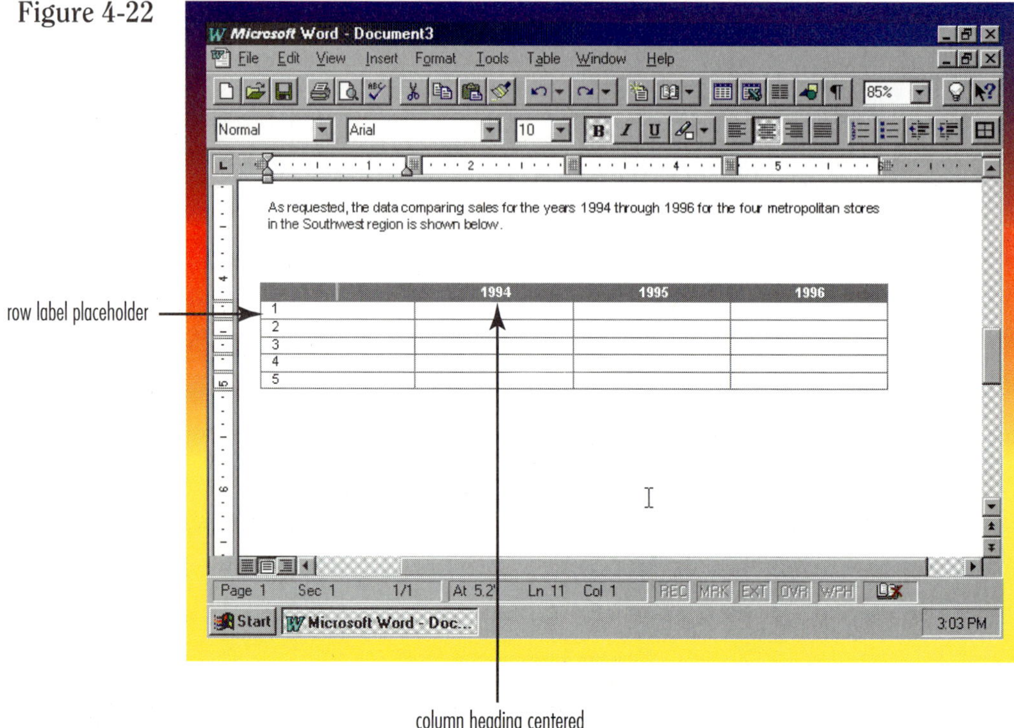

A table with the settings you specified using the Table Wizard is inserted into the memo at the location of the insertion point. It consists of four columns and six rows (counting headings). The column headings display the years center-aligned, and the row headings consist of left-aligned number placeholders. Each cell contains a single line space where you can enter data.

You can move from one cell to another by using the arrow keys or by clicking on the cell. In addition, you can use Tab to move to the right one cell and Shift + Tab to move to the left one cell. The mouse pointer may also appear as an arrow when positioned in the table. When it is an arrow and you click on a cell, the entire cell is highlighted, indicating that it is selected. You will learn more about this feature shortly.

Entering Data in a Table

Now you want to replace the numbers in the first column with row labels.

You can select and edit data in a cell like any other Word entry.

Do not press Enter to complete an entry. If you do, a new line is created in all cells of that row. Press Backspace while on the line in the cell in which it was created to remove the line.

Move to: cell A2

Replace the number 1 with the label Store 48.

Press: →

Your screen should be similar to Figure 4-23.

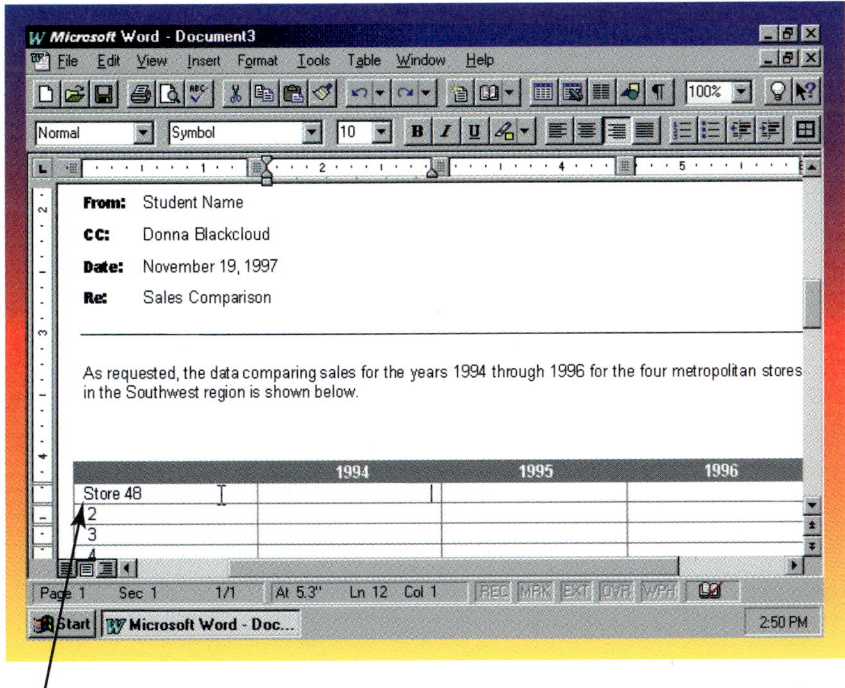

Figure 4-23

The new row label is left-aligned in the cell space and the insertion point is in cell B2, where you will enter the sales number for 1994 for store 48.

Type: **749300**

The number entry is right-aligned in the cell space as you specified using the Table Wizard.

Press: Tab

To complete the data for Store 48,

Type: **778800**
Press: Tab
Type: **789900**

Next you will enter data for Store 55. To move to the first cell in the current row,

Press: Alt + Home

Once a cell contains an entry, using → and ← moves the insertion point through the entry before moving it to the next cell.

The insertion point is back in cell A2, the leftmost cell in the current row. To move down one row,

Press: ↓

Replace the number placeholder with the label **Store 55**.

Press: Tab

To enter the sales for 1994 for Store 55,

Type: **544900**
Press: Tab
Type: **589800**
Press: Tab
Type: **592800**
Press: Tab

The insertion point moves to the first cell in the next row and selects the text. Once a cell contains an entry, using Tab and ⇧Shift + Tab both moves the insertion point to the cell and selects the entry.

Replace the number placeholders in column A and enter the data for stores 57 and 62 using the following information:

Col A	1994	1995	1996
Store 57	620700	633800	631700
Store 62	578900	569400	565300

In cell A6, replace the number 5 placeholder with the label **Total**.

Press: Tab

Your screen should be similar to Figure 4-24.

Figure 4-24

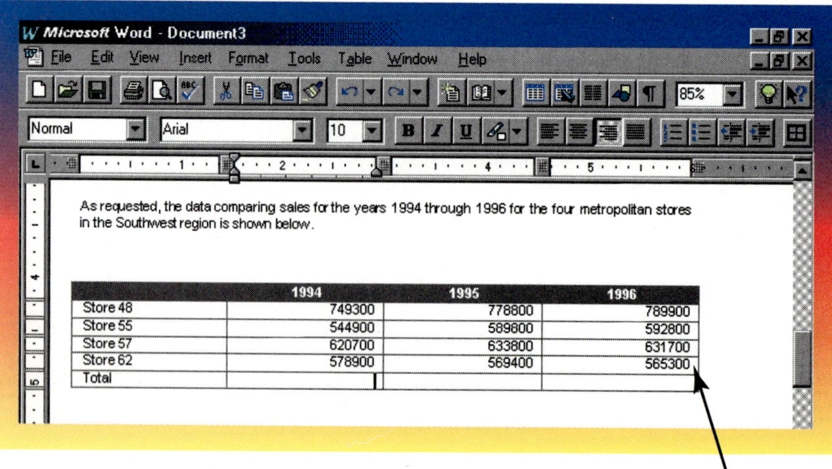

numbers right-aligned

Entering a Formula

Now you are ready to enter the data for the totals. Rather than adding the values for each column of data and entering them in the Total row, you can enter a formula to make this calculation for you.

Concept 4: Formulas and Functions

Formulas and functions are used to perform calculations. A **formula** is a field that contains any combination of numbers, fields resulting in numbers, table references, and operators. Operators are used to specify the type of calculation to perform. The most common operators are:

Operator	Type of Calculation
+	add
–	subtract
*	multiply
/	divide

To use the operators, follow the common arithmetic laws: multiply and divide before adding and subtracting, and calculate whatever is in parentheses first. For example, the formula, 125 + D3 * D5 will multiply the value in cell D3 by the value in cell D5 and then add 125. If you want to add 125 to D3 and then multiply the result by D5, put 125 and D3 in parentheses: (125 + D3) * D5.

A **function** is a predefined formula. One function you may use frequently is the SUM function. SUM adds the numbers directly above the current cell. Other functions include:

Function	Description
AVERAGE	Calculates the average of a column of numbers
COUNT	Totals the number of cells in the column
MAX	Displays the maximum value in the column
MIN	Displays the minimum value in the column

The field result is displayed in the cell containing the field formula or function.

The formulas and functions in Word let you create simple tables and spreadsheets for your documents. For larger, more complex spreadsheets, use Excel and then paste the spreadsheet into your document.

To enter the formula to sum the values in the 1994 column of data,

Choose: **Table/Formula**

Your screen should display the Formula dialog box shown in Figure 4-25.

Figure 4-25

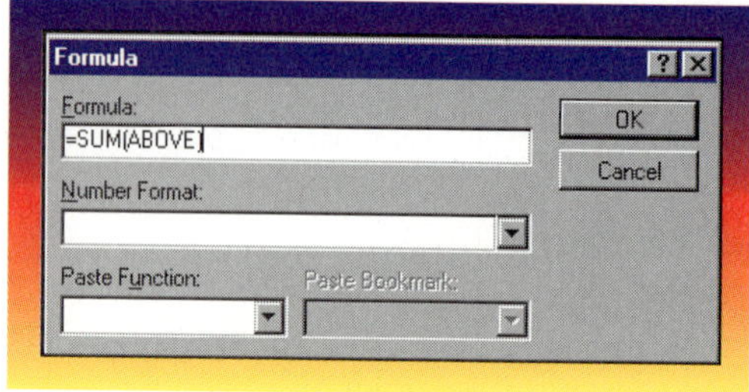

In the Formula text box, Word has proposed the function =SUM[ABOVE]. This is the field code that will be entered in the document to calculate the field result. To use this function to calculate the total of all values in the cells above the function,

Choose: **OK**

Your screen should be similar to Figure 4-26.

Figure 4-26

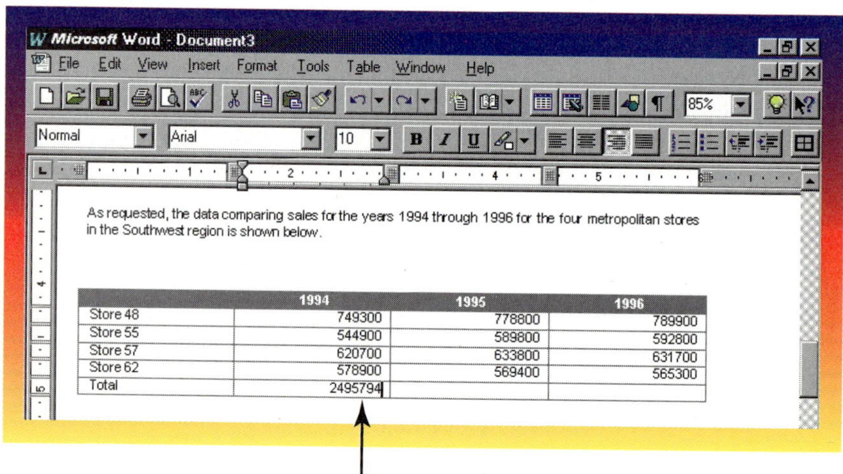

The field result displays the calculated value 2495794 in cell B6; however, the calculated value for this column should be 2493800.

Because the function calculates the sum of all the numbers above the current cell, it included the value in cell B1, the year 1994 column heading, making the total incorrect. To correct this, you need to specify which cells to use in the function. To do this, you will delete the formula from the cell, and reenter the formula using the specific table references.

You can double-click the entry to select it.

Delete the entry in cell B6.

To reenter the formula,

Choose: **Table/Formula**

In place of the word [Above] in the function, you need to specify cells B2 through B5 containing the values to be summed. To enter this,

Select: ABOVE (do not include the brackets)
Type: B2:B5
Choose: OK

The colon (:) indicates "through."

The formula recalculates the result, and the calculated value 2493800 is displayed in cell B6. The formula calculates the result using the values in the specified cells of the table.

If the values in the cells referenced by a formula change, the field result will reflect the new correct result when the document is opened or printed or if the Update Field command is used.

If the cell displays "syntax error," you entered the function incorrectly. Clear the cell and reenter the function.

The function to calculate the total for 1995 needs to be entered in cell C6. This function will sum the values in cells C2 though C5.

Enter this function in cell C6.

In a similar manner, enter the function in D6 to sum the values in D2 through D5.

Do not press ←Enter when you are in the last cell of the table or a new row will be inserted.

Your screen should be similar to Figure 4-27.

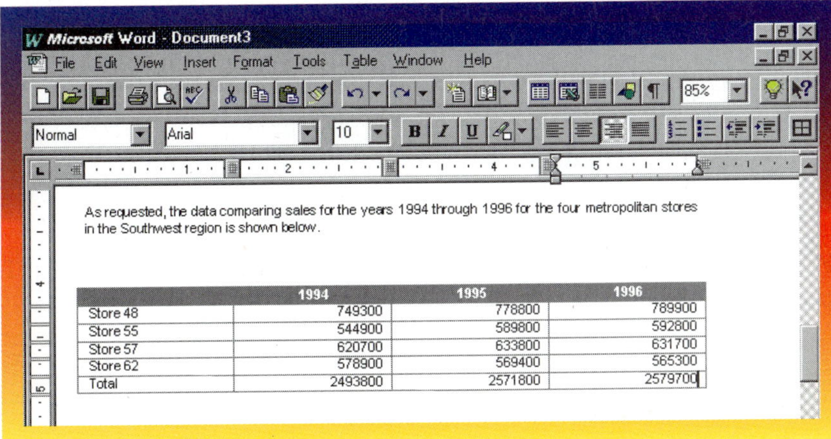

Figure 4-27

Inserting a Row

After looking at the table, you decide it may look better if it included a table heading. To do this, you need to insert a blank row at the top of the table. To quickly move to cell D1 and insert the blank row,

Press: Alt + Page Up
Choose: Table/Insert Rows

A blank row is inserted above the current row with the same format (shading) as the current row. In addition, the entire row is selected. Because this new row will display a table heading, it does not need the column dividers. To clear the selected row of the column dividers,

Choose: **Table/Merge Cells**

Your screen should be similar to Figure 4-28.

Figure 4-28

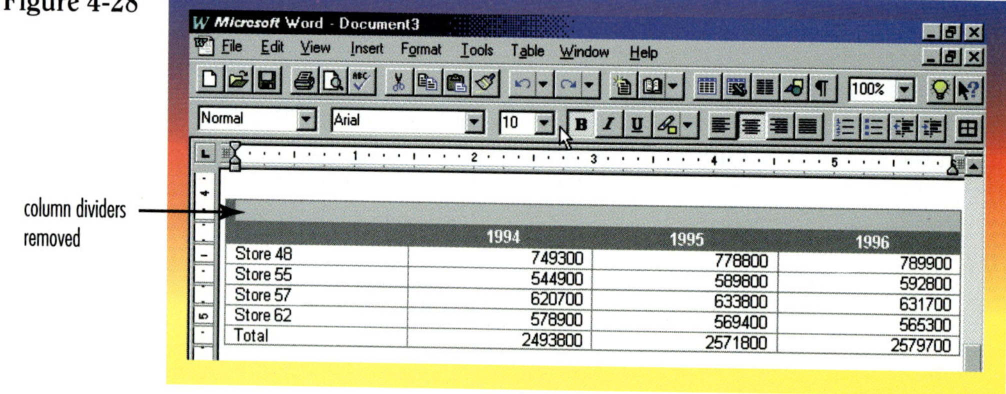

The three column dividers are eliminated, and the top row is one cell.

Now you are ready to add the text for the heading. To enter the table title,

Press: Caps Lock
Type: **ANNUAL SALES**
Press: Caps Lock

Finally, you think the table would look better if the grid lines were heavier. To change the weight of the grid lines,

Choose: **Format/Borders and Shading**

Select 3 pt line style from the Borders tab.

Choose: **OK**

The outline border and the grid lines are now thicker and should be easier to see when the document is printed. The memo is now complete.

Save the document as Sales Comparison Memo.

Preview the memo. Zoom the window to 50 percent.

> As a safeguard to prevent you from saving over the original template file, Word proposes the filename of Professional Memo 1.

Your screen should be similar to Figure 4-29.

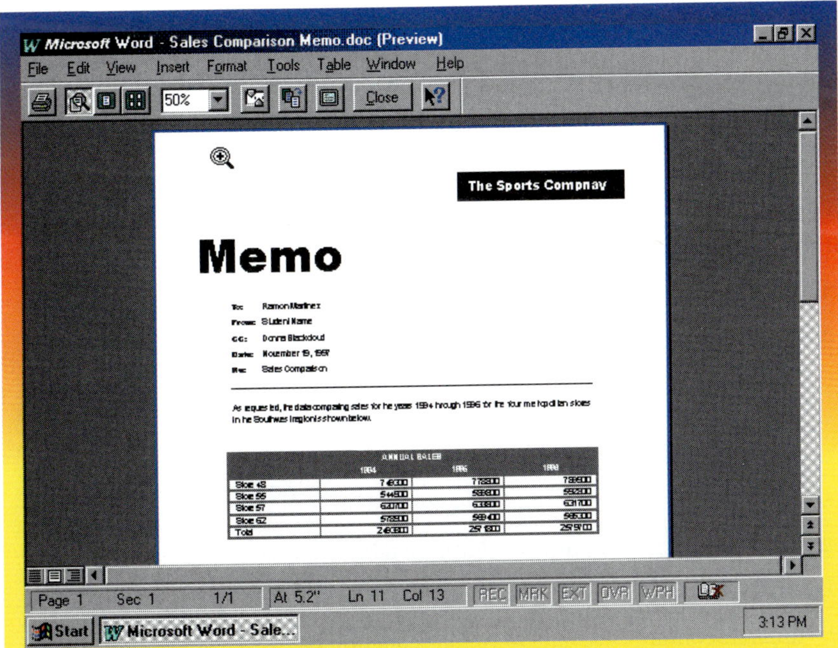

Figure 4-29

Print the document (select the appropriate printer). Close the Preview window.

Return the zoom to 100 percent. Return to Normal view. Close and save any open files. Exit Word and Windows.

LAB REVIEW

Key Terms

address file (WP 157)
cell (WP173)
click and type (WP171)
column (WP173)
data field (WP157)
data source (WP157)
formula (WP181)
function (WP181)
landscape (WP177)
Mail Merge (WP156)
main document (WP157)
merge field (WP157)
placeholder text (WP171)
portrait (WP177)
record (WP157)
row (WP173)
table (WP173)
table reference (WP173)

Command Summary

Command	Action
Tools/Mail Merge	Opens Merge menu
Table/Insert Table/Wizard	Starts the Table Wizard
Table/Formula	Inserts a formula into a table
Table/Insert Rows	Inserts new rows in a table
Table/Merge Cells	Merges cells in a table

Matching

1. merge field	_____	**a.** data that runs vertically in a table
2. template	_____	**b.** function that adds the numbers directly above the current cell
3. column	_____	**c.** intersection of a row and a column in a table
4. table	_____	**d.** data that runs horizontally in a table
5. record	_____	**e.** file that contains the data for a main document
6. =SUM [ABOVE]	_____	**f.** display of data that contains rows and columns
7. main document	_____	**g.** controls what information is used from the data source and where it is entered in the main document
8. row	_____	**h.** all the fields of data that are needed to complete the information for one entity
9. data source	_____	**i.** a predesigned document
10. cell	_____	**j.** the basic form letter that directs the merge process

Discussion Questions

1. Describe how the Mail Merge feature works. What are some advantages of using Mail Merge?

2. What steps are used to create the data source file? How can the data be used in a main document?

3. How does the Table Wizard speed up the design of a table? If you did not use the Table Wizard, describe the process you would use to create and design a table.

4. What is the significance of using a column and row format in tables? How are the rows and columns labeled?

5. Describe the use of formulas and functions in tables. How are they an advantage over entering fixed values?

Fill-In Questions

1. Complete the following statements by filling in the blanks with the correct terms.

- **a.** To create a merged document you need a __________ file and a __________ file.
- **b.** The data source consists of ____________ made up of ________________.
- **c.** A __________________ can be a maximum of 40 characters and cannot contain spaces.
- **d.** The ______________ identifies the cells in a table.
- **e.** ______________ and ______________ are used to perform calculations in tables.

Hands-On Practice Exercises

Step by Step

Rating System

1. To complete this exercise, you must have completed Practice Exercise 4 in Lab 1. In this exercise, you will create a form letter to be sent to the friends and relatives who want a copy of Grandma Gertie's cookie recipes.

- **a.** Open the file COOKIE LETTER from your data disk.
- **b.** Follow the example in Lab 4 to define the document in the active window as the main document, and create the data source. Assign the file name COOKIE DATA SOURCE. Enter the following records and at least three more of your own choice:

  Susan
  Wagner
  463 E. Tioga Ave.
  Forty Fort
  PA
  18704

  George
  Peterson
  832 Colonial Dr.
  Wellesley
  MA
  02181

- **c.** When you are finished entering the records, view the data source file. Save the data source file again.
- **d.** In the COOKIE LETTER document, create an inside address by inserting data source merge fields above the salutation. In the salutation, replace "Friends and Family" with the FirstName merge field.
- **e.** Insert the current date as a field above the inside address and right-align it.
- **f.** Increase the font size for the letter to 12 pt. Justify the letter. Center your return address. When you are finished, document the file and save the letter as COOKIE MAIN DOCUMENT.
- **g.** Merge the data source and main document files. Document the merge file and save the merged letters as COOKIE MERGE DOCUMENT. Print the letters.

2. To complete this exercise, you must have completed Practice Exercise 2 in Lab 2. In this exercise, you will modify the document ACCEPTANCE LETTER to be a form letter.

- **a.** Open the file ACCEPTANCE LETTER from your data disk. Define ACCEPTANCE LETTER as the main document, and create a data source named STUDENT DATA SOURCE consisting of the following fields:

  Title
  FirstName
  LastName
  Address1
  City
  State
  PostalCode
  Major

Hint: After you have removed all unnecessary fields, enter the field name Major in the Field Name text box. Then, click the Add Field Name button.

b. Enter information that pertains to you as record 1 of the data source, and then enter records for three of your friends. When you have finished entering records, view the data source. Document the file and resave it.

c. Modify the ACCEPTANCE LETTER to contain appropriate merge fields where your name, address, or major appears throughout the letter. Insert the current date as a field. You might have to right-align the date again. Increase the font size to 12 pt. for the entire letter. Use the Shrink to Fit command if the entire letter does not fit on one page. Document and save the modified main document as STUDENT MAIN DOCUMENT.

d. Merge the letters. Document and save the file as STUDENT MERGE DOCUMENT. Print the letters.

3. Murphy's Department Store is holding a private sale for its preferred customers. As CEO, you are sending a "personal" letter to each of these customers inviting them to the sale.

a. Open the file PREFERRED CUSTOMER from your data disk. Cut the first line ("Murphy's") to the Clipboard, and paste it (use Ctrl + V) into the WordArt Enter Your Text Here dialog box. Create a title using the WordArt features you learned. Center the title, and enter another blank line below it.

b. Go to the line of text below the title. Set a centered tab at position 3", and a right-aligned tab at 6". Move the street address to the centered tab, and move the city, state, and zip code information to the right tab. Draw a box around this line.

c. Use Find and Replace to locate and replace "preferred customer" with "Special Preferred Customer" in the first and third paragraphs only. Bold and italicize those two occurrences of "Special Preferred Customer." Italicize the text "Any day this month" at the beginning of the second paragraph.

d. Use the Insert Date and Time command to replace [Current Date] at the top of the document.

e. Use the active document to create a form letter. Create a data source named CUSTOMER DATA SOURCE that contains the following fields:

Title

FirstName

LastName

Address1

City

State

PostalCode

f. Enter the following records:

Mr. Joel Allen
316 River St.
Wilkes-Barre, PA 18702

Ms. Ronnie Lee
452 Valley View Dr.
Shavertown, PA 18706

Mr. Dean Walter
409 Laurel Rd.
Mountain Top, PA 18707

g. When you are finished entering records, view the data source. Document the file and resave it.

h. In the main document, insert fields representing the customers' names and addresses above the salutation line. Remove "Preferred Customer" from the salutation, and replace it with the customer's FirstName merge field. Remove [Customer's First Name] from the third paragraph, and replace it with the appropriate merge field code. Insert your name as the CEO in the closing.

i. Document the file and save the main document as CUSTOMER MAIN DOCUMENT. Merge the main document and the data source. Document the merged letter file and save it as CUSTOMER MERGE DOCUMENT. Print the letters.

4. In this exercise, you will create a memo informing employees that a new time sheet form will be used effective next Monday.

a. Create the memo below using the Professional Memo template.

Note: You will only have to press [←Enter] once after each paragraph in the body of the memo. If you open the Paragraph dialog box and look at the Indents and Spacing tab, you will notice that this template includes 11 pt. spacing after each paragraph. If you set up your document in this manner before typing, you can eliminate the need to press [←Enter] two times after each paragraph.

To: [Student's Name]
From: Mr. J. B. Biggs
C.C.: Payroll Department
Date: [Current Date]
RE: New Time Sheets

This Friday will mark the last day that you will use the old time sheets. Below is a sample of the new time sheets we will be using effective next Monday.
Please make sure that your time sheet is turned in no later than 9:00 a.m. the Monday after each pay period ends so that Payroll can process your check on time.
Thank you for your cooperation in this matter.

b. Select and delete the "Company Name Here" box in the upper right corner.

	Date	Time In	Time Out	Regular Hours	Overtime Hours	Total Hours
Monday	1/6/97	8:00	5:00	8	0	8
Tuesday	1/7/97	8:00	5:00	8	0	8
Wednesday	1/8/97	8:00	5:00	8	0	8
Thursday	1/9/97	7:00	6:00	8	3	11
Friday	1/10/97	7:00	6:00	8	3	11
Total Hours						**46**

c. Use the Table Wizard to create the sample time sheet (as shown above) below the memo. Apply the format Grid 1. Make sure all numbers are right-aligned.

d. Use formulas to calculate the total hours column.

e. Bold and italicize entries as shown. Use the Cell Height and Width command to automatically size all columns of the table. Delete column dividers for all but the first cell of the Total row.

f. Document the file and save it as TIME SHEET MEMO. Print the document.

5. As the owner of Susie's Sundries, you are replenishing your stock of some very popular items: widgets, gadgets, smidgens, and do-dads. In this exercise you will create an order form.

Item	Vendor	Quantity	Unit Cost	Total Cost
Widgets	Wonder Widgets	100	.50	
Gadgets	Gadgets Galore	100	2.00	
Smidgens	Smidgen Sensations	50	12.00	
Do-Dads	Do-Dad Delights	250	10.00	
Grand Total				

a. Use the Table Wizard to create the table shown above. Apply the AutoFormat Style List 8 to the table.

b. Enter the formula =c2*d2 to calculate a total for widgets. While you are in the Formula dialog box, use the Number Format drop-down list to apply the second format (#,###.00) to the value. Using this logic, calculate totals and apply the same number format to all values representing total amounts for gadgets, smidgens, and do-dads.

Note: If you accidentally click OK before you are finished in the Formula dialog box, you can always choose Table/ Formula to modify the formula or edit the number format.

c. Calculate a grand total at the bottom of the Total Cost column. Format the grand total amount to display a dollar sign (third Number Format option). Bold the grand total value.

d. Select the entire table and use the AutoFit option from the Column tab of the Cell Height and Width dialog box to accommodate the widest entry in each column.

e. Insert a row at the top of the table. Remove the column dividers and enter the title "Order Form" in a different font that is larger than the text in the rest of the table. Center this title.

f. Make sure all entries in the first two columns are left-aligned, and that the number entries (and their column headings) in subsequent columns are right-aligned.

g. Insert your name and the current date below the table.

h. Document the file and save it as ORDER FORM TABLE. Print the form.

On Your Own

6. Use the Table Wizard to create a schedule of your classes for the semester. Use any style or format you want. The column headings should display the days of the week, and the row headings should display hours. The cells below the column headings should display the classes you have on those days. Document and save the file as SCHEDULE. Print the document.

7. To complete this exercise, you must have completed Practice Exercise 7 at the end of Lab 1. Open the file COVER LETTER from your data disk. In this exercise, you will create a data source and convert the COVER LETTER to a main document file.

Create the data source containing at least three prospective employers, using information of your own choice. Use the fields that are described in the return address of the Lab 1 exercise. Save the file as COVER DATA SOURCE.

Insert the data source fields into the appropriate locations of the COVER LETTER to create a main document. Increase the font size of the letter to 12 and change the font.

Hint: Use a font for the cover letter and resume that is conservative and easy to read. When in doubt, use Times New Roman and/or Arial. Fancy fonts (script, for example) can be difficult to read, and Courier looks as though you just "cranked it out" on a typewriter. You're better than that!

Save the file as COVER MAIN DOCUMENT.

Merge the two files. Document the merged letter file and save it as COVER MERGE DOCUMENT. Print the letters.

8. In this exercise, you will use the table feature to create a resume.

Use the Table Wizard to create a table using Style 1 and specify the following options:

What kind of column headings do you want?
No headings, just 2 columns.

What kind of row headings do you want?
No headings, just 16 rows.

What will most or all of the table cells contain?
Text: left-aligned

In which direction do you want to print your table?
Portrait

Select the Grid 1 format and clear the Borders check box under Formats to Apply so that no borders will print.

Note: When the table is displayed, dotted grid lines will be displayed for you to use as a guide. These lines will not print, however.

Career Objective	Type your objective(s) here.
Education	
Date: [Enter Date Here]	Institution City Degree Courses included:
Work Experience (most recent first)	
Date: [Enter Date Here]	Your Job Title Name of Company Duties Included:
Activities	List Activities
Honors and Awards	List Honors and Awards (Dean's List, Who's Who)
Special Skills	List skills that would enhance your job performance
References	List References or "Available upon request from..."

Enter the resume headings in column A as displayed in the table above.

Enter resume information into column B. Cells follow the same formatting rules as a paragraph. If you right-align a cell, all entries in the cell will be right-aligned.

When listing information that exceeds the width of a cell, overflow information will wrap to the next line. You can press ←Enter to add multiple lines (e.g., the date, job title, company, and duties) to a cell. If you had more than one job or graduated from more than one school, you can enter additional information below the first set of information in the same cell.

When you are finished, increase the font size to 12 pt. The default font size (10 pt.) is much too small for such an important document!

Create a centered return address above the table. The return address should contain your name, address, city, state, zip code, and phone number(s). It can be slightly larger than the resume text, and you can use a different font to attract attention. Just don't get too carried away! Remember . . . keep it conservative!

If the document does not fit on one page, reduce the margins to 1" all around. If the document still does not fit, use the Shrink to Fit command.

When you are finished, document and save the file as RESUME. Print the resume.

9. Now that you have created letters, memos, time sheets, newsletters, and resumes "the long way," try some of the Wizards to create similar documents. Save the completed files with names that reflect the type of document you created. Print the document(s).

Concept Summary

4 Merging Documents and Creating Tables

Data Source

FirstName	LastName	Address	City	State	PostalCode
Anthony	Manahan	2931 E. Campus Dr.	Mesa	AZ	85202
Corey	Owens	3857 W. University Ave.	Temp e	AZ	85285
Student	Name	89 Any Street	Mesa	AZ	85202

Main Document

April 7, 1997

<<FirstName>> <<LastName>>
<<Address1>>
<<City>>, <<State>> <<PostalCode>>

Dear <<FirstName>>:

Thank you for opening a new credit card account with The Sports Company and becoming one of our most valued customers. Here's your new Sports Company credit card! Using your new card is as easy as 1-2-3.

1. ***Please sign your new card in ink with your usual signature.***
2. ***If you have an old card, destroy it immediately.***
3. ***Always carry your new Sports Company credit card with you.***

Your new card identifies you as a Preferred Customer and guarantees you a quick and convenient shopping experience at any of The Sports Company stores located throughout the country.

You can begin using your new Sports Company credit card with your very next purchase. In appreciation for becoming a new Sports Company credit card customer, you will receive 10% off the first purchase you make with your new card. Please turn in this letter at the time the discount is given.

Additionally, each month you will receive The Sports Company Update, a newsletter about new products, sports trends, sports safety tips, and upcoming events. The newsletter will also include announcements of special sale days for our preferred customers only. If you have questions about an event, call 1-800-555-9839 or come in and speak to the Customer Service representative.

We are the leading sports store in the Southwest with a tradition of personal, friendly service. As you use your new Sports Company credit card, you will discover the many conveniences that only our credit customers enjoy.

We are delighted with the opportunity to serve you and we look forward to seeing you soon.

Sincerely,

Merged Documents

April 7, 1997

Anthony Manahan
2931 E. Campus Dr.
Mesa, AZ 85202

Dear Anthony:

Thank you for opening a new credit card acco
becoming one of our most valued customers. Here's yo
Using your new card is as easy as 1-2-3.

1. ***Please sign your new card in ink with y***
2. ***If you have an old card, destroy it imme***
3. ***Always carry your new Sports Company***

Your new card identifies you as a Preferred C
convenient shopping experience at any of The Sports C
country.

You can begin using your new Sports Compa
In appreciation for becoming a new Sports Company cr
off the first purchase you make with your new card. Ple
discount is given.

Additionally, each month you will receive Th
new products, sports trends, sports safety tips, and upco
include announcements of special sale days for our pref
questions about an event, call 1-800-555-9839 or come
representative.

We are the leading sports store in the Southw
service. As you use your new Sports Company credit c
conveniences that only our credit customers enjoy.

We are delighted with the opportunity to serv
soon.

April 7, 1997

Corey Owens
3857 W. University Ave.
Tempe, AZ 85285

Dear Corey:

Thank you for opening a new credit card account with T
becoming one of our most valued customers. Here's your new Sp
Using your new card is as easy as 1-2-3.

1. ***Please sign your new card in ink with your usual***
2. ***If you have an old card, destroy it immediately.***
3. ***Always carry your new Sports Company credit ca***

Your new card identifies you as a Preferred Customer ar
convenient shopping experience at any of The Sports Company st
country.

You can begin using your new Sports Company credit c
In appreciation for becoming a new Sports Company credit card c
off the first purchase you make with your new card. Please turn in
discount is given.

Additionally, each month you will receive The Sports C
new products, sports trends, sports safety tips, and upcoming even
include announcements of special sale days for our preferred custo
questions about an event, call 1-800-555-9839 or come in and spe
representative.

We are the leading sports store in the Southwest with a t
service. As you use your new Sports Company credit card, you wi
conveniences that only our credit customers enjoy.

We are delighted with the opportunity to serve you and
soon.

Since

Student Name
89 Any Street
Mesa, AZ 85202

Dear Student:

Thank you for opening a new credit card account with The Sports Company and becoming one of our most valued customers. Here's your new Sports Company credit card! Using your new card is as easy as 1-2-3.

1. ***Please sign your new card in ink with your usual signature.***
2. ***If you have an old card, destroy it immediately.***
3. ***Always carry your new Sports Company credit card with you.***

Your new card identifies you as a Preferred Customer and guarantees you a quick and convenient shopping experience at any of The Sports Company stores located throughout the country.

You can begin using your new Sports Company credit card with your very next purchase. In appreciation for becoming a new Sports Company credit card customer, you will receive 10% off the first purchase you make with your new card. Please turn in this letter at the time the discount is given.

Additionally, each month you will receive The Sports Company Update, a newsletter about new products, sports trends, sports safety tips, and upcoming events. The newsletter will also include announcements of special sale days for our preferred customers only. If you have questions about an event, call 1-800-555-9839 or come in and speak to the Customer Service representative.

We are the leading sports store in the Southwest with a tradition of personal, friendly service. As you use your new Sports Company credit card, you will discover the many conveniences that only our credit customers enjoy.

We are delighted with the opportunity to serve you and we look forward to seeing you soon.

Sincerely,

Mail Merge

The Mail Merge feature combines a list of data, typically names and addresses, that are contained in one file with a document, commonly a form letter, in another file to create a new document.

Field Names

Field names are used to label each data field in the data source.

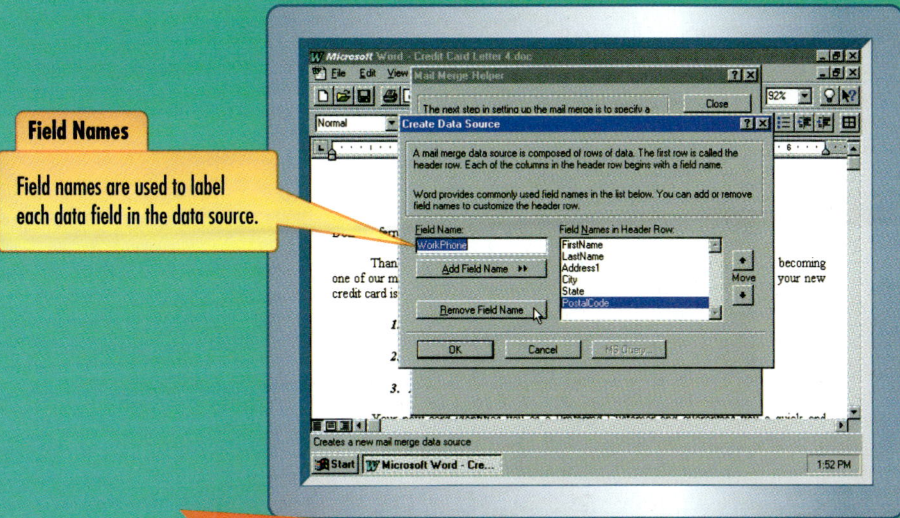

Concepts

- Mail Merge
- Field Names
- Tables
- Formulas and Functions

Tables

A table consists of rows, which run horizontally, and columns, which run vertically. The intersection of a row and column creates a cell in which you can enter data or other information.

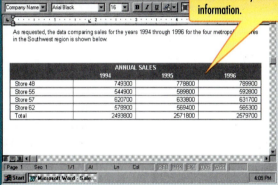

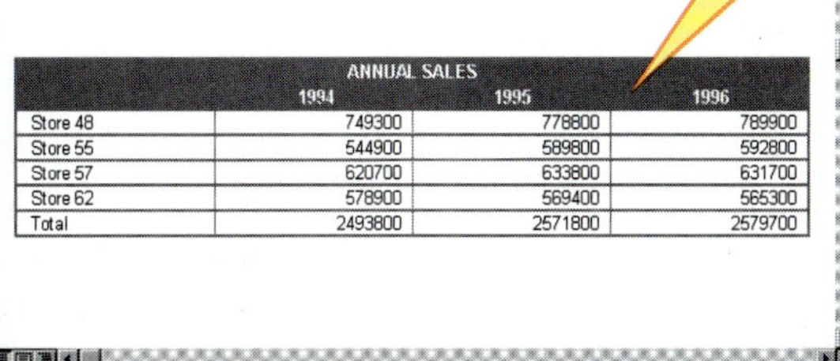

ANNUAL SALES	1994	1995	1996
Store 48	749300	778800	789900
Store 55	544900	589800	592800
Store 57	620700	633800	631700
Store 62	578900	569400	565300
Total	2493800	2571800	2579700

Formulas and Functions

Formulas and functions are used to perform calculations.

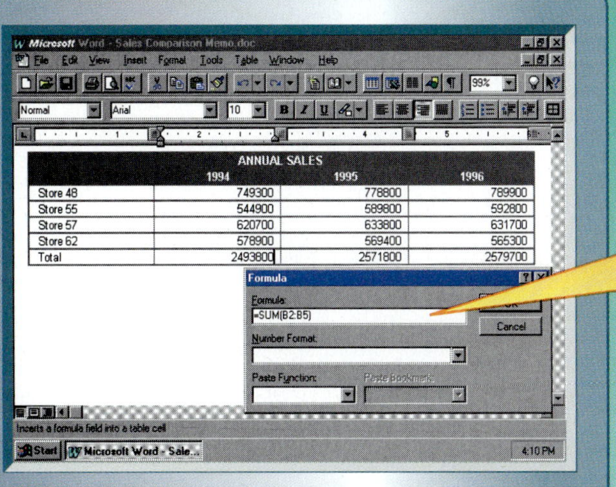

Case Project

Introduction

This project is designed to reinforce your knowledge of the word processing features used in the four Microsoft Word 7.0 for Windows 95 labs. You will also be expected to use Help to learn more about advanced features available in Word for Windows.

Case

Marianne Virgili is the Director of the Glenwood Springs Chamber Resort Association. Semiannually, the chamber produces a newsletter called *Trends,* which reviews the latest economic indicators for Garfield county. It is sent to all chamber members. Marianne has compiled much of the data to be included in the next issue and has asked you to work on several of the articles.

Part I

a. Open the file TRENDS. This file contains some of the text that will be used in the newsletter.

b. The first paragraph contains many errors. Use the editing techniques you learned in the labs to correct the paragraph.

c. Spell-check the document. Check that the document has a single space between words and following a period at the end of a sentence.

d. Search for the word "TRENDS" throughout the document and change it to be displayed in italics. Locate all occurrences of incorrect capitalization for Glenwood Springs and replace them with the correct capitalization.

e. Delete the paragraph about school attendance in the Population, Housing, and Construction section. In the same section, move the paragraph about commercial construction below the paragraph on residential construction.

f. Bold the section headings throughout the document. Change the font type, bold, and enlarge the main heading "Trend Indicators."

g. Save and replace your document. Print the document.

Part II

This issue of *Trends* will contain two tables. The first table will provide employment information for 1996 to 1997 for Garfield county. The second table will provide information on gross sales.

a. The employment information is shown below. Use the Table Wizard to create a table from this data in a new document. Use the List 8 table AutoFormat.

Job Category	1996	1997	% Change
Agr., For., Fish.	141	174	23.4
Mining	705	813	15.3
Construction	856	1,171	36.8
Manufacturing	284	327	15.1
Trans., Comm., Util.	443	504	13.8
Wholesale Trade	338	410	21.3
Retail Trade	2,580	2,859	10.9
Fin., Ins., Real Est.	522	601	15.1
Services	2,679	2,767	3.3
Government	2,234	2,328	4.2
TOTAL			

b. Right-align the entries in the three data columns, including the column heads. Left-align the row heads. Bold and underline the column heads.

c. Enter functions to sum the 1996 and 1997 columns of data, and average the % Change column. *Hint:* You will need to exclude the cells containing the date column headings from being included in the calculated total. Bold the total row.

d. Insert a new row above the table. Remove the column dividers. Add the title "Table 1: JOBS IN GARFIELD COUNTY." Center and bold the title.

e. Enhance the appearance of the table by appropriately sizing the columns and making the grid lines thicker.

f. Save the table. Print the table.

The second table will display the percent of gross sales for the first half of 1998 for the five major cities in the county.

g. Open a new document file. Use the Table Wizard to create a table from the following data. Select a table AutoFormat of your choice.

City	Sales	% of Total
Glenwood Springs	165.7	61.0
Parachute	2.3	0.8
Silt	3.4	1.3
Carbondale	19.3	7.1
Rifle	34.7	12.8
Remainder of County	46.1	17.0
TOTAL 1st Half		

h. Enter formulas to total the two columns of data.

i. Insert a new row above the table. Clear the column dividers. Enter the title "Table 2: TOTAL GROSS SALES" on the first line, "JANUARY–JUNE 1998" on the second line, and "(In millions of dollars)" on the third line. Center the title lines.

j. Right-align the data columns. Left-align the City column.

k. Enhance the appearance of the table by adding bold and making other format changes as you like. Appropriately size the table columns.

l. Save the table. Print the table.

Part III

You need to create the newsletter headline next.

a. The headline should display the following information:

Newsletter name: TRENDS

Subheadings: A Semiannual Review of Economic Indicators

Glenwood Springs Chamber Resort Association

Your Name

Current Date

b. Use the following features when designing the headline:

- centered text
- font and type sizes of your choice
- italics
- bold
- borders with different line weights
- WordArt

c. Save the headline as a separate document file.

Part IV

Now you are ready to create the newsletter.

a. Copy the headline to the top of the text file, TRENDS. Change the newsletter text display to two columns. Make the page margins 0.5 inch. Make the space between columns 0.25 inch.

b. Copy each table into the newsletter near the reference to the table in the text. Size the tables to fit within the column widths.

c. Hyphenate the newsletter.

d. Display the last paragraph of text in a shaded text box.

e. Save the newsletter. If necessary, select another printer and adjust the newsletter layout (you may need to change font and type sizes, adjust columns, or change the placement of the tables). Print the newsletter.

Part V

The final document you need to create is a cover memo to the Director to accompany a sample copy of the newsletter.

a. Open a memo template of your choice.

b. Enter the information that is needed to complete the template. (Use your name following FROM:.)

c. Enter the body of the memo. The memo should introduce the newsletter and indicate that you can revise the newsletter as needed.

d. Save the memo. Print the memo.

Glossary of Key Terms

Active window: The window you can work in. It is identified by a highlighted title bar, the insertion point, and scroll bars. It is the topmost window in the desktop.

Address file: The data source file used in a merge; it typically contains name and address data to be combined with the main document.

Alignment: Positioning of text on a line, such as flush left, centered, flush right, or justified.

Bold: Printed text that appears darker than surrounding text as a result of printing over the text several times.

Case-sensitive: Capable of distinguishing between uppercase and lowercase characters.

Cell: The space created by the intersection of a vertical column and a horizontal row.

Character styles: A combination of any character formats that affect selected text.

Click and type: A feature found in many templates that lets you click on the placeholder and replace it with the text you type.

Clip Art: A collection of graphics that usually is bundled with a software application.

Column: A vertical block of cells one cell wide in a table.

Cursor: The blinking vertical bar that shows you where the next character you type will appear. Also called the insertion point.

Custom Dictionary: A dictionary of terms you have entered that are not in the main dictionary.

Data field: Each piece of information in the data source that creates a record.

Data source: The file that supplies the data.

Default: Initial word settings that can be changed to customize documents.

Document pane: When footnotes are created, the upper portion of the window that displays the document.

Drag-and-drop: A mouse procedure that moves or copies a selection to a new location.

Drawing objects: Simple objects consisting of shapes such as lines and boxes.

Drop cap: Special effect that is applied to a single character.

Edit: The process of changing and correcting existing text in a document.

Embedded object: Text added to a document that can be enclosed in a frame, edited, or moved and sized to any location in the document.

Endnotes: Reference notes that are displayed at the end of the document.

End-of-file marker: The horizontal line that marks the end of a file.

Field: Special codes that instruct Word to insert information in a document.

Field code: The code containing the instructions about the type of information to insert in the document.

Field result: The results displayed in a field according to the instructions in the field code.

Font: The different type sizes and styles that can be selected to improve the appearance of the document.

Footnotes: A note of reference in a document displayed at the bottom of the page where the reference occurs.

Formatting: Features that enhance the appearance of the document to make it more readable or attractive.

Formatting toolbar: The toolbar, displayed below the Standard toolbar, that contains buttons representing the most frequently used text-editing and text-layout features.

Formula: Table entry that does arithmetic calculations.

Frame: A box containing text, a table, a graphic or another object that you can move freely on a page.

Functions: A set of built-in formulas that perform calculations automatically.

Graphics: Non-text elements in a document.

Handles: Small boxes surrounding a selected object that allow you to manipulate its size and placement.

Heading style: A style that is designed to identify different levels of headings in a document.

Hyphenation zone: An unmarked space along the right margin that controls the amount of white space in addition to the margin that Word will allow at the end of a line.

Insert mode: Method of text entry in which new characters are inserted into existing text, which moves to the right to make space for the new characters; the text on the line is reformatted as necessary.

Insertion point: The blinking vertical bar that shows you where the next character you type will appear on the line. Also called the cursor.

Italics: Printed text that appears slanted.

Landscape: Text that is printed across the length of the paper.

Mail Merge: Combining a text document with a data document or file containing names and addresses to produce a merged document or form letter.

Main dictionary: The dictionary of terms that comes with Word 7.0.

Main document: Document that contains the basic form letter in a merge operation.

Manual page break: Begins a new page regardless of the amount of text on the previous page.

Merge fields: Fields that control what information is used from the data source and where it is entered in the main document.

Monospaced: A font that uses the same amount of space for every character.

Newpaper columns: Display text so that it flows from the bottom of one column to the top of the next column.

Note pane: Lower portion of the window that displays footnotes.

Note separator: The horizontal line separating footnote text from main document text.

Note text: The text in a footnote.

Optional hyphen: Hyphen inserted by Word when a word is broken between two lines because the full word didn't fit.

Overtype mode: Method of text entry in which new text types over the existing characters.

Paragraph mark: Special hidden character that indicates the end of a paragraph.

Paragraph styles: A combination of any character formats and paragraph formats that affects all text in a paragraph.

Picture: A graphic that has been created using a drawing tool or other graphic application.

Placeholder text: Text that marks the space and provides instructions for the text that should be entered at that location.

Points: Measure used for height of type: 1/72 of an inch.

Portrait: Text that is printed across the width of the paper.

Proportional: A font that varies the amount of horizontal space given to each character.

Record: All the fields of data that are needed to complete the main document for one entity in a merge operation.

Reference mark: A numbered mark or a custom mark that references a footnote.

Row: The horizontal line in a table.

Ruler: The ruler located below the Formatting toolbar that shows the line length in inches.

Sans serif fonts: Fonts that do not have a flair at the base of each letter, such as Arial or Helvetica.

Scalable: A font that can be printed in nearly any point size.

Selecting: Highlighting text.

Selection bar: The unmarked area to the left of the document area where the mouse can be used to highlight text lines.

Serif fonts: Fonts that have a flair at the base of each letter, such as Roman or Times New Roman.

Server: The application used to create the embedded object.

Shortcut menu: Menu that displays options related to the current selection; accessed by clicking the right mouse button.

Soft spaces: A space automatically entered by Word to align the text properly on a single line.

Spelling tool: Word tool that locates spelling errors and proposes alternative spellings.

Standard toolbar: The toolbar, displayed below the menu bar, that gives quick access to editing features.

Status bar: The line of information at the bottom of the screen.

Styles: Attributes that can be associated with fonts, such as bold and italics.

Tab: A predefined stopping point along a line to which text will indent when you press Tab.

Tab leaders: Series of dots between a heading and the page number in the table of contents.

Tab stop: The tab stopping points along the ruler that mark the locations of the tabs.

Table: A grid of horizontal rows and vertical columns; the intersection of rows and columns creates cells in which you can enter text.

Table references: The column letter and row number that identify cells in a table.

Template: A prewritten blank worksheet that is used repeatedly to enter text.

Text area: The center area of the Word screen, where documents are displayed in windows.

Thesaurus: The file of synonyms and antonyms provided with Word.

Typeface: Another word for font, a set of characters with a specific design.

Type size: The height of a character.

Wizards: A Word feature that asks questions and uses your answers to the questions to automatically create a layout and format for a document.

WordArt: A supplementary application included with the Word program that is used to enhance a document by changing the shape of text, adding 3-D effects, and changing the alignment of text on a line.

Word wrap: Feature that automatically determines where to begin the next line of text; the user does not press Enter at the end of a line unless it is the end of a paragraph or to insert a blank line.

Command Summary

Command	Shortcut Keys	Button	Action
File/New	Ctrl + N		Opens new document template
File/Open	Ctrl + O		Opens selected file
File/Close			Closes active file
File/Save	Ctrl + S		Saves file using same filename
File/Save As			Saves file using a new filename
File/Properties			Shows the properties of the active document
File/Page Setup			Changes layout of page including margins, paper size, and paper source
File/Print Preview			Displays document as it will appear when printed
File/Print	Ctrl + P		Prints file using selected print settings
File/Exit	Alt + F4		Exits Word program
Edit/Undo	Ctrl + Z		Restores last editing change
Edit/Redo or Repeat	Ctrl + Y		Restores last Undo; Repeats last command or action
Edit/Cut	Ctrl + X		Removes selection and copies it to Clipboard
Edit/Copy	Ctrl + C		Copies selection to Clipboard
Edit/Paste	Ctrl + V		Inserts contents of Clipboard into document
Edit/Select All	Ctrl + A		Selects entire document
Edit/Find	Ctrl + F		Locates specified text or formatting
Edit/Replace	Ctrl + H		Locates and replaces specified text or formatting
Edit/Go To	Ctrl + G		Moves insertion point to specified location in document
View/Normal			Displays document in Normal view
View/Outline			Displays the structure of the document as an outline

Command	Shortcut Keys	Button	Action
View/Page Layout			Displays the page as it will appear when it is printed
View/Master Document			Shows several documents organized into a master document
View/Full Screen			Shows the document without Word's toolbars, menus, scroll bars, and other screen elements
View/Toolbars			Displays or hides selected toolbars
View/Footnote			Hides or displays the footnote pane
View/Zoom		100%	Changes onscreen character size
View/Zoom/Whole Page			Displays entire page onscreen
Insert/Break	Ctrl + ←Enter		Inserts manual page break
Insert/Page Numbers			Specifies page number location
Insert/Date and Time			Inserts current date or time maintained by computer system in selected format
Insert /Footnote	Alt + Ctrl + F		Inserts footnotes into document
Insert/Index and Tables			Inserts an index or a table of contents, figures, or authorities
Insert/Frame			Inserts a frame around selected object
Insert/Picture			Inserts a graphic figure into document
Insert/Object			Inserts objects into document
Format/Font			Changes appearance of selected characters
Format/Font/Font Style/Italic	Ctrl + I		Makes selected text italic
Format/Font/Font Style/Bold	Ctrl + B		Makes selected text bold
Format/Font/Underline/Single	Ctrl + U		Adds single underline below selection
Format/Paragraph			Changes appearance of selected paragraphs
Format/Paragraph/Indents and Spacing			Sets indentation, spacing, and alignment for selected paragraphs
Format/Paragraph/Indents and and Spacing/Alignment			
/Left	Ctrl + L		Aligns text to left margin
/Centered	Ctrl + E		Centers text between left and right margins
/Right	Ctrl + R		Aligns text to right margin
/Justified	Ctrl + J		Aligns text equally between left and right margins
Format/Tabs			Specifies types and position of tab stops
Format/Borders and Shading			Adds borders and shading to selected paragraphs or objects

Command	**Shortcut Keys**	**Button**	**Action**
F**o**rmat/**C**olumns			Specifies number, spacing, and size of columns
F**o**rmat/Change Cas**e**/**U**PPERCASE	Ctrl + Shift + A		Changes selected text to uppercase
F**o**rmat/**D**rop Cap/**D**ropped			Changes selected letter to a drop cap
F**o**rmat/Bullets and **N**umbering			Inserts and removes bullets or numbers from selection
Tools/Sp**e**lling	F7		Starts the Spelling tool
Tools/**T**hesaurus	Shift + F7		Turns on Thesaurus tool
Tools/**H**yphenation			Specifies hyphenation settings
Tools/Mail Me**r**ge			Produces merged documents
Tools/**O**ptions/View/**S**paces/Paragraph **M**arks			Displays or hides nonprinting characters
T**a**ble/**I**nsert Table/Wi**z**ard			Starts the Table Wizard
T**a**ble/**I**nsert Rows			Inserts new rows in a table
T**a**ble/**M**erge Cells			Merges cells in a table
T**a**ble/F**o**rmula			Inserts a formula into a table
Window/**A**rrange All			Displays all open document windows without overlapping
Window/**#**filename			Makes selected window active
Help/**M**icrosoft/Word Help Topics	F1		Displays Word online Help

Windows 95 Review

The following is an alphabetical arrangement of the most common Windows 95 features. The features are described in general. Wherever applicable, a How To section discusses how to perform the task.

Arranging Windows: There are two ways to arrange windows: cascade and tile.

Cascade	Layers open windows, displaying the active window fully and only the title bars of all other open windows behind it.
Tile	Resizes each open window and arranges the windows vertically or horizontally on the desktop

Cascading windows is useful if you want to work primarily in one window but you want to see the title of other open windows. Tiling is most useful when you want to work in several applications simultaneously, because it allows you to quickly see the contents of all open windows and move between them. However, the more windows that are open, the smaller the space available to display the tiled window contents.

The commands to tile windows on the Windows 95 desktop are displayed in the taskbar shortcut menu. In most Windows 95 applications, the commands are found in the Window menu.

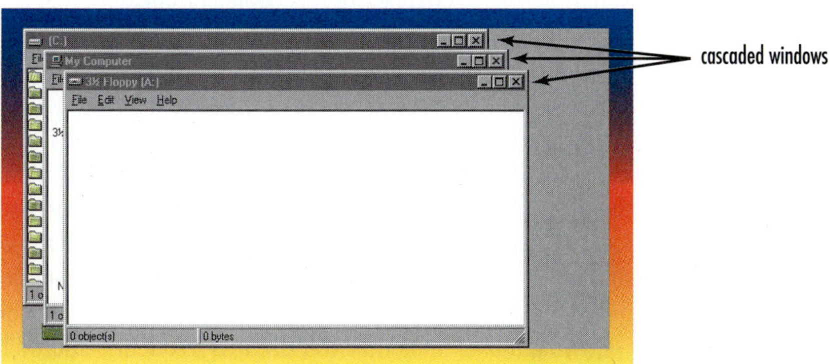

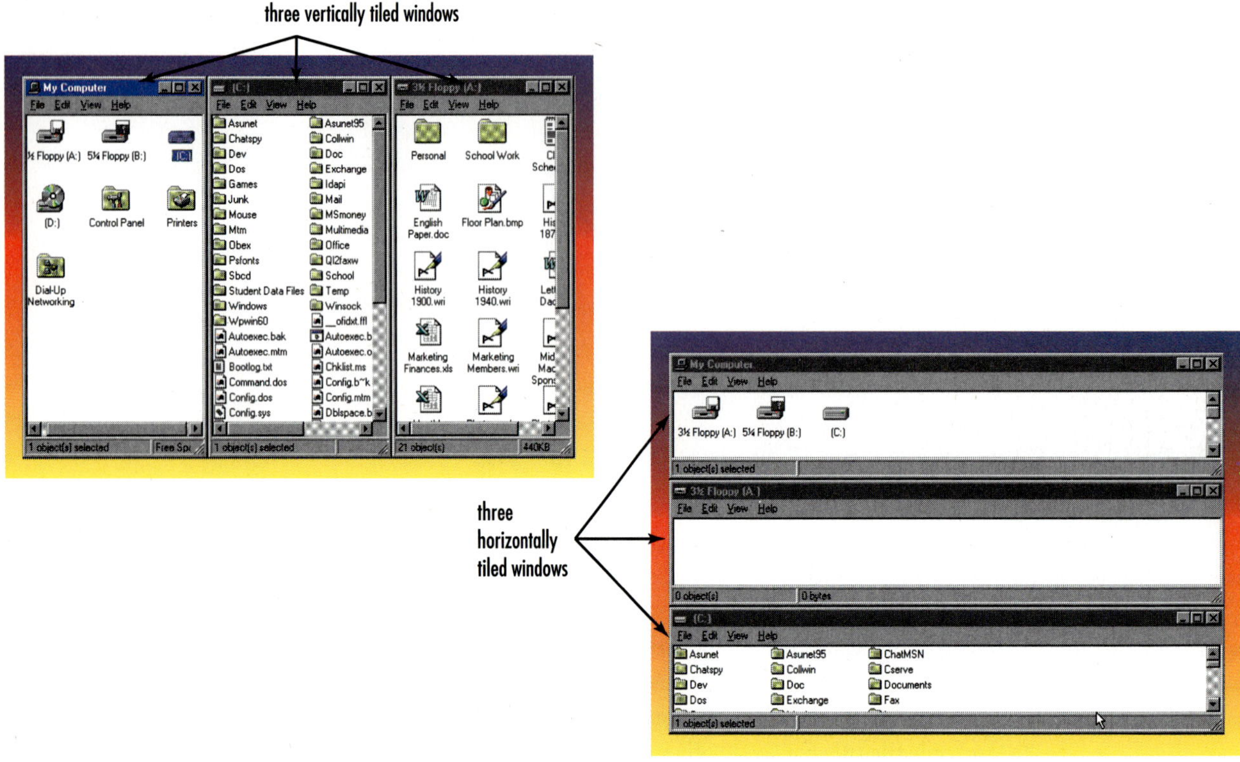

Cut, Copy, and Paste: All Windows applications include features that allow you to remove (cut), duplicate (copy) and insert (paste) information from one location to another. The location that contains the information you want to cut or copy is called the source. Then the command to cut or copy the selection is used, and the selection is stored in a temporary storage area in your computer's memory called the Clipboard. Finally, you select the location, called the destination, where you want to insert a copy of the information stored in the Clipboard and use the Paste command.

How To: The commands to perform these tasks are found in the Edit menu. The toolbar equivalents are Cut, Copy, Paste, and the keyboard shortcuts are Ctrl + X to Cut, Ctrl + C to Copy and Ctrl + V to Paste. The information must be selected before it is copied or cut.

Desktop: The Windows 95 screen is called a desktop. It displays icons that represent various tools and features. Like your own desk at home, you can add and remove items from the desktop, rearrange items, or you can get rid of them by throwing them away in the "trash." You can also open items and, much like a drawer in your desk, find other tools or materials you have stored. You can place these items on the desktop or take items off the desktop and place them in the "drawer." Just like your own desk, your most frequently used items should be on the desktop so you can quickly begin work, while those items that you use less frequently should be put away for easy access as needed.

Dialog Box: A dialog box is how Windows programs provide and request information from you in order to complete a task. All dialog boxes have a title bar at the top of the box that displays a name identifying the contents of the dialog box. Inside the dialog box are areas to select or specify the needed information and command buttons.

How To: Select an item in a dialog box by clicking on the item, by pressing Alt and the underlined letter, or by tabbing to the item. Type information in a text box. Select (highlight) an item in a list box. Click on option buttons and check boxes to turn on/off the item.

Tab dialog box: Many dialog boxes include tabs that open to display options related to the feature in the tab. The tab names appear across the top of the dialog box and indicate the different categories of tabs. The tab name of the active tab is displayed in bold. The options displayed in the open tab are the available options for the feature.

How To: To select and open a tab in a tab dialog box, click on it with the mouse or move to the tab using Ctrl + Tab to select the tab to the right or Ctrl + Shift + Tab to select the tab to the left.

Dialog Box features: The features shown in the table below are found in dialog boxes. However, not all features are found in every dialog box.

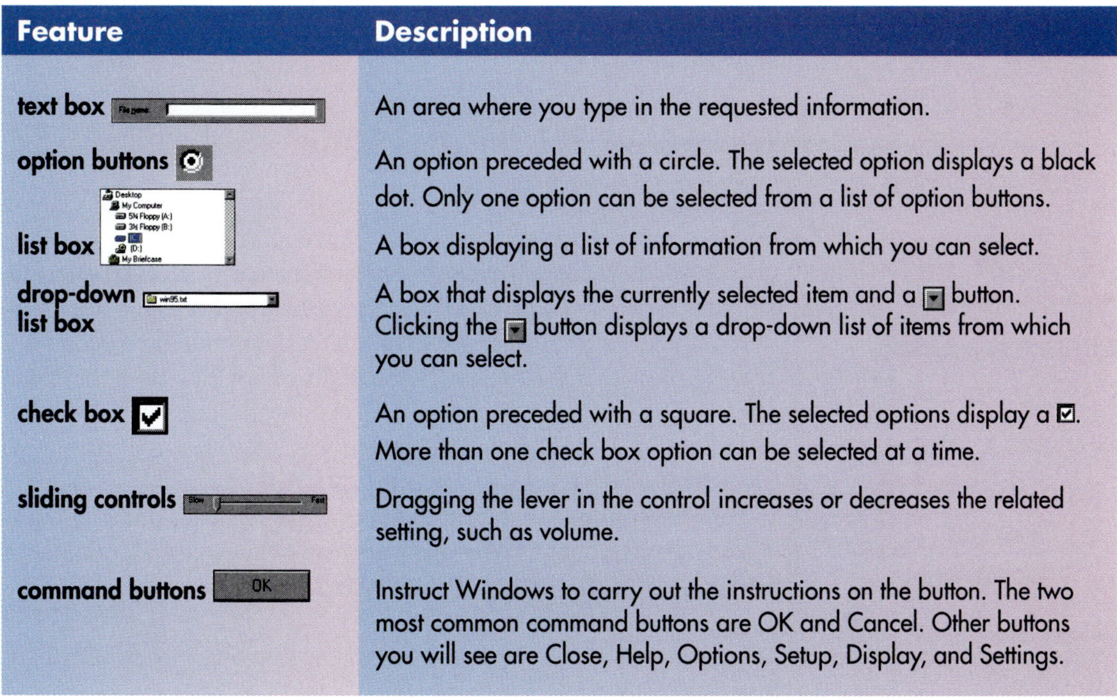

Feature	Description
text box	An area where you type in the requested information.
option buttons	An option preceded with a circle. The selected option displays a black dot. Only one option can be selected from a list of option buttons.
list box	A box displaying a list of information from which you can select.
drop-down list box	A box that displays the currently selected item and a ▾ button. Clicking the ▾ button displays a drop-down list of items from which you can select.
check box	An option preceded with a square. The selected options display a ☑. More than one check box option can be selected at a time.
sliding controls	Dragging the lever in the control increases or decreases the related setting, such as volume.
command buttons	Instruct Windows to carry out the instructions on the button. The two most common command buttons are OK and Cancel. Other buttons you will see are Close, Help, Options, Setup, Display, and Settings.

Drag and Drop: Common to all Windows applications is the ability to copy or move selections by dragging and dropping. This feature is most convenient for copying or moving short distances or when the place you want to drag and drop to is visible onscreen. Using drag and drop does not copy to the Clipboard.

How To: First select the item to be copied or moved. Then point to the selection and drag. A drag-and-drop insertion point + appears while dragging to show where the selection will be pasted. When you release the mouse button, the selection is copied or moved to the new location. To copy, hold down Ctrl while dragging. The mouse pointer displays a + when you copy.

Editing: Making changes to or correcting existing entries is called editing. Editing is commonly performed in all applications as well as within text boxes used in dialog boxes or Wizards.

How To: Generally, editing is performed by moving the insertion point to the location of the error, deleting the text that needs to be modified, and retyping the entry correctly. Two frequently used keys to delete entries are the Backspace key (removes characters to the left of the insertion point) and the Delete key (removes characters to the right of the insertion point). You can also select the text to be removed and replace it with existing text as you type.

Files and Folders: The information your computer uses is stored in files. The instructions used to run a program are stored in program files. For example, the word processing program on your computer consists of many files that contain the program statements required to use the program. The information you create while using a program is stored in data files. For example, if you write a letter to a friend using the word processing program, the contents of the letter are stored as a data file.

In addition, you can create folders and subfolders in which you store files that are related. Storing related files in folders keeps the disk organized and makes it much easier to locate files. Both files and folders are identified by names that are descriptive of the contents of the file or folder.

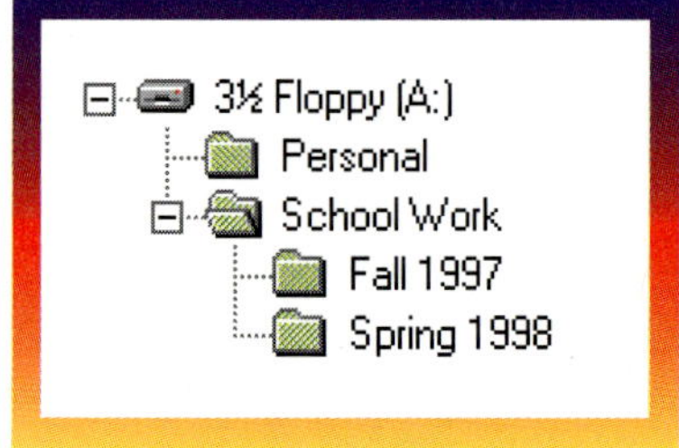

The organization of folders, subfolders, and files on your disk is called a hierarchy or tree. The top-level folder of the disk is the main or root folder. This folder is created when the disk is formatted. All folders are branches from the main folder. Subfolders are branches under a folder. Files can be stored in the root folder, a folder, or a subfolder. The figure in (left) is a graphical representation of folders and subfolders.

Help: The Windows Help facility is a quick way to find out information about commands or features. The Help menu is always the last menu in the menu bar and always contains a Help Topics command. This command opens the Help Topics tab dialog box. The three tabs, Contents, Index, and Find, provide different methods of getting help information. The Find tab allows you to select a word from a list that you need help on and then locates and displays all topics containing the word. The Contents tab displays broad Help categories preceded with book icons. Clicking on the book opens the book and displays additional books or specific Help topics. Topics are preceded with a ? icon, and when selected open the related Help window. The Index tab area allows you to select a topic from a list that you need help on. Windows Help can also display brief screen tips.

How To: Select Help Topics from the Help menu to open the Help dialog box. Clicking [?] What's this? in a dialog box and then clicking on the area in the box that you want Help information on displays a Screen Tip for the item. Clicking the [?] button in the toolbar displays Help Screen Tips on toolbar buttons, commands, or other items on the screen.

Insertion Point: The insertion point appears in a text entry area to show your location within the text. It appears as a vertical blinking bar.

How To: The insertion point is moved using the directional keys or by clicking in the text at the location you want the insertion point to appear. The mouse pointer appears as an I-beam when positioned in text, to make it easy to indicate where to move the insertion point.

Menus: A menu is one of many methods you can use to tell the program what you want it to do.

Start menu: The Start menu is a special Windows 95 menu that is used to access and begin all activities you want to perform on the computer.

How To: Click the Start button on the taskbar to open the Start menu.

Menus bars: Most menus are displayed in the menu bar immediately below the title bar of the window. When opened, a menu displays a list of commands, called a drop-down menu. Horizontal lines within many menus divide the commands into related groups.

How To: Most menu bar menus can be opened simply by clicking on the menu name. Using the keyboard, you need to press Alt or F10 and type the underlined letter of the menu name. To clear a menu without making a selection, click anywhere outside the menu or press Esc.

Shortcut menus: Other menus, called Shortcut menus, pop up when you right-click on an item. They contain commands related to the object you were pointing to when you right-clicked.

How To: Right-click an item to display its Shortcut menu.

Selecting and Choosing commands: Once a menu is open, you can select and choose commands from the menu. Selecting indicates a command is "ready" to be used. Choosing a command performs the action associated with the command.

How To: You select a command by moving the highlight bar, called the selection cursor, to the command. Simply pointing to the command moves the selection cursor to it. (You can also move the selection cursor with the directional keys on your keyboard if it is more convenient.) You choose the selected command by clicking on it, or by typing the underlined command letter, or by pressing ←Enter. When the command is chosen, the associated action is performed.

Menu features: The features shown in the tables below are found on menus. However, not all features are found on every menu.

Feature	Description
ellipses (...)	Indicates that a dialog box will be displayed for you to specify additional information needed to carry out the command.
▶	Indicates a submenu of commands will be displayed.
dimmed command	Indicates that the command is not available for selection until certain other conditions are met.
shortcut key	A key or key combination that can be used to execute a command without using the menu.
checkmark (✓)	Indicates a toggle type command. Selecting it turns the feature on and off. The checkmark indicates the feature is on.
Bullet (•)	Indicates that the commands in that group are mutually exclusive: only one can be selected. The bullet indicates the currently selected feature.

A mouse

Mouse: The mouse is a hand-held hardware device that is attached to your computer. It controls an arrow called the mouse pointer that appears on your screen. The pointer movement is controlled by the rubber-coated ball on the bottom of the mouse. This ball must move within its socket in order for the pointer to move on the screen. The ball's movement is translated into signals that tell the computer how to move the onscreen pointer. Some computers use a track ball to move the mouse pointer. The direction the ball moves controls the direction the pointer moves.

The mouse pointer changes shape on the screen depending on what it is pointing to. Some of the most common shapes are shown in the table on the next page (right).

How To: Moving the mouse across your desktop moves the pointer in the direction you are moving the mouse. The mouse is held in the palm of your hand with your fingers resting on the buttons. If you pick up the mouse and move it to another location on your work surface, the pointer will not move on the screen.

On top of the mouse are two buttons. You use these buttons to choose items on the screen. The mouse actions and descriptions are shown in the next table.

Action	Description
Point	Move the mouse so the mouse pointer is positioned on the item you want to use.
Click	Quickly press and release the left mouse button.
Double-click	Quickly press and release the mouse button twice.
Drag	Move the mouse while holding down a mouse button.
Right-click	Quickly press and release the right mouse button.

Pointer Shape	Meaning
	Select
	Horizontal Resize
	Vertical Resize
	Diagonal Resize
	Move
	Help Select
	Unavailable
	Wait
	Text Select

Moving Windows: When open, windows may appear in different locations on your desktop. Sometimes the location of the window is inconvenient. Moving a window simply displays the window at another location on the desktop. It does not change the size of the window.

How To: A window is moved by clicking on the title bar and dragging an outline of the window to the new location on the desktop.

Naming Files: To save your work as a file on the disk, you must assign it a filename. The filename should be descriptive of the contents of the file. Windows 95 applications allow you to use long filenames of up to 255 characters. A filename can contain the letters A to Z, the numbers 0 to 9, spaces, and any of the following special characters: underscore (_), caret (^), dollar sign ($), tilde (~), exclamation point (!), number sign (#), percent sign (%), ampersand (&), hyphen (-), braces ({}), parentheses (), "at" sign (@), apostrophe ('), and the grave accent (`). Filenames cannot contain commas, backslashes, periods or any the following characters: \/ : * ? " < > |.

In addition to a filename, a filename extension can be added. A filename extension is up to three characters and is separated from the filename by a period. Generally a filename extension is used to identify the type of file. It is not always necessary to enter a filename extension, because most application programs automatically add an identifying filename extension to any files created using the program. For example, Word 7.0 files have a filename extension of .doc. The parts of a file name are shown below:

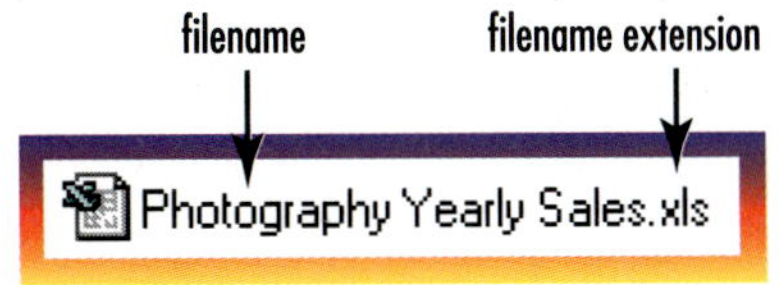

Properties: Properties are the settings associated with objects and files.

How To: An object's properties can be viewed using the View/Properties command or the Shortcut menu. A file's properties are viewed and changed using the File/Properties command. The Properties command is also commonly located on the Shortcut menu. The Property sheet displays the property settings.

Saving Files: While using any application, the document you are creating is stored in your computer's temporary memory as you work. It is lost if you do not save your work to a file on a disk. The file is a permanent copy of your document that is named and can be accessed at a later time. Although many programs create automatic backup files if your work is accidentally interrupted, it is still a good idea to save your work frequently.

How To: Two commands on the File menu of all Windows programs can be used to save a file: Save and Save As. The Save command saves a document using the same path and filename by replacing the contents of the existing disk file with the changes you have made. The Save As command allows you to select the path and provide a different filename. This command lets you save both an original version of a document and a revised document as two separate files. When you save a file for the first time, either command can be used.

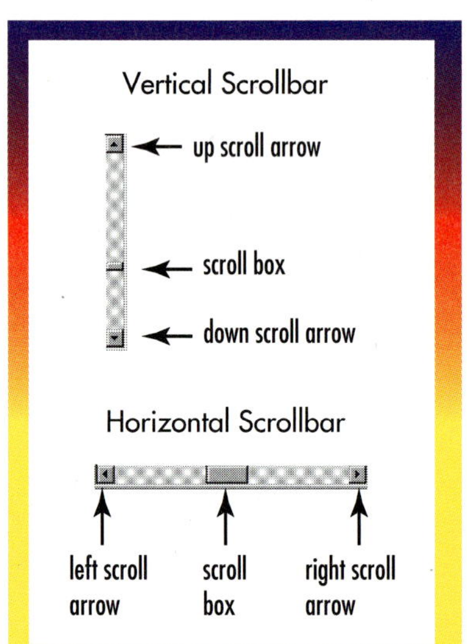

Scroll Bar: Whenever there is more information than can be displayed in a window or list box, a scroll bar is displayed. It is used with a mouse to bring additional lines of information into view. The vertical scroll bar is used to move vertically, and the horizontal scroll bar moves horizontally in the space. All scroll bars have scroll arrows and a scroll box. The location of the scroll box on the scroll bar shows your relative position within the area of available information. In many scroll bars, the size of the scroll box also indicates the relative amount of the information that is available. For example, a small box indicates that only a small amount of the total available information is displayed, whereas a large box indicates that almost all or a large portion of the total amount of available information is displayed.

How To: Clicking the scroll arrows in the vertical scroll bar scrolls the information in the window line by line vertically in the direction of the arrows. Clicking the scroll arrows in the horizontal scroll bar moves the information in the window horizontally. Dragging the scroll box moves vertically or horizontally to a general location within the area. Clicking above or below the scroll box moves information by screenfuls within the window.

Selecting: When an item is selected, it is highlighted and will be affected by the next action that is performed.

How To: Clicking an item on the screen selects the item. The keyboard can also be used to select items. Generally, pressing Tab moves the highlight forward to the next item and Shift + Tab moves it backward.

Selecting Text: Selecting text expands the highlight to cover the area of text that will be affected by your next action. Selecting text is commonly used to modify existing entries in a dialog box and in most applications.

How To: There are many methods you can use to select an area of text. The most common method is to drag the mouse across the text. You can drag in any direction in the document to extend the highlight. You can drag diagonally across text to extend the highlight from the character the insertion point is on to the last character in the selection. You can also drag in the opposite direction to deselect text. Additionally, you can use the keyboard to select text by holding down Shift while pressing a directional key. Either method requires that you move the insertion point to the beginning or end of the area to be selected before you select it. You can also select the entire document using the Select All command on the Edit menu in all Windows 95 applications. Pressing Delete removes all selected text. Typing new text automatically replaces all selected text.

Sizing Windows: A window may appear on the desktop in different sizes, and sometimes the current size is too small or too large. A window can be changed to just about any size you want.

How To: Clicking the Maximize button enlarges a window to its largest possible size, and clicking the Minimize button reduces a window to a button. A window can be custom sized by pointing to the window border and dragging the border. Dragging inward decreases the size, and dragging outward increases the size. Dragging a corner increases or decreases the size of the two adjoining borders at the same time.

Status Bar: A status bar at the bottom of the window displays information about program settings you are using and the task being performed.

Toolbar: The toolbar is a bar of button icons displayed below the menu bar. Toolbar buttons replace menu selections for many of the most common commands. The icons graphically represent the feature that is activated when selected.

How To: Click on the button to activate the command. A Tooltip consisting of the button name and a brief description displayed in the status bar can be displayed for each toolbar button by pointing to the button.

Undo: Common to all Windows applications is the ability to undo the effects of last action or command. However, some actions you perform cannot be undone. If the Undo command is unavailable, it appears dimmed and you cannot cancel your last action. Some programs allow you to undo multiple actions, up to a certain limit.

How To: Choose the Undo command from the Edit menu. The keyboard shortcut is Ctrl + Z, and the toolbar button equivalent is Undo. If the Undo button displays a ▾, clicking it displays a drop-down list of the most recently performed actions that can be undone. Selecting from the list reverses the selected action as well as all subsequent actions.

Window: A window is a rectangular section of the screen that is dedicated to a specific activity or application. The window border outlines the window. All windows have the basic parts shown below:

Feature	Description
title bar	A bar located at the top of the window that displays the application name.
Control-menu box	An icon located on the left end of the title bar that when opened displays the Control menu. This menu consists of a list of commands that are used to move, size and otherwise control the window.
Minimize button	Used to reduce a window to a button.
Maximize	Used to enlarge a window to its maximum size.
Restore button	Returns the window to its previous size.
Close button	Used to exit the application running in the window and close the window.
menu bar	Displays a list of menus that can be used within the application displayed in the window.
scroll bar	Whenever the window cannot fully display the information, a scroll bar is displayed.

Windows 95: Windows 95 is an operating system program that controls all the parts of your computer. It uses a graphical user interface (GUI, pronounced "gooey") that displays pictures called icons representing the items you use. The icons are buttons that when "pushed" activate the item.

All Windows programs have a common user interface, which makes it easy to learn and use all types of programs that run under Windows. A common user interface means that programs have common features, such as menu commands and toolbars. For example, a command such as Save in a spreadsheet program is also found on the same menu (File), has the same toolbar button, and performs the same action as it does in a word processing program.

Index

Notes